MW00744930

BIG
BOOK OF
KNOWLEDGE

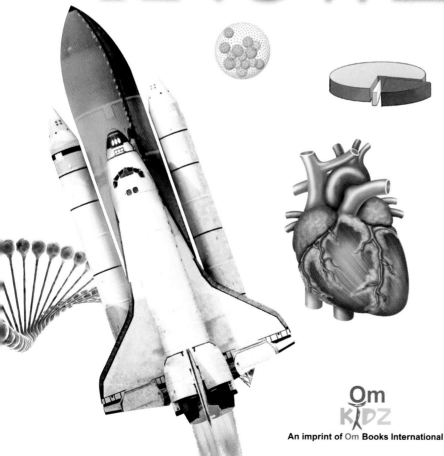

Om
KIDZ
An imprint of Om Books International

First Published in 2021 by

 Om **Books International**

Corporate & Editorial Office
A-12, Sector 64, Noida 201 301
Uttar Pradesh, India
Phone: +91 120 477 4100
Email: editorial@ombooks.com
Website: www.ombooksinternational.com

Sales Office
107, Ansari Road, Darya Ganj
New Delhi 110 002, India
Phone: +91 11 4000 9000
Email: sales@ombooks.com

© Om Books International 2021

Editor: Anjana Saproo
Design: Dipankar Manna

ISBN: 978-93-53761-06-6

Printed in India
10 9 8 7 6 5 4 3 2 1

Contents

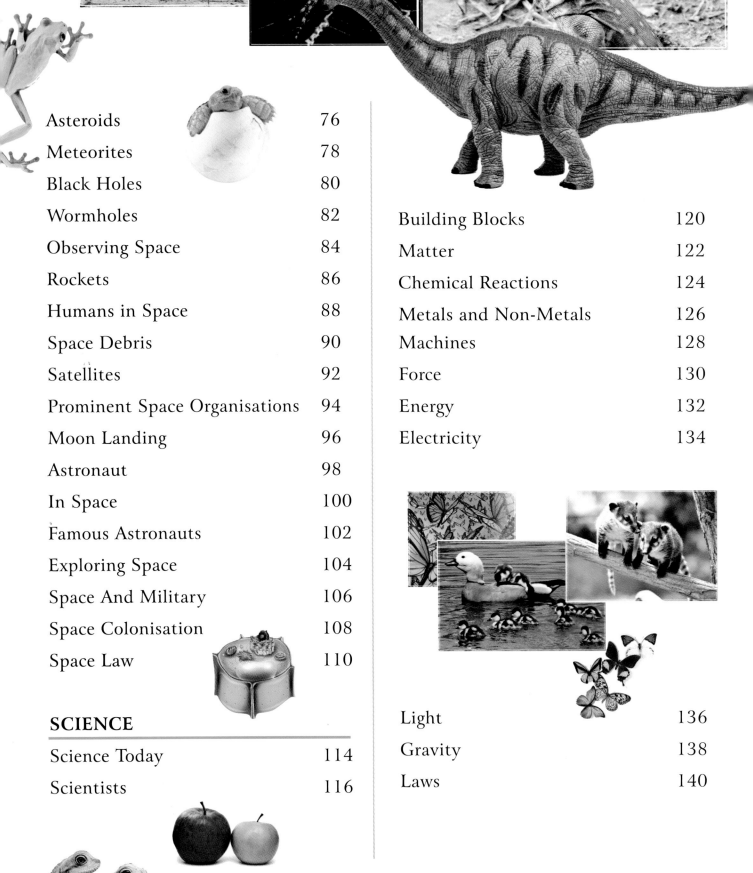

SCIENCE

GEOGRAPHY

HISTORY

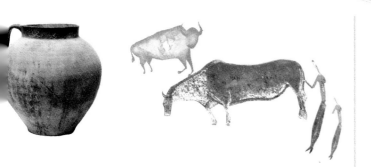

How to use the book

This *Big Book of Knowledge* is a fascinating visual experience of the world around us. The visually stimulating photographs, graphics and illustrations make the book an interesting experience of discovery and exploration.

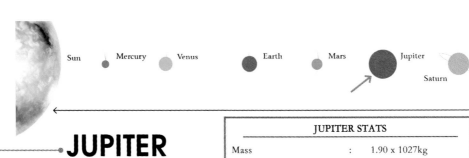

Sun   •Mercury   Venus   Earth   Mars   Jupiter
                                              Saturn

Heading:
The headings are titles of the broader subject.

JUPITER

Jupiter is the largest planet in the solar system. It is two and a half times the total mass of all other planets in the solar system combined. It is the third brightest object in the night sky after the Moon and Venus. Jupiter has 67 known moons. Some of the known moons include Io, Europa, Ganymede and Callisto. The distance of Jupiter from the Sun is 778.5 km.

SPACE

JUPITER STATS		
Mass	:	1.90 x 1027kg
Diameter	:	142,800 km
Average distance from Sun	:	778,412,020 km
Rotation period	:	0.41 (9.8 Earth hours)
Mean surface temperature	:	120 K (cloud tops)

The Great Red Spot is a huge storm on Jupiter that has raged for at least 350 years. It is so huge that three Earths could fit within it.

Jupiter

The Romans named the planet after the roman god Jupiter

Fast facts:
Realistic images that make the facts about the related topics appear more interesting.

M:
Ju
str
me
1.4
it t

At
Ju
of
mi
sur
lay
me
hy
son
anc
pre
hy

Captions:

These are concise explanatory descriptions of the images to make the understanding of the topic more engaging and comprehensive.

Neptune

BIG BOOK OF KNOWLEDGE

...tic field is 14 times as ..s, ranging from 0.42 ... the equator to 1.0 – ...e at the poles, making ... in the solar system.

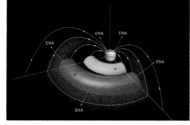

The dipole magnetic field of Jupiter

Rotation

Jupiter's rotation is the fastest amongst all the planets in our solar system. It completes a rotation on its axis in a little less than 10 hours.

The planetary rings of Jupiter: The inner halo, the bright main ring and the outer gossamer ring

Rings

...ht to consist ... with a ...ents, a

...yer ... of molecular

Jupiter has a faint planetary ring system of three main segments: an inner "torus" of particles known as the "halo", a relatively bright main ring and an outer gossamer ring. These rings appear to be made of dust.

The four largest moons of Jupiter orbit within this magnetosphere, which protects them from the solar wind

Cloud layers

Core

Metallic hydrogen

Liquid hydrogen

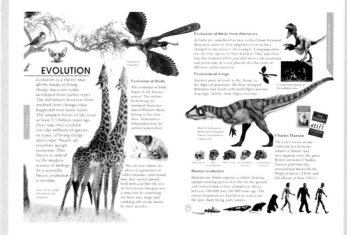

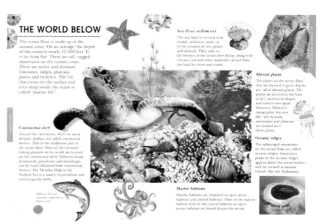

SPACE

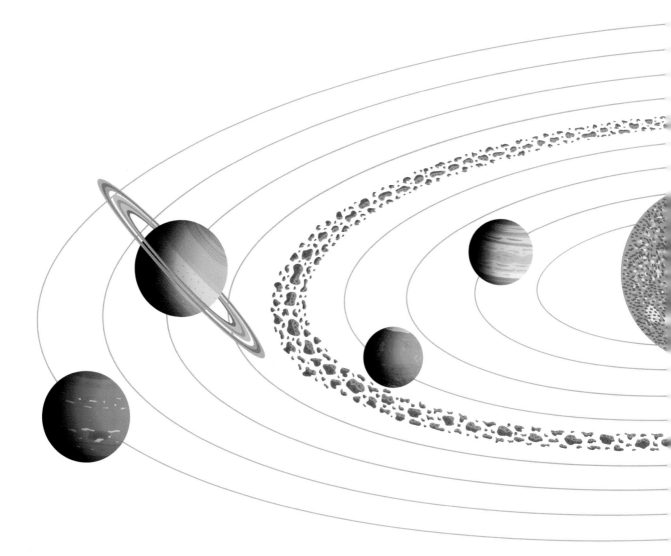

What lies beyond the Sun, the Moon, and stars is a three-dimensional area called space. Space is the final frontier that has everything in the universe beyond the top of the Earth's atmosphere – the Moon, where the GPS satellites orbit, Mars, other stars, the Milky Way, black holes, and the distant quasars.

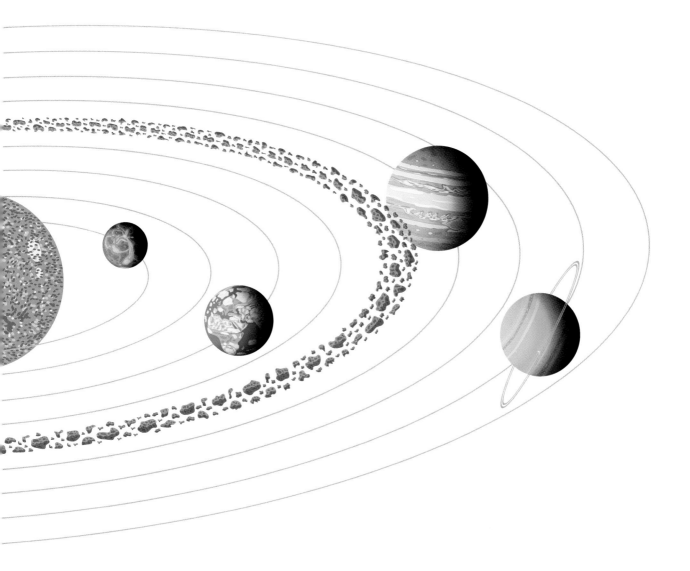

SPACE

Space begins where Earth's atmosphere ends. Although it is considered to be a void, outer space can be thought of as an environment in itself. Radiation and objects pass freely through it.

Chacteristics

• Vacuum

Space is mostly made up of vacuum. Vacuum is a completely empty space with no air. Humans find it difficult to survive in space as they there is no air. The molecules present in vacuum are spaced out and sound does not get transmitted either.

Pluto

Neptune

• Gravity

Gravity in space is the force that holds the Sun, the moons, the stars, the planets and galaxies in their place. But, gravity becomes weaker with distance. It is possible for a spacecraft to go far enough from Earth and the passengers inside would feel very little affects of gravity.

• Celestial bodies

Besides vacuum and gravity, space consists of planets, stars, several hundred galaxies, matter, dust, and gases. There are also solar winds in space.

Uranus

Saturn

• Dark matter

Dark matter is material that makes up most of the matter in our universe. It is composed of particles that do not absorb or reflect or even emit light. Hence, dark matter cannot be seen directly. We know it exists because it affects objects that can be directly observed.

Sun

Mercury

Venus

• Pressure

In space, the pressure is almost zero. With no external pressure, the air within human lungs need to be exhaled out immediately so that the human lungs don't rupture.

Earth

Mars

• Temperature

Space itself has no temperature since space is made up of empty space or vacuum. So, one cannot feel the heat or coldness of space. But there are several thermal effects going on like radiation. The Sun radiates huge amounts of energy in the form of light and other electromagnetic radiation.

Jupiter

Stars have different colours depending on how hot they are. They can be brown, red, orange, yellow, white or even blue in colour.

13

BEGINNING OF THE UNIVERSE

The Big Bang Theory is a scientific theory on how our universe, our stars and galaxies were formed. The universe was originally a hot dense superforce known as the singularity. Then, about 13.8 billion years ago, it started expanding rapidly, quickly forming atoms which in turn led to the formation of stars and galaxies.

This image is an artist's rendition of what different universes being born rapidly would look like. This collection of multiple universes is known as a multiverse.

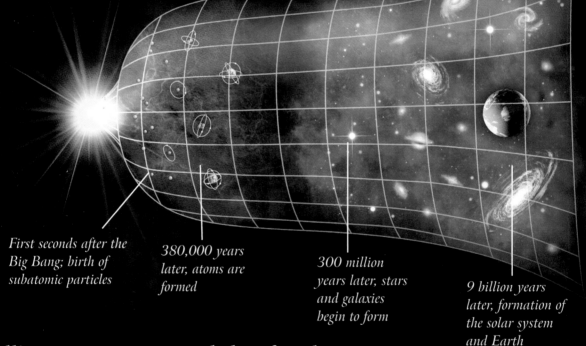

First seconds after the Big Bang; birth of subatomic particles

380,000 years later, atoms are formed

300 million years later, stars and galaxies begin to form

9 billion years later, formation of the solar system and Earth

Falling temperatures and the afterglow

The Big Bang theory predicted that the early universe was a very hot place. As the universe expanded, the gas within it started cooling down. Thus, the universe was filled with radiation that was actually remnant heat left over from the Big Bang. This primary light, or the "afterglow", is known as the Cosmic Microwave Background Radiation (CMBR).

An artist's rendition of the afterglow of the bang starting to leak into the universe.

Oscillation Model Theory

According to this theory, the universe goes thorugh a cyclic process. It started with a Big Bang and will continue till the universe expands to its maximum size. At this point, there will be a rapid contraction, called the Big Crunch, until the universe contracts back to a single point. This singularity would then explode again, restarting the cycle.

An artist's rendering of an oscillating universe

This cone is supposed to represent the space-time continuum. The direction of the arrow shows how it progresses. It starts as time moves up along the height of the cone while space moves around the width of the cone. As a result, at the tip, both space and time meet at a single point. This point is known as the "singularity"

The Hawking-Turok Theory

Rather than explaining the Big Bang itself, this theory tries to explain that the Big Bang needed an impetus which was provided by a particle described as an "instanton". The instanton is a hypothetical particle that has the mass of a pea but is much, much smaller in size.

Neil Turok and Stephen Hawking, authors of the Hawking-Turok theory

Eternal Inflation Theory

According to this theory, the rapid expansion, following the Big Bang, never stopped. It continued in other universes. Thus, this inflation is "eternal". In theories of eternal inflation, the phase of the inflation of our universe's expansion will never end. This is true for only some regions of our universe.

WILL THE UNIVERSE END?

There are several theories that predict the end of the universe. Scientists have been researching this and have come up with three theories as to how our universe could come to an end.

Open universe

Studies suggest that the universe will expand forever. As it expands, the matter it contains will spread and become thinner. The galaxies will exhaust their resources to make new stars. The existing stars will slowly fade. The universe will become dark, cold and eventually, lifeless.

Closed universe

Astronomers believe that a closed universe will reduce its pace until it reaches its maximum size. Then it will collapse on itself. The universe will become denser and hotter until it ends in a hot and dense singularity. A closed universe will lead to what is called a "big crunch".

Interestingly, for the first 380,000 years or even more, the universe was extremely hot for light to shine.

Flat universe

The universe will consume all the energy from the Big Bang, and then the universe will come to a stop. This is a contrast to the Open Universe theory because it will take an infinite amount of time for the universe to reach the equilibrium point of the consumption of energy.

Multiverse

The multiverse theory states that there will be no real end to the universe. It states that when our universe was created, there were multiple more universes created and that they are all at different stages of their existence. When our universe ends, there will be other universes that will still go on and newer universes that will be created.

The Big Bounce

According to one version of the Big Bang Theory of cosmology, in the beginning, the universe had infinite density. The Big Bounce consists of multiple repetitions of the Big Bang followed by big crunches.

False vacuum

In a false vacuum a lower energy state can be reached wherein some usable energy is left. This theory believes that every time we reach such a false vacuum, the universe decays to reach a true vacuum and begins multiple new universes in the process.

A multiverse is a portmanteau of the words "multiple" and "universe".

GALAXIES

A galaxy is a massive, gravitationally bound system consisting of stars, interstellar mediums of gas, dust and dark matter. Galaxies contain multiple planets, star systems, and many types of interstellar clouds. Many galaxies are believed to have supermassive black holes at their centre. There are more than in the universe! Each one of these 2 trillion galaxies has hundreds of billions of stars.

This image shows Earth at night with trillions of stars that form our galaxy.

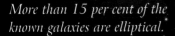

More than 15 per cent of the known galaxies are elliptical.

Spiral galaxy

Spiral galaxies make up 72 percent of the galaxies observed by scientists. Most of them have a flat rotating disk having stars, gas and dust. They also have a concentration of stars in the centre known as the bulge. The Milky Way which includes our Earth and the solar system is a spiral galaxy.

The Milky Way is a spiral galaxy. It has over 200 billion stars!.

Elliptical galaxy

This is the most abundant type of galaxy found in the universe. They are in the shape of an ellipse, a stretched-out circle. They are made up of older lower mass stars. Elliptical galaxies range in size from tens of millions to over one hundred trillion stars.

Barred spiral galaxy ——————————

A barred spiral galaxy is one with a bar through the centre. Their spiral arms emerge from the two ends of the bar that guide gases and dust towards the central bulge. The flow of this matter results in many barred spirals to have active nuclei. New stars are born as a result of gases and dust from these galaxies.

Messier 109 is a barred spiral galaxy.

Irregular galaxy

Irregular galaxies are born out of collisions with regular galaxies. They are unique in shape, age and structure. Often, irregular galaxies orbit regular galaxies. For example, the Magellanic Cloud galaxy orbits the Milky Way.

About 3 per cent of all galaxies are irregulars.

Lenticular galaxy

They contain a large-scale disc but do not have large-scale spiral arms. They however, have a significant amount of dust in their disks. As a result, they mainly consist of aging stars.

Lenticular galaxy in space surrounded by thick dust lanes

COLLIDING GALAXIES

Since several galaxies are members of a group or a cluster, and are close together, they tend to collide with each other. When two galaxies interact, the clouds of gas inside each galaxy may compress. This causes the clouds to collapse under their own gravity, transforming them into stars.

Messier 64 (M64) or the Black eye galaxy.

Black Eye galaxy

The Black Eye galaxy, is also known as Evil Eye galaxy or Sleeping Beauty . This spiral galaxy lies at a distance of 24 million light years from Earth. It is known for the enormous light-absorbing dust band in front of its central region, which has earned the galaxy the names "black eye" or "evil eye".

Mice galaxies right before their collision.

Cartwheel galaxy

This galaxy is a lenticular and ring galaxy. It is slightly larger than the Milky Way.

Cartwheel galaxy

Mice galaxies

These galaxies get their name because the long streams of stars, gas and dust thrown off of each other as a result of their interaction resemble the tails of a pair of mice. The tails are the remains of their spiral arms.

Interacting galaxies

ARP 272 is a pair of interacting galaxies, which consists of two spiral galaxies, NGC 6050 and IC 1179 The galaxies are a part of the Hercules Cluster. The two galaxies in ARP 272 are in physical contact through their spiral arms.

ARP 272 in the Hercules constellation.

Antennae galaxies

These two galaxies are known as the Antennae Galaxies. The two long tails of the stars, gas and dust ejected due to the collision resemble an insect's antennae. The nuclei of these two galaxies will eventually join to become one giant galaxy.

The Antennae Galaxies in collision.

This image is part of a large collection of 59 images of merging galaxies taken by the Hubble Space Telescope.

ACTIVE GALAXIES

Active galaxies have very bright cores and they emit up to thousands of times more energy than a normal galaxy. Most of this energy is released in the form of radio waves to gamma rays. Such galaxies also spew long jets of gas at nearly the speed of light. This activity is driven by a massive black hole in the galaxy's nucleus.

Radio galaxy

A radio galaxy serves as a strong source of electromagnetic radiation or radio waves. Compared to ordinary galaxies, a radio galaxy emits as much as a thousand to a million times more energy per unit time.

The power of a quasar originates from supermassive black holes that are believed to exist at the core of all galaxies.

Radio galaxy

Quasars

Quasars are the farthest objects that can be seen from our galaxy. They are extremely bright masses of energy and light. Quasar is short for "quasi-stellar radio source" or "quasi-stellar object". They are the brightest objects in our universe. They emit radio waves, X-rays and

Blazar

A blazar is a dense energy source fuelled by supermassive black holes. They are considered to be one of the most dangerous phenomena in space. They are characterised by their high speed and energy. They are also extremely powerful.

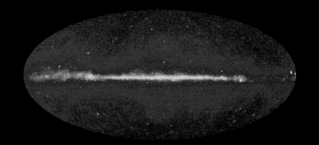

3C 454.3 is one of the brightest gamma ray sources in the sky. It appears in Pegasus, near Alpha Pegasi.

The difference between Quasar, radio galaxy and a Blazar is the angle of the stream. If the stream is straight up, it is a radio galaxy and Earth is not in the firing line. If the stream is angled slightly towards Earth, then its a Quasar. But if the stream is angled directly towards Earth, its a Blazar.

Seyfert galaxy

Almost all Seyfert galaxies are spiral galaxies. The striking feature of these galaxies is that their luminosity can change rapidly. In the constellation Pegasus, NGC 7742 is known to be a Seyfert galaxy. It resembles a fried egg, with a very bright nucleus that is visible at all wavelengths. It is ringed by blue-tinted stars forming regions and faintly visible spiral arms.

PARTS OF THE MILKY WAY

The Milky Way is the galaxy that contains our Solar System. The name describes the galaxy's appearance from Earth. It can be seen as a hazy band of light in the night sky. The newer stars formed in this spiral disc. The galaxy formation process has not stopped. The Milky Way has already swallowed several galaxies and is expected to collide with the nearest galaxy Andromeda in a few billion years.

Halo

The halo primarily contains single old stars and clusters of old stars. It also contains dark matter. The dark matter halo around the Milky Way may span as much as 2 million light years.

Bulge

The bulge is a round structure made primarily of old stars, gas and dust. The bulge of the Milky Way is roughly 10,000 light years across.

Spiral arms

The spiral arms are curved extensions. They begin at the bulge of a spiral galaxy, appearing like a "pinwheel". The spiral arms contain a lot of gas and dust as well as young blue stars. They are found only in spiral galaxies.

Disc

The disc is a flattened region that covers the bulge in a spiral galaxy. It is shaped like a pancake. The Milky Way's disc is 100,000 light years across and 1,000 light years thick. It consists of mostly young stars, gas and dust, which are concentrated in its spiral arms. Some old stars are also present.

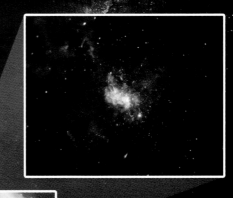

A vector of the supermassive black hole at the centre of the Milky Way

Chandra X-ray observatory image of Sagittarius A*, the radio source corresponding to the supermassive black hole of the Milky Way galaxy.

Stars, gas and dust

Stars come in a variety of types. Blue stars, which are very hot, tend to have shorter life spans than red cooler stars. The regions of galaxies where stars are currently forming are bluer than the regions where there has been no recent star formation. Spiral galaxies have a lot of gas and dust, whereas elliptical galaxies contain very little of it.

NEBULA

The literal translation of nebula is "cloud". Planetary nebulae are the leftovers of stars like the Sun. They consist of a cloud of gas and dust surrounding a slowly cooling white dwarf star. The best-known planetary nebula is the Ring Nebula in the constellation Lyra. It was once a sun-like star that gently blew its outer atmosphere to space as it aged.

Images showing the varied rich colours of Nebulae, like the Crab, Eagle, Orion, Pelican, Ring and Rosette Nebulae.

Importance of Nebula

About 1,500 nebulae are known to exist in the Milky Way Galaxy. Planetary nebulae are important objects in astronomy because they play an important role in the chemical evolution of the galaxy. In other galaxies, planetary nebulae may be the only objects that can be observed by humans and yield useful information about chemical abundances.

The nebula cycle

Interestingly, nebulae are not just the starting points of star formation. Ironically, they can also be the end points. This could be thought of as the nebula – star – nebula cycle. Stars that evolve into red giants can lose their outer

layers during pulsations in their outer layers, known as their atmospheres. It is this released matter that forms a planetary nebula. The planetary nebula is just one of four major types of nebulae. The other three are H II regions, supernova remnant and dark nebula.

Composition

They show swirls of light. Stars with different elements inside these nebulae cause them to glow with beautiful red, blue and green hues. Most nebulae are composed of approximately 90 per cent hydrogen, 10 per cent helium and 0.1 per cent heavy elements such as carbon, nitrogen, magnesium, potassium, calcium and iron. Some of the prominent nebulae are the Crab, Eagle, Orion, Pelican, Ring and Rosette Nebulae.

STARS

Stars are born in a cluster of gas and dust called a 'nebula'. Once pressure builds up in the nebula, it will bring the gas and dust together and produce what is called a protostar. The heat inside this is pretty intense and when it gets hot enough, it can explode into a star. The Sun is a star.

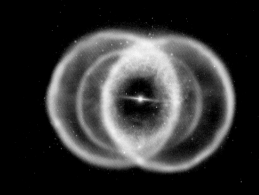

The Cat's Eye Nebula is so called as the intersection of the two halos formed by the nebula looks like a cat's eye

Stages that every star undergoes

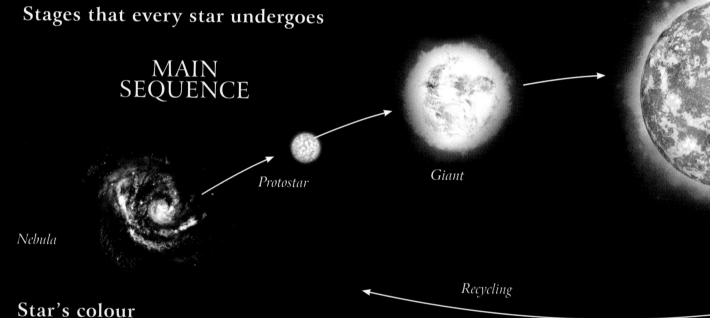

MAIN
SEQUENCE

Protostar

Giant

Nebula

Recycling

Star's colour

A star's colour is determined by its temperature. The hottest stars have temperatures of over 40,000 K, and the coolest stars have temperatures of about 2000 K. Blue stars are the hottest. Red stars are the coolest. Our Sun's surface temperature is about 6000 K. It is slightly greenish-yellow. In space, the Sun would look white, shining with about equal amounts of reddish and bluish wavelengths of light.

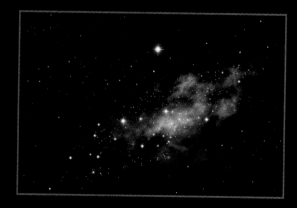

Growth

Stars expand as they grow old. As the core exhausts its hydrogen and then helium, it contracts and the outer layers expand, cool and become less bright. It will finally collapse and explode. Depending on the original mass of the star, it will either become a black dwarf, a neutron star or a black hole.

Supergiant

Type II Supernova

Supernova Remnant

Rigel

This is a blue star that is the brightest as well in the constellation Orion. We couldn't live as close to Rigel as we do to our Sun as its surface temperature is much hotter, about 21,000 degrees Fahrenheit. Rigel emits about 120,000 times more energy than the Sun. Yet, you might be surprised to find that Rigel has only 21 times more mass, and is 79 times the diameter of the Sun. Someday, it will explode as a supernova.

Neutron Star

Black Hole

Brightness

The most luminous stars emit more than six million times the Sun's light and the least luminous ones emit less than one ten-thousandth of it. It is an indication of a star's actual brightness as viewed from Earth.

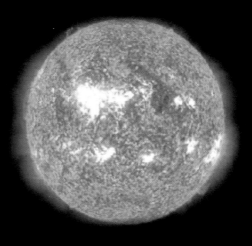

Rigel, a star larger than the Sun

NOVA AND SUPERNOVA

A nova and supernova are both bright events in the sky that are generally visible during the night to the naked eye.

Nova

Nova is the name for the white dwarf star whose surface has exploded. Nova means a 'newly born star.' A white dwarf star explodes because they are very hot. This liberates an enormous amount of energy, blowing the remaining gases away from the white dwarf's surface and producing an extremely bright outburst of light.

The white dwarf star owing to the gravitational pull between the stars is able to pull some of the hydrogen from the red giant.

Nova Eridani 2009 as seen on the night of a full moon.

Supernova

A supernova is a huge explosion of a star towards usually towards the end of the star's lifecycle. A supernova burns for only a short period of time. When the star explodes, it shoots elements and debris into space. These elements travel on to form new stars, planets and everything else in the universe.

A nova as represented by an artist

The earliest recorded supernova was SN 185, which was viewed by Chinese astronomers in 185 AD. SN 1006 is the brightest recorded supernova in human history.

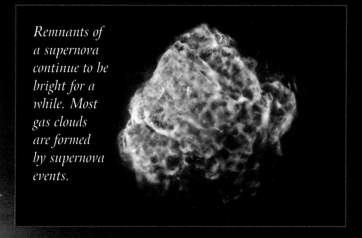

Remnants of a supernova continue to be bright for a while. Most gas clouds are formed by supernova events.

Supernovae are relatively rare events within a galaxy, occurring about thrice in a century in the Milky Way. One of the last supernovas in the Milky Way took place about 340 years ago. It happened in the constellation of Cassiopeia, so it is known as Cassiopeia A (Cas A).

RED GIANT

A red giant is a big giant star that weighs about one-half to ten times as much as the Sun. Red giants get their name because they appear to be red in colour and they are very large. Many red giants could fit thousands and thousands of suns like ours inside of them. A star with a solar mass between 0.3 and 8.0 will evolve into red giant.

Formation

All stars start the same way when gravity causes hydrogen to fuse into helium. But in larger stars, the hydrogen gets depleted over time. Lack of hydrogen fusion means that the core can no longer counteract gravity, and the outer layers contract inwards.

This causes the temperature and pressure in the core increases. The increase in temperature causes hydrogen fusion in the outer shells, which then expand into a red giant or a larger red giant depending on size. The outer layers which are far from the core burn cooler (3500-4500K), causes the star to appear red.

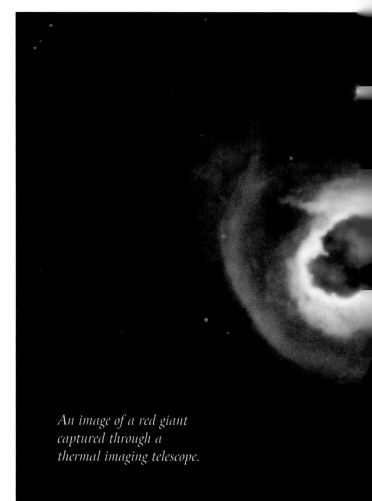

An image of a red giant captured through a thermal imaging telescope.

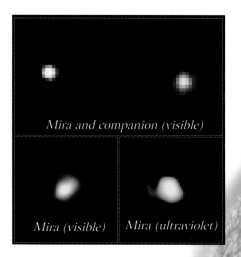

Mira and companion (visible)

Mira (visible)

Mira (ultraviolet)

The bright yellow dot in the top left corner is a star the size of the Sun. It serves as a comparison to show how big a red giant could be.

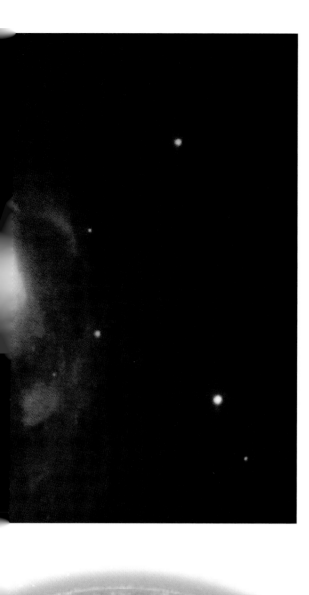

Characteristics

Since the expansion of the star greatly increases its surface area, red giants tend to be cooler and burn with an orange hue. Despite their name, they are closer to orange in reality.

In 2017, an international team of astronomers identified the surface of the red giant π Gruis in detail . They found that the red giant's surface has just a few convective cells, or granules, that are each about 75 million miles across. By comparison, the Sun has about two million convective cells about 930 miles across.

The five largest known supergiants in the galaxy are red supergiants: VY Canis Majoris, Mu Cephei, KW Sagitarii, V354 Cephei, and KY Cygni.

An artist's conception of a red giant at sunset on one of its orbiting worlds.

THE SOLAR SYSTEM

A solar system refers to a star and all the objects that orbit around it. Our solar system consists of the Sun, which is our star, eight planets and their natural satellites, dwarf planets, an asteroid planet and many moons. It was formed approximately 5 billion years ago.

Inner planets

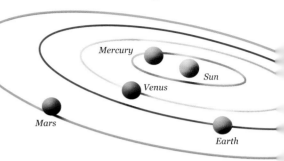

The Sun is vital for life on Earth

Inner planets

Mercury

Mercury is the closest planet to the Sun and it is also the smallest of the eight planets in the solar system.

Venus

Venus is the second planet from the Sun and the third brightest object in Earth's sky after the Sun and the Moon.

Earth

Earth is the third planet from the Sun and the largest of the terrestrial planets.

Mars

Mars is the fourth planet from the Sun. It is sometimes called the Red Planet because of the brownish-red colour of its urface.

SPACE

Sun

Inner Planets

The inner planets are rocky, sometimes all the way to their core. Size is the most obvious difference between the inner and outer planets. The outer planets are huge! Our largest inner planet is Earth, and Earth is only 1/4 the size of the smallest outer planet, Neptune.

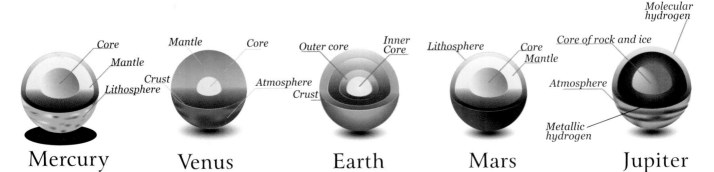

Mercury   Venus   Earth   Mars   Jupiter

The outer planets

The outer planets are called the jovian planets, meaning huge gas giants. These planets in order are Jupiter, Saturn, Uranus, and Neptune. Pluto comes after Neptune, but it is no longer considered a planet. It is now a dwarf planet.

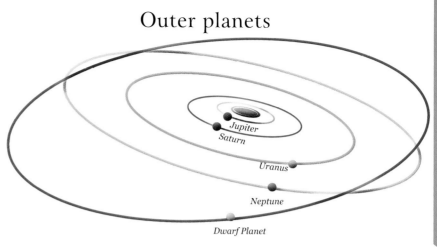

Outer planets

Jupiter
Saturn
Uranus
Neptune
Dwarf Planet

Outer planets

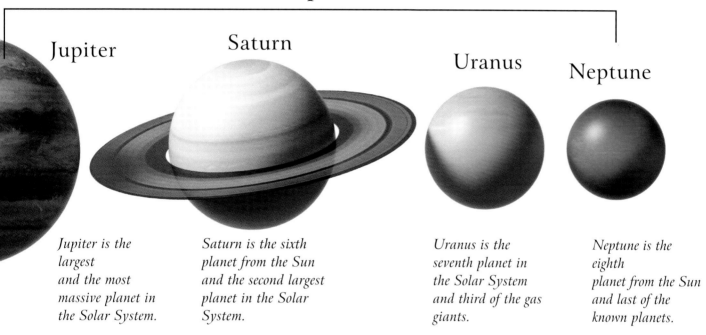

Jupiter

Saturn

Uranus

Neptune

Jupiter is the largest and the most massive planet in the Solar System.

Saturn is the sixth planet from the Sun and the second largest planet in the Solar System.

Uranus is the seventh planet in the Solar System and third of the gas giants.

Neptune is the eighth planet from the Sun and last of the known planets.

Most of the planets in the solar system rotate on their axes in the same direction that they move around the Sun. Uranus, though, is tilted on its side so it rotates like a top that was turned so that it was spinning parallel to the floor. Scientists think that Uranus was probably knocked over by a collision with another planet-sized object billions of years ago.

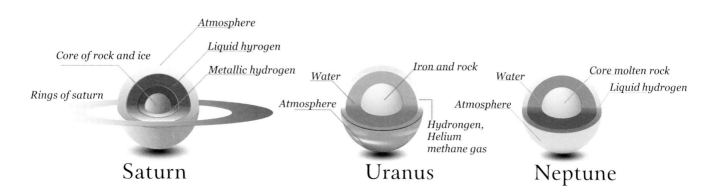

Atmosphere
Liquid hyrogen
Core of rock and ice
Metallic hydrogen
Rings of saturn

Water
Iron and rock
Atmosphere
Hydrongen, Helium methane gas

Water
Core molten rock
Liquid hydrogen
Atmosphere

Saturn

Uranus

Neptune

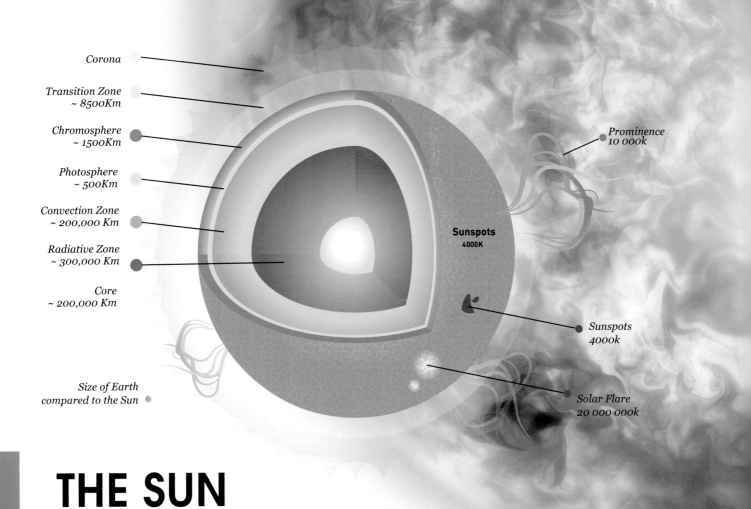

Corona

Transition Zone
~ 8500Km

Chromosphere
~ 1500Km

Photosphere
~ 500Km

Convection Zone
~ 200,000 Km

Radiative Zone
~ 300,000 Km

Core
~ 200,000 Km

Size of Earth
compared to the Sun

Prominence
10 000k

Sunspots
4000K

Sunspots
4000k

Solar Flare
20 000 000k

THE SUN

The Sun is at the centre of our solar system. It is an almost perfect sphere of super-hot gases whose gravity holds the solar system together. The energy produced by the Sun is essential for life on Earth and is a driving force behind the Earth's weather. It has a diameter of about 1,392,684 kilometres. The Sun takes 225 – 250 million years to revolve around the centre of the Milky Way.

It is an almost perfect sphere of super-hot gases whose gravity holds the solar system together. The energy produced by the Sun is essential for life on Earth and is a driving force behind the Earth's weather.

The Sun is composed of hydrogen (70%) and helium (28%).

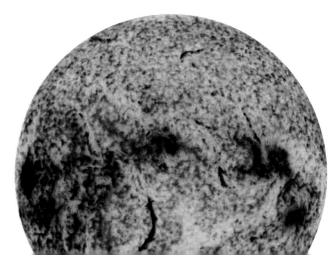

Eventually, the Sun will swell to become a red giant. Then, it will shed its outer layers and the remaining core will collapse to become a white dwarf. Slowly, this will fade and enter its final phase as a dim, cool object known as a black dwarf.

Sunspots viewed against their natural light

Sunspots

Sunspots are regions on the solar surface that seem dark as they are cooler than the surrounding photosphere. The largest sunspots observed had diameters of about 50,000 kilometres, which makes them so large that they can be seen with the naked eye.

Photosphere

The photosphere is the solar "surface" that we see when we look at the Sun in visible light. The Sun's surface, like that of a boiling pot, is constantly changing. Solar granulation refers to the cell structure, or bubbly appearance, of the photosphere.

Chromosphere

Chromosphere, the lowest layer of the Sun's atmosphere, is located above the photosphere. It contains comparatively cool columns of ascending gas known as "spicules".

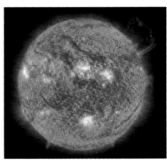

Solar flares rarely occur during the three or four years of sunspot.

Corona

Corona is the outermost region of the Sun's atmosphere. Solar flares occur above the surface in the corona, and energy deposited at the surface raises a superhot cloud, of about 100 million °C. This is a strong, long-lasting source of X-rays.

Photosphere

Chromosphere

Corona

37

SOLAR ECLIPSE

A solar eclipse is a natural event that occurs on Earth when the Moon moves in its orbit between the Sun and Earth. This is also known as an occultation. It happens at New Moon, when the Sun and the Moon are in conjunction with each other. During an eclipse, the Moon's shadow (which is divided into two parts: the dark umbra and the lighter penumbra) moves across Earth's surface.

Types of solar eclipses

An annular eclipse occurs when the Sun and the Moon are exactly in line, but the size of the Moon is smaller than the Sun. Hence, the Sun appears as a very bright ring, or annulus, surrounding the dark disc of the Moon. A partial eclipse occurs when the Sun and the Moon are not exactly in line. A total eclipse occurs when the dark silhouette of the Moon completely obscures the intensely bright light of the Sun, allowing the much fainter solar corona to be visible.

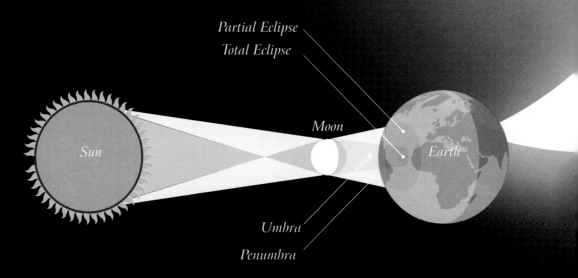

The Moon covers the Sun. This is visible as a total eclipse in some parts of Earth and partial eclipse in others. Some parts of Earth will not see an eclipse at all.

Partial Eclipse
Total Eclipse
Sun
Moon
Earth
Umbra
Penumbra

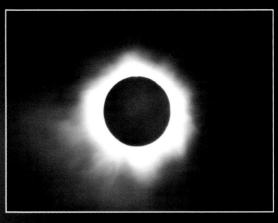

A total eclipse of the Sun. The Sun has been covered by the Moon.

Observation

Looking directly at the photosphere of the Sun can cause permanent damage to the retina of the eye even if we look at it just for a few seconds. This is because of the intense visible and invisible radiation that the photosphere emits. Viewing the, Sun during partial and annular eclipses as well as during total eclipses outside the brief period of totality, requires special eye protection, or indirect viewing methods, if eye damage is to be avoided. The Sun's disc can be viewed using appropriate filtration to block the harmful part of the Sun's radiation.

Phases observed during a total eclipse

First contact:	*Second contact:*	*Totality:*	*Third contact:*	*Fourth contact:*
When the Moon's limb (edge) is exactly tangential to that of the Sun's.	Starting with Bailey's Beads and the diamond ring effect, almost the entire disc is covered.	The Moon obscures the entire disc of the Sun and only the solar corona is visible.	When the first bright light becomes visible and the Moon's shadow is moving away from the observer. Again, a diamond ring may be observed.	When the trailing edge of the Moon ceases to overlap with the solar disc and the eclipse ends.

The Moon covering the Sun in a partial eclipse. This happens when the Moon passes in front of the Sun and hides it from being viewed by Earth.

MERCURY

Mercury is the smallest planet in the Solar System. It is closest to the Sun. Mercury orbits the Sun within Earth's orbit as an inferior planet. Its apparent distance from the Sun as viewed from Earth never exceeds 28°C. This proximity to the Sun means the planet can only be seen near the western horizon after sunset or eastern horizon before sunrise, usually in twilight.

MERCURY STATS		
Mass	:	3.3 x 1023 kg
Diameter	:	4879 km
Average distance from Sun	:	57,909,175 km
Rotation period	:	58.65 Earth days
Surface temperature	:	100-700 K

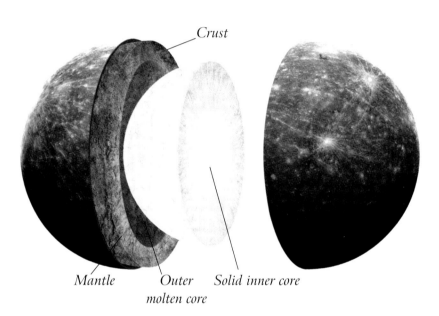

Crust

Mantle   Outer   Solid inner core
          molten core

Internal structure

Mercury consists of approximately 70 per cent metallic and 30 per cent silicate material. Mercury possesses a "dorsa" or "wrinkle-ridges", montes (mountains), planitiae (plains), rupes (escarpments) and valles (valleys). There are craters on Mercury, the largest one known is "Caloris Basin", with a diameter of 1,550 kilometres.

Unlike the Moon whose one side faces Earth at all times, Mercury rotates twice for every revolution around the Sun.

Mercury   *Moon*

SPACE

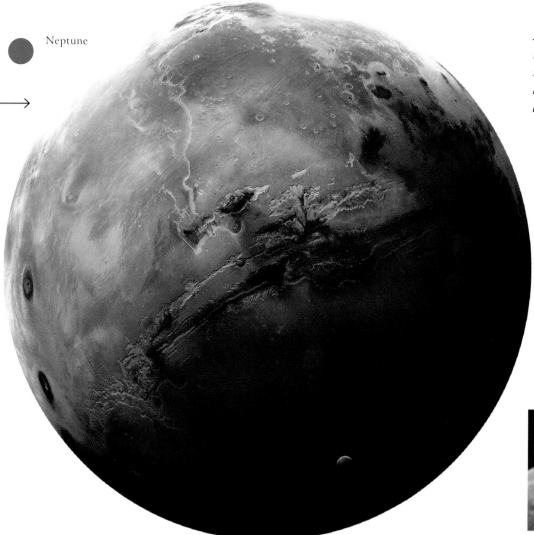

Neptune

An image of the planet Mercury as captured by a space probe of NASA. It appears red because it is covered in red soil.

Temperature

Mercury is only the second hottest planet in the solar system despite being the closest to the Sun, with the hottest planet being Venus. The surface temperature of Mercury ranges from 100 K to 700 K at the most extreme place. Mercury has a significant magnetic field.

Atmosphere

At certain points on Mercury's surface, you would be able to see the Sun rise about halfway, then reverse and set before rising again, all within the same Mercurian day. To a hypothetical observer on Mercury, the Sun appears to move in a backward direction.

The surface of the planet Mercury is very similar to that of the Moon, in the sense that it is rough and full of craters and rocks. It is also dry and dusty seeing that it is the closest planet to the Sun.

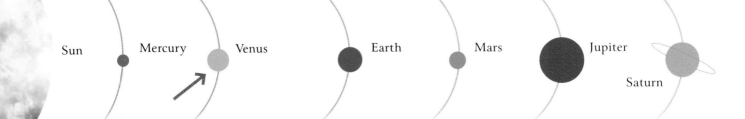

VENUS

Venus is the second planet from the Sun and the second brightest object in the night sky, after the Moon. It can also be seen during daytime from Earth. It is the hottest planet in the solar system. Venus is sometimes called the Earth's "sister planet" because of their similar size, mass, proximity to the Sun.

VENUS STATS		
Mass	:	4.87 x 1024 kg
Diameter	:	12104 km
Average distance from Sun	:	108,208,930 km
Rotation period	:	243.02 Earth Days (retrogade)
Surface temperature	:	737 K

Named after the Roman goddess of love and beauty, Venus is the second largest terrestrial planet

Atmospheric pressure on Venus is 92 times greater than Earth's.

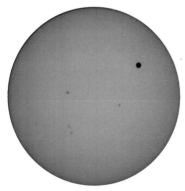

Transits of Venus are among the rarest of predictable astronomical phenomena. We see the shadow of Venus falling on the Sun.

42

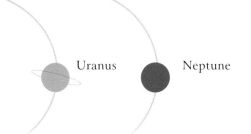

Uranus   Neptune

Internal Structure

The similarity in size and density between Venus and Earth suggests they share a similar internal structure: a core, a mantle, and crust. Like that of Earth, the Venusian core is at least partially liquid because the two planets have been cooling at about the same rate. The slightly smaller size of Venus means pressures are 24% lower in its deep interior than Earth's.

Mantle   *Atmosphere*

Core   *Crust*

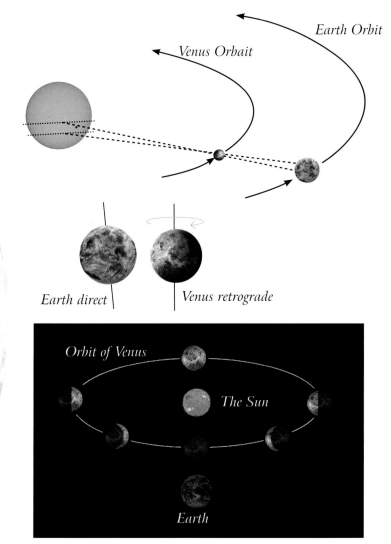

Earth Orbit

Venus Orbait

Earth direct   *Venus retrograde*

Orbit of Venus

The Sun

Earth

The different phases of Venus as seen from Earth. Just like the Moon, the Sun illuminates parts of Venus as it orbits around it.

Orbit

All the planets of the solar system orbit the Sun in an anti-clockwise direction as viewed from Earth's North Pole, but Venus rotates clockwise, called "retrograde" rotation, once every 243 Earth days. As it moves around its orbit, Venus displays phases like those of the Moon in a telescopic view. The planet presents a small "full" phase when it is on the opposite side of the Sun. It shows a larger "quarter phase" when it is at its maximum elongation from the Sun and at its brightest in the night sky.

EARTH

It is the only astronomical object known to harbour life. The first life forms appeared between 3.5 and 3.8 billion years ago. Earth is the third planet from the Sun. Earth's circumference at the equator is about 40,075 kilometres, but from pole to pole, it is only 40,008 kilometres around. This shape, caused by the flattening at the poles, is called an "oblate spheroid".

EARTH STATS		
Mass	:	5.98 x 1024 kg
Diameter	:	12756 km
Average distance from Sun	:	149,597,890 km
Rotation period	:	23.93 hours
Mean surface temperature	:	281K

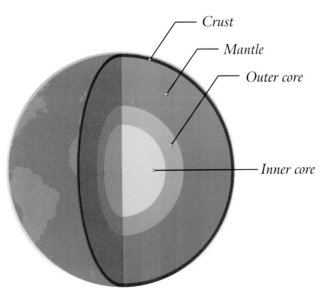

Hadean	Archean	Proterozoic	Paleozoic (Part 1)

~4,600   4,000   3,600   3,200   2,800   2,500   1,600   1,000   541   485   443   419

Paleozoic (Part 2)	Mesozoic	Cenozoic

419   358   298   252   201   145   66   23   2.6   0

Internal Structure

Earth is the densest planet in the solar system because of its metallic core and rocky mantle. The outer layer is a chemically distinct silicate solid crust, which is underlain by a highly viscous solid mantle. The crust is separated from the mantle. The thickness of the crust varies from about 6 kilometres under the oceans to 30–50 kilometres for the continents. The crust and the cold, rigid, top of the upper mantle are collectively known as the Lithosphere. Beneath it is the Asthenosphere on which the lithosphere rides.

Crust

Mantle

Outer core

Inner core

Uranus   Neptune

Earth's ability to support life depends on its atmosphere.

Atmosphere

The atmosphere of Earth has a layer of gases, commonly known as air. The atmosphere of the Earth protects life by creating pressure on this planet, for liquid water to exist on the Earth. By volume, dry air contains 78.09% nitrogen, 20.95% oxygen, 0.93% argon, 0.04% carbon dioxide, and small amounts of other gases. Air also contains a variable amount of water vapour. Air composition, temperature, and atmospheric pressure vary with altitude. Air which is suitable for use in photosynthesis, and breathing of terrestrial animals is found only in Earth's atmosphere.

Formation of the Moon

Earth's one and only natural satellite is the Moon. Radiometric dating of rocks from the Moon has shown that it was formed at least 30 million years after the solar system.

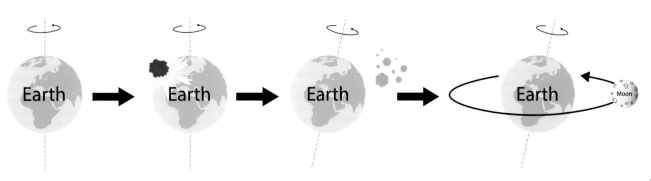

MARS

Mars is the fourth planet from the Sun in our solar system.Mars is also known as the 'Red Planet' since it is red in colour. This signature colour comes from the large amount of a chemical called iron oxide or 'rust' as you might know it in its rocks and soil. It has two moons Phobos and Deimos.

MARS STATS		
Mass	:	6.42 x 1023 kg
Diameter	:	6787 km
Average distance from Sun	:	227,936,640 km
Rotation period	:	1.026 Earth Days
Surface temperature	:	150-310 K

It is described as the "Red Planet", because the iron oxide prevalent on its surface gives it a reddish appearance.

Internal Structure

Mars has approximately half the diameter of Earth. The average thickness of the planet's crust is about 50 kilometres, as compared to the 40-kilometres crust of Earth.

Mars, Earth and the Moon in space

Martian Terrain

Mars is one of the terrestrial planets and consists of minerals containing silicon and oxygen, metals and other elements that rocks are ideally made of. The surface of Mars is primarily composed of tholeiitic basalt.

Atmosphere   Mantle   Crust
      Core

Uranus   Neptune

→

Martian soil is slightly alkaline and contains elements such as magnesium, sodium, potassium and chlorine. These nutrients, necessary for plant growth, are found in the soils found on Earth.

The atmospheric density of the planet of Mars is lowered because of the impact that the solar winds have on it.

Atmosphere

Liquid water cannot exist on Mars due to its low atmospheric pressure, which is about 100 times thinner than the Earth's. But the polar ice caps seem to be made mainly of water.

The atmosphere of Mars comprises about 96 per cent carbon dioxide, 1.93 per cent argon and 1.89 per cent nitrogen with traces of oxygen and water.

Martian soil has a basic pH of 7.7 and contains 0.6 per cent of salt perchlorate.

During the transit, Earth passes between the Sun and Mars.

JUPITER

Jupiter is the largest planet in the solar system. It is two and a half times the total mass of all other planets in the solar system combined. It is the third brightest object in the night sky after the Moon and Venus. Jupiter has 67 known moons. Some of the known moons include Io, Europa, Ganymede and Callisto. The distance of Jupiter from the Sun is 778.5 km.

JUPITER STATS		
Mass	:	1.90 x 1027kg
Diameter	:	142,800 km
Average distance from Sun	:	778,412,020 km
Rotation period	:	0.41 (9.8 Earth hours)
Mean surface temperature	:	120 K (cloud tops)

The Great Red Spot is a huge storm on Jupiter that has raged for at least 350 years. It is so huge that three Earths could fit within it.

Jupiter

The Romans named the planet after the Roman god Jupiter.

SPACE

48

Uranus   Neptune

Magnetic field

Jupiter's magnetic field is 14 times as strong as Earth's, ranging from 0.42 metric tonne at the equator to 1.0 – 1.4 metric tonne at the poles, making it the strongest in the solar system.

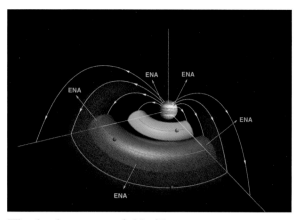

The dipole magnetic field of Jupiter

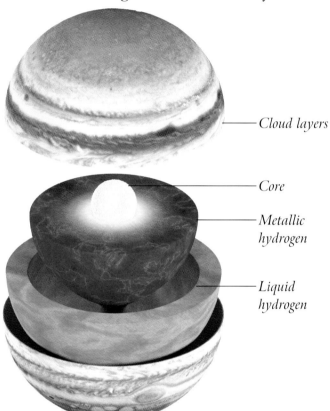

— Cloud layers

— Core

— Metallic hydrogen

— Liquid hydrogen

Rotation

Jupiter's rotation is the fastest amongst all the planets in our solar system. It completes a rotation on its axis in a little less than 10 hours.

The planetary rings of Jupiter: The inner halo, the bright main ring and the outer gossamer ring.

Atmosphere

Jupiter is thought to consist of a dense core with a mixture of elements, a surrounding layer of liquid metallic hydrogen with some helium and an outer layer predominantly of molecular hydrogen.

Rings

Jupiter has a faint planetary ring system of three main segments: an inner "torus" of particles known as the "halo", a relatively bright main ring and an outer gossamer ring. These rings appear to be made of dust.

The four largest moons of Jupiter orbit within this magnetosphere, which protects them from the solar wind

SATURN

Saturn is the sixth
planet from the Sun.
Saturn is a gas giant
with an average radius
around nine times that
of Earth. One-eighth the
average density of Earth,
Saturn is just over 95
times bigger. Saturn
appears to the naked
eye in the night sky as a
bright, yellowish point
of light. It has more
than 30 rings around
it. The notable moons
include Titan, Rhea and
Enceladus.

SATURN STATS		
Mass	:	5.69 x 1026kg
Diameter	:	120660 km
Average distance from Sun	:	1,426,725,400 km
Rotation period	:	0.44 (10.2 Earth hours)
Mean surface temperature	:	88 K (1 bar level)

Saturn's interior

Saturn's interior
is composed of
a core of iron–
nickel and rock. Its
core is surrounded
by a deep layer
of metallic hydrogen,
an intermediate
layer of liquid
hydrogen and liquid
helium, and finally a
gaseous outer layer.

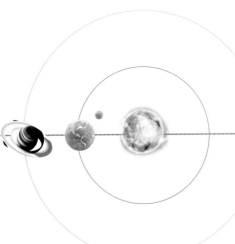

*Saturn orbits the Sun once every
29.4 Earth years.*

*Comparison between Saturn
and Earth*

Uranus Neptune

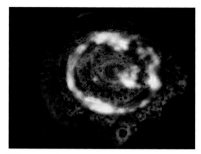

Density

Saturn is the only planet in the solar system that is less dense than water (about 30 per cent less).

Atmosphere

Saturn has a pale yellow hue due to ammonia crystals in its upper atmosphere. It's magnetic field is weaker than the Earth's, but it has a magnetic moment that is 580 times that of Earth due to Saturn's larger size.

The planet chiefly consists of hydrogen.

Rotation

It spins very fast, completing its rotation every 10.7 hours. Saturn has a prominent ring system that consists of nine continuous main rings and three discontinuous arcs, composed chiefly of ice particles and some rocky debris and dust.

Saturn is named after the Roman god of agriculture

Cloud layers

Core

Metallic hydrogen

Liquid hydrogen

Saturn is also known as the gaseous giant as it is majorly made of gases.

A few moons on the outer edge of Saturn's rings keep the rings from expanding and are known as shepherd moons.

URANUS

Uranus is the seventh planet from the Sun. Uranus is the third largest planet in our Solar System in relation to diameter. It is the fourth biggest planet in our Solar System. Saturn, it is also the first planet that was actually discovered in what we call "modern history" by William Herschel. It has 27 known moons and 13 known rings. Some notable moons include Oberon, Titania, Miranda, Ariel and Umbriel.

URANUS STATS		
Mass:	:	8.68 x 1025kg
Diameter	:	51118 km
Average distance from Sun	:	2,870,972,200 km
Rotation period	:	30,685 (84 Earth years)
Mean surface temperature	:	59 K

Uranus makes one trip around the Sun every 84 Earth years.

Internal Structure

The Uranus' internal structure consists of three layers: a rocky core made up of of silicate, iron and nickle. It has an icy mantle in the middle and an outer gaseous hydrogen/helium envelope. The core is relatively small, with a mass of only 0.55 Earth masses and the mantle comprises its bulk.

A rendering of the gas planet Uranus in a clear night sky.

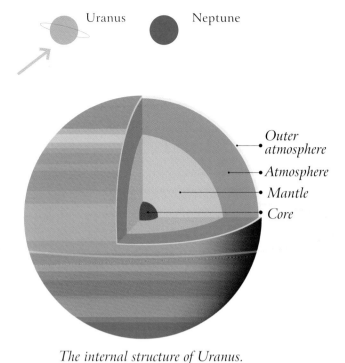

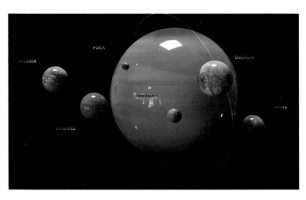

The internal structure of Uranus.

Atmosphere

The methane gas present in the atmosphere absorbs the red wavelengths in sunlight, which makes the planet appear blue.Uranus has a ring system, a magnetosphere and numerous moons. Its axis of rotation is tilted sideways. Its north and south poles, therefore, lie where most other planets have their equators.

It is mainly made of various ices, such as water, ammonia and methane. Hydrogen and helium constitute only a small part of the total.

The stripes on Uranus are not visible because of the methane gas clouds that absorb the red light from the sunlight and reflect only the blue spectrum.

While Uranus appears blue, it has stripes similar to Jupiter and Saturn.

Rotation

Uranus' axis has an almost 98 degree tilt. This means that it rotates on its side. The resulting situation is that it's north pole points only half of the year towards the sun and the south pole points the other half of its year. Daytime on one of the hemisphere means night on the other for 42 Earth years at a time.

Uranus appears blue when observed from Earth.

NEPTUNE

Neptune is the eighth and farthest planet from the Sun. It is 17 times the mass of Earth.

It has fourteen known moons and five rings. Triton one of its well-known moons.

NEPTUNE STATS		
Mass:	:	1.02 x 1026 kg
Diameter	:	49528 km
Average distance from Sun	:	4,498,252,900 km
Rotation period	:	0.67 (19.1 hours)
Mean surface temperature	:	48 K

*Helium and hydrogen
in liquid state*

*Core full
of rocks*

*Liquid water and
ammonia in an extremely
compressed state*

Atmosphere

Neptune's atmosphere is composed primarily of hydrogen and helium, along with traces of hydrocarbons and possibly nitrogen. It contains a higher proportion of "ices" such as water, ammonia and methane. The interior of Neptune is primarily composed of ices and rock.

Neptune has 14 moons.

*Bands of high-altitude clouds
cast shadows on Neptune's
lower cloud deck.*

SPACE

Uranus   Neptune

Its atmosphere forms about five to 10 per cent of its mass and extends perhaps 10 to 20 per cent of the way towards the core, where it reaches pressures of about 100,000 times that of Earth's atmosphere.

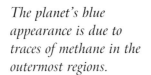

The planet's blue appearance is due to traces of methane in the outermost regions.

At high altitudes, Neptune's atmosphere is 80 per cent hydrogen and 19 per cent helium along with a trace amount of methane.

Its atmosphere is divided into two regions: the lower troposphere, where the temperature decreases with altitude, and the stratosphere, where the temperature increases with altitude. The stratosphere gives way to the thermosphere that gradually transitions to the exosphere.

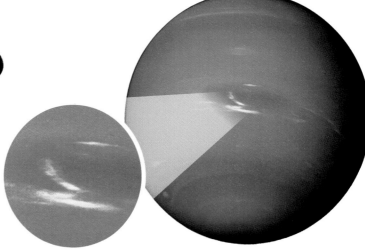

Climate

Neptune has a very active climate. Large storms whirl through its upper atmosphere and high-speed winds blow around the planet at up to 1,300 mph. One of the largest storms ever seen was called the "Great Dark Spot".

VOLCANOES IN SPACE

A volcano is a mountain that faces downward towards a pool of molten rock below the Earth's surface. When pressure builds, eruptions occur. Gases and rocks shoot up through the opening and spill over or fill the air with lava debris. Eruptions cause lateral blasts, lava flows, hot ash flows, mudslides, avalanches, falling ash and floods.

Olympus Mons

Olympus Mons is a shield volcano on Mars. It resembles the shape of the large volcanoes making up the Hawaiian islands. It consists of a central structure that is 22 kilometres high and 700 kilometres wide. It is thrice as high as Mount Everest, making it the tallest mountain in the solar system.

Without magma, Olympus Mons stopped increasing in length and size.

Venus's highest volcano Maat Mons

Volcano Types

Shield Volcano

This type of volcano tends to erupt as basalt lava. Since basalt is more watery, it can flow on the surface better. When these types of volcanoes erupt, the lava flows outwards over or across large distances.

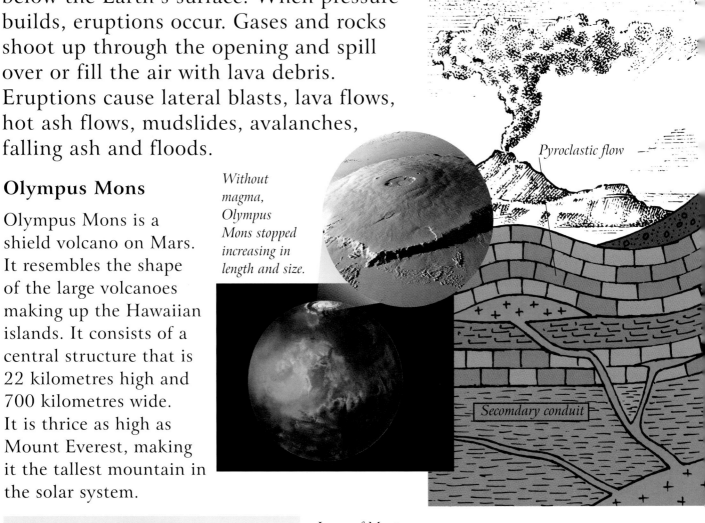

Pyroclastic flow

Secomdary conduit

Image of Maat Mons on Venus created by NASA using data from the Magellan spacecraft's radar.

Maat Mons

More than three-fourths of Venus's surface consists of volcanic plain, where the lava flow hardened more than 80 million years ago. There are several hundreds of volcanoes around the planet. Maat Mons is the highest. Its peak is five kilometres above the surface.

SPACE

Stratovolcano

Ash-cinder
Volcano

Cinder cones form out of ejected
tephra, magma and ash.
When cinder cones spew out lava, it
splatters across the air. Eventually, it
settles and cools down, becoming part
of the cone-like features.

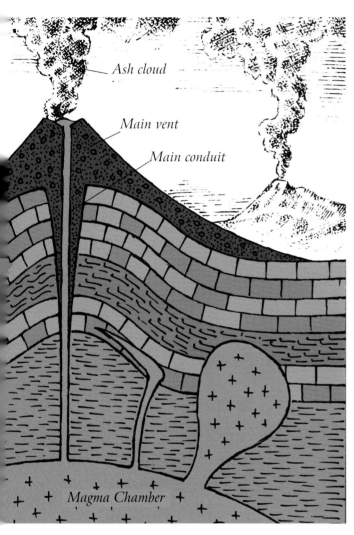

Ash cloud

Main vent

Main conduit

Magma Chamber

Volcanic Io

Io is the most active volcano in the solar system. There are no signs of impact craters on its surface. This is because they are rapidly filled with volcanic material the moment that they appear.

This image shows two volcanic plumes
on Io, a moon of Jupiter.

Triton

When the Voyager 2 spacecraft flew past Triton, Neptune's moon, it discovered geyser-like plumes ejecting from its surface. These occurred as the result of "cryovolcanism". This activity is triggered in regions where the Sun's light pierces the frozen nitrogen ice covering its surface. The material is heated and vaporised, thereby creating a greenhouse effect.

Triton, moon of planet Neptune

RINGS OF SPACE

There are huge rings of material that encircle the four largest planets in our solar system. The rings of Jupiter, Saturn, Uranus and Neptune are made of different gases. Saturn's rings are the biggest and brightest. The planetary rings must constantly be refilled with new dust from the planet's moons to exist.

An artist's representation of the rings of Saturn showing the division of the rings as shown by images from the NASA spacecraft, Cassini.

SPACE

Saturn's Rings

An astronomer named Galileo was the first person to see Saturn's rings. He spotted them while looking into space through a telescope in 1610. That's almost 400 years ago! Saturn's mesmerizing rings are made of ice and rock of various sizes.

Some pieces are as small as a grain of sand. Others as large as a house. But scientists aren't sure when or how Saturn's rings formed. They believe the rings might have something to do with Saturn's many moons.

Saturn has the largest rings in our solar system spanning up to 175,000 miles

Encke Division

Cassini Division

A Ring

B Ring

C Ring

D Ring

E Ring

F Ring

G Ring

Saturn's B-ring is its largest and brightest, also in terms of mass.

Jupiter rings

Jupiter is circled by three rings. The innermost, cloud-like ring is called the "halo ring". Next is the main ring, narrow and thin. Beyond the main ring are the two nearly transparent gossamer rings. Its rings are made of tiny rock fragments and dust.

Neptune's rings

Neptune has six rings. These unusual rings are not uniform, but possess bright thick clumps of dust called "arcs". The rings are thought to be relatively young. Earth-based observations of the year 2005 found Neptune's rings far more unstable than previously thought, some dwindling away rapidly. NASA's Voyager 2 satellite was the first and as yet only spacecraft to visit Neptune on Aug. 25, 1989.

Rings of Uranus

Uranus's Rings

The rings of Uranus were discovered on March 10, 1977, by James L. Elliot, Edward W. Dunham, and Jessica Mink. They are very dark and faint. The majority of Uranus's rings are opaque and only a few kilometres wide. The ring system contains little dust overall; it consists mostly of large bodies 20 cm to 20 m in diameter.

CRATERS

These are geologic structures that form when a large meteoroid, asteroid or comet crashes into a planet or satellite. When an asteroid strikes the solid surface of a planet, it generates a shock wave. This wave spreads outwards from the site of the impact. It breaks the rock, resulting in a large cavities.

Asteroid

Lunar crater(Earth's moon)

Manicouagan Impact Crater in Quebec, Canada, is one of the largest known terrestrial impact craters. It is 65 kilometers (40 miles) in diameter.

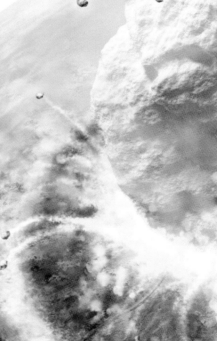

SPACE

Endurance crater (Mars)

Parts of a Crater

Floor – It is the bottom of a crater that is either bowl-shaped or flat. It is usually below ground-level.

Central peaks – For larger craters, of a few tens of kilometers in diameter the excavated crater becomes so great it collapses on itself. This material hat falling back into the crater forces itself it up the mound, forming the central peak.

Walls – These are the steep interior sides of a crater. They may have huge stair-like terraces that are created by collapsing walls.

Rim – It is the edge of the crater. It is elevated above the nearby terrain as it is composed of material that is pushed up at the edge.

Ejecta – It refers to the rock material thrown out of the crater in the event of an impact. It is distributed outwards from the crater's rim onto the planet's surface as debris.

Rays – These are bright streaks that extend away from the crater. At times, these extend for great distances and are composed of ejecta debris and material.

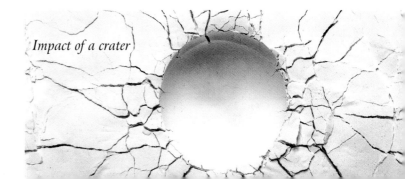

Impact of a crater

WATER AND SPACE

Extraterrestrial liquid water is liquid found beyond Earth. It is one of the key prerequisites for the existence of extraterrestrial life. Earth is the only planet known to have stable bodies of liquid water, which is essential to support all known life forms.

Reservoirs of ice still hidden below Mars' surface.

Enceladus

Enceladus, a moon of Saturn, has geysers of water and a subsurface ocean. The blue-green "tiger stripes" are thought to be the source of Enceladus's water jets.

Ganymede

The subsurface saline ocean theorised to exist on Ganymede is estimated to be 100 kilometres deep. The surface lying below is a crust of 150 kilometres of ice.

Scientists using the Hubble Space Telescope have discovered that Jupiter's largest natural satellite, Ganymede, has an ocean buried beneath its icy surface.

Europa

It is predicted that the outer crust of solid ice on Europa (one of Jupiter's smallest moons) is approximately 10–30 kilometres thick. This puts the volume of Europa's oceans at slightly more than twice the volume of Earth's oceans.

Icy Mars

Water on Mars exists almost entirely as ice, with a small amount present in the atmosphere as vapour. No large standing bodies of liquid water exist because the atmospheric pressure at the surface is only 0.6 per cent of Earth's mean sea level pressure. The global average temperature is far too low for water in its liquid form, leading to either rapid evaporation or freezing (210 K or −63 °C).

The icy surface of Europa is strewn with cracks, ridges and chaotic terrain, where the surface has been disrupted and ice blocks have moved around.

DWARF PLANETS

Dwarf planets are similar to the eight planets, but are smaller. Like planets, they are large, roundish objects that orbit the Sun. Our solar system has six dwarf planets, namely, Eris, Pluto, Ceres, Makemake, Haumea and the unnamed V774104.

Eris

Eris was only discovered in the year 2003.

Eris

Studies show that this dwarf planet has a surface even more reflective than Earth's snow, suggesting that it's covered in a thin layer of ice.

Theoretical structure of Pluto

Pluto

Pluto

Pluto is the second largest dwarf planet after Eris. Pluto's orbit is a long way from elliptical, which implies that its distance from the Sun can change significantly. Pluto's surface is one of the coldest places in the solar system at roughly -225 °C.

Ceres

Close up of the dwarf planet Ceres.

Ceres

Ceres is the smallest dwarf planet. It is the largest object in the asteroid belt, which lies between the orbits of Mars and Jupiter. It is composed of rock and ice. Approximately a quarter of its weight is water. The surface contains iron-rich clays. Ceres is a possible destination for human colonisation given its abundance of ice, water and minerals.

Comparison of the size of Ceres with Earth and the Moon

Haumea

Image of Haumea and its two moons, Hi'iaka (below) and Namaka (above)

Haumea

It is one of the fastest rotating objects in our solar system. It completes a rotation on its axis every four hours. The rapid spinning has elongated the dwarf planet into a unique shape. It is one of the densest dwarf planets.

Makemake

Makemake is the second brightest object in the Kuiper belt, after Pluto.

Makemake

Makemake is a dwarf planet in the outer solar system. It is reddish brown in colour, leading scientists to conclude that it contains a layer of methane on its surface.

EARTH'S MOON

The Moon is Earth's only natural satellite. It is a cold, rocky body that is about 3,476 kilometres in diameter. It does not have a light of its own, but shines by the sunlight reflected from its surface. The Moon is thought to have formed nearly 4.5 billion years ago.

Phases of Earth's moon.

Outer core
Inner core
Crust
Mantle
Inner mantle

Internal Structure

The Moon has a distinct crust, mantle and core. The core mostly contains of iron, but also contain large amounts of sulphur and other elements. Its mantle is made up of dense rocks rich in iron and magnesium. The outermost part of the crust is broken due to large impacts.

The Moon

Earth

The Sun

Due to its reddish colour, a totally eclipsed Moon is sometimes referred to as "Blood Moon".

Moon's surface

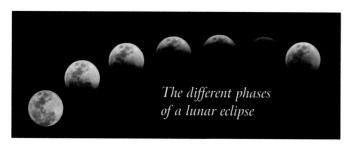

The different phases of a lunar eclipse

Lunar Tides

The Moon's gravity pulls at Earth, causing rises and falls in sea levels known as "tides". High tides are when water bulges upward and low tides are when water drops down. High tides result on the side of Earth nearest to the Moon.

The Earth' Moon is the second densest of all known satellites.

Unlike a solar eclipse, lunar eclipses are safe to view without any special precautions.

Lunar Eclipse

A lunar eclipse occurs when the Moon passes directly behind Earth, into its umbra (shadow). This can occur only when the Sun, Earth and the Moon are aligned exactly with Earth in the middle.

A lunar eclipse may be viewed from anywhere on the night side of Earth. A lunar eclipse lasts for a few hours.

Lunar eclipse

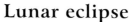

Penumbra

Earth's orbit

Umbra

SUN

EARTH

Moon

Moon's orbit

Gravity

The Moon has a much weaker gravity than Earth, due to its smaller mass, so one would weigh about one-sixth (16.5%) of their weight on Moon.

Atmosphere

The Moon has a very thin atmosphere. Temperatures range from 134 °C to -153 °C.

A solar eclipse occurs in the day time, when the Moon is between Earth and the Sun, while a lunar eclipse occurs at night when Earth passes between the Sun and the Moon.

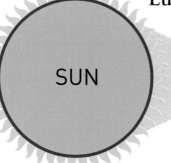

MARTIAN MOONS

Mars has two moons, Phobos and Deimos. Phobos and Deimos resemble asteroids more than moons. They are two of the smallest moons in the solar system.

Phobos

Mars is described as the "Red Planet", because the iron oxide on its surface gives it a reddish appearance.

Phobos (Mars I) is the larger and closer of the two natural satellites of Mars. A small, irregularly shaped object with a mean radius of 11 kilometres, it is seven times more massive than Mars's outer moon, Deimos.

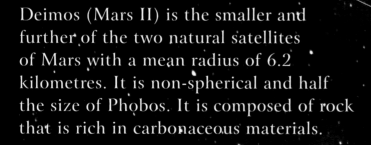

Deintos, the smaller moon of Mars

Deimos (Mars II) is the smaller and further of the two natural satellites of Mars with a mean radius of 6.2 kilometres. It is non-spherical and half the size of Phobos. It is composed of rock that is rich in carbonaceous materials.

Deimos looks like a smaller irregular moon.

An artist's representation of the planet Mars along with one of its moons, Phobos, orbiting around it.

Phobos is heavily cratered, with the most prominent crater being Stickney. Many grooves and streaks cover the oddly–shaped surface. The grooves are typically less than 30 metres deep, 100–200 metres wide and up to 20 kilometres long.

Both moons are tidally locked, always presenting the same face towards Mars.

Mars

Deimos is cratered, but the surface is noticeably smoother than that of Phobos. This is due to the partial filling of craters with regolith (a layer of loose, heterogeneous material covering solid rock). The regolith is highly porous.

JOVIAN MOONS

Jupiter has a total of 67 known moons. Due to its large size, Jupiter has a large area of gravitational stability to support many moons. The moons of Jupiter have orbital periods ranging from seven hours to almost three Earth years.

A series of dark lines known as lineae are seen across the surface of Europa.

Comparison between Jupiter and its moons

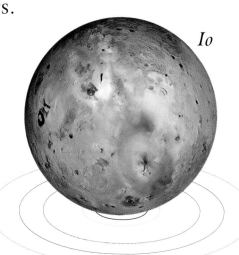

Io

Io

It is the driest known object in the solar system. Io has over 400 active volcanoes that produce plumes of sulphur and sulphur dioxide that climb as high as 500 kilometres above the surface. Io's surface is also dotted with more than 100 mountains.

The four Galilean moons orbiting Jupiter.

Europa

Europa

This is the smallest of the four Galilean satellites. Europa has an outer layer of water around 100 kilometres thick; some in the form of frozen ice above the crust and some as liquid ocean beneath the ice. Europa is one of the smoothest objects in the solar system.

The crust and the interior of the Galilean moon Callisto.

Callisto

Callisto is the most heavily cratered object in the solar system. Its composition consists of magnesium and iron-bearing hydrated silicates, carbon dioxide, sulphur dioxide and possibly ammonia and other organic compounds.

Scientists have observed oceanic movements on the surface of Ganymede through the Hubble Space Telescope.

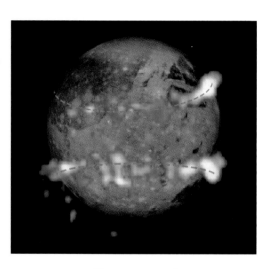

Ganymede

It is the largest moon in the solar system. Its average density suggests a composition of approximately equal parts rocky material and water, mainly ice. Some additional volatile ices such as ammonia may also be present.

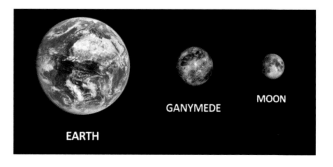

GANYMEDE

MOON

EARTH

Ganymede compared with Earth and the Moon

SATURN'S MOONS

Saturn has 62 moons. The moons of Saturn range from tiny moonlets less than one km in length, to the gigantic Titan, which is larger than Mercury.

Titan comprises more than 96 per cent of the mass in orbit around Saturn.

Titan has an atmosphere thicker than Earth's.

Titan

An image showing the bright trailing hemisphere, with part of the dark area appearing on the right.

Iapetus

Iapetus

Iapetus is the third-largest moon of Saturn. It is known to be composed primarily of water, with fewer rocks. The most striking feature of Iapetus is its dual colouration. The leading hemisphere of the satellite is coal-black, while its rear is brighter.

Titan

It is the only object besides Earth, where clear evidence of stable bodies of surface liquid has been found. Large areas of Titan's surface are covered with sand dunes made of hydrocarbon.

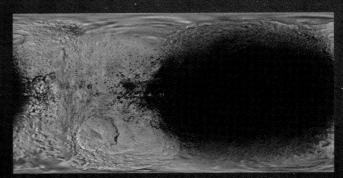

An image providing a closer look at the dark side of Iapetus, that helps it hide when observing from Earth.

Saturn along with its satellites in space

NASA's Cassini spacecraft found a Pac-Man-like shape on Tethys.

Tethys

Tethys is made of water ice. The frigid surface is highly reflective. A giant crater known as the "Odysseus Crater" covers almost two-fifth of the moon's diameter. Tethys is the third closest of the major moons.

Tethys

Rhea

Rhea

Virtual image of Rhea, named after the Titan Rhea of Greek mythology, "mother of the gods".

Dione

Fractures dividing older craters on Dione. The ones running from upper right to lower left are the Carthage Fossae, while Pactolus Catena runs horizontally on the lower right.

Rhea

Rhea is the second-largest moon of Saturn. It is the only moon that has oxygen in its atmosphere. In addition to the oxygen, carbon dioxide has also been found in traces, indicating that it could support life.

Dione

Dione is the 15th largest moon in the solar system. It is composed primarily of water ice, but since it is the third densest moon of Saturn, it has denser material like silicate rock in its interior.

Rhea, mid-sized moon of Saturn

An artist's representation of Dione in comparison to the other moons of Saturn.

COMETS

Comets are cosmic snowballs of frozen gases, rock and dust that orbit the Sun. When frozen, they are the size of a small town. When a comet's orbit brings it close to the Sun, it heats up and spews dust and gases into a giant glowing head larger than most planets. The dust and gases form a tail that stretches away from the Sun for millions of miles. There are likely billions of comets orbiting our Sun in the Kuiper Belt and the even more distant Oort Cloud.

Nucleus

The nucleus is a solid, core structure of a comet. It is composed of an amalgamation of rock, dust, water ice and frozen gases such as carbon dioxide, carbon monoxide, methane and ammonia.

The astronomical symbol for comets also consists of "a small disc with three hair-like extensions",.

Coma or Tail

The force exerted on the comet by the Sun's radiation, pressure and solar wind causes streams of dust and gas to be released. These form a huge and thin atmosphere called the "coma". As it approaches, a huge "tail" is formed. When a comet moves in space, it forms two distinct tails; one each for the trail of dust and gas.

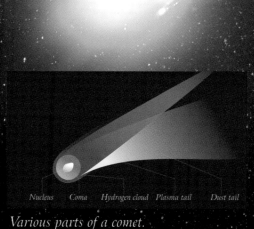

Nucleus   Coma   Hydrogen cloud   Plasma tail   Dust tail

Various parts of a comet.

The nucleus of Comet 103P/ Hartley as seen during a spacecraft flyby. This nucleus is about two kilometres in length.

The Giotto Photo of Halley's.

A comet, an asteroid, a meteorite glows, enters the Earth's atmosphere.

Halley's Comet

Halley's Comet or Comet Halley is a short-period comet visible from Earth every 75 –76 years. Halley's Comet is the only short-period comet that is clearly visible to the naked eye from Earth. Halley's Comet has hills, mountains, ridges, depressions and at least one crater. It consists of water, carbon monoxide, carbon dioxide and other ices as well as coal.

Edmund Halley, the one who discovered Halley's comet.

ASTEROIDS

Asteroids are minor planets. They are comets found in the inner solar system. The term "asteroid" has now increasingly come to refer to "the small bodies of the inner solar system outside of the orbit of Jupiter".

Origin

There are millions of asteroids. Many of these are thought to be the shattered remnants of planetesimals. Planetesimals were bodies within the Sun's solar nebula that didn't grow large enough to form planets.

A representation of the impact that will cause the mass extinction of life on Earth

Composition

A large majority of known asteroids orbit in the asteroid belt which lies between Mars and Jupiter. The majority of the asteroids fall into three main groups: C-type, S-type and M-type. They are named for their compositions. They are generally identified by carbon-rich, stony and metallic compositions, with the same initials, respectively.

Extinction

An extinction event is a widespread and rapid decrease in the amount of life on Earth. The most recent extinction occurred approximately 66 million years ago. This was the Cretaceous – Paleogene extinction event, which was mostly caused by asteroid impacts.

An artist's rendition of an impact event: Dinosaurs were killed by the Cretaceous-Paleogene extinction event.

The asteroid belt that lies between the orbits of Mars and Jupiter.

METEORITES

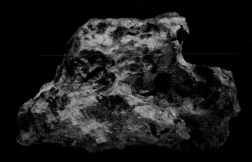

Iron meteorite Gibeon which impacted Namibia.

Meteorites are fragments of rock and/or metal that fall from space to Earth. They break away from large extraterrestrial bodies and can measure anything from a fraction of a millimetre to the size of a football pitch and bigger.

If a meteoroid, comet, asteroid or any piece withstands the wear from its atmospheric entry and impacts the ground, it is called a meteorite.

A meteoroid is a small, rocky or metallic body travelling through space. Objects that are smaller than one metre are classified as micrometeoroids.

Hoba meteorite Grootfontein, Grootfontein District Otjozondjupa Region, Namibia

Meteor shower

A meteor shower is caused by an interaction between a planet such as Earth and streams of debris from a comet. These streams are also known as a "dust trail". Millions of meteors arrive in Earth's atmosphere daily. Most of them are about the size of a grain of sand. Meteors may occur in showers. A meteor shower is "a celestial event in which a number of meteors are observed to radiate or originate from one point in the night sky".

Shooting star

A meteor or a "shooting star" is the passage of a meteoroid or micrometeoroid into Earth's atmosphere. Here, it becomes incandescent from air friction and starts shedding glowing material in its wake. This is sufficient to create a visible streak of light.

BLACK HOLES

We've seen that medium stars die off by fading into black dwarfs, and giants and supergiants explode into supernovas. It is interesting to know that such explosions don't dissipate all the matter of the star. The largest stars can leave behind a core larger than four times the mass of our Sun. These remnants of stars may form black holes. A black hole is mathematically defined as a region of space so dense that nothing can escape its gravitational field.

Many spiral galaxies may have black holes at their centre.

Depicting a black hole that would theoretically allow for faster than speed of light travel. Due to the fact that nothing escapes the field of a black hole, including light, X-rays, radio waves and other forms of electromagnetic radiation, they are very hard to detect.

Distorting space-time

An interesting fact about black holes is their distortion of space and time as a by-product. They tend to warp the space around them as well as cause time dilation, causing time to pass slower as matter gets closer to the black hole. As a result, they may create wormholes that allow faster-than-light time travel.

An artist's impression of an accretion disc. An accretion disc is formed due to the heating of matter as it enters the black hole. It is a bright phenomenon.

At the centre of our galaxy lies the supermassive black hole Sagittarius A*, often abbreviated Sgr A*. This giant hole is about 4 million times the mass of the Sun and about 23.6 million kilometers in diameter. Around Sgr A* swirls a ring of debris known as an accretion disk.

A diagrammatic representation of the fabric of time.

Event horizon

The event horizon is a boundary in space-time through which matter and light can only pass inward towards the black hole. Not even light can escape from within the event horizon. The boundary is named as an event horizon because no information about an event occurring inside this horizon will pass outside.

A black hole keeps sucking in light as well as everything that lies within its gravitational reach.

A wormhole, showing both the mouths and throat.

Mouth of the wormhole

Throat of the wormhole.

Mouth of the wormhole

WORMHOLES

Wormhole is just a theory. No evidence exists proving wormholes exist or existed in the past.

1. Researchers believe a wormhole could connect different parts of the universe that are billions of light-years away, to different points of time (time travel) or even an alternate universe.

2. A wormhole in theory could be used to travel faster than the speed of light, allowing humans to explore the galaxy and the observable universe. The term wormhole was coined in 1957 by American theoretical physicist John Archibald Wheeler in a paper that was co-authored by American physicist Charles Misner.

What do wormholes look like?

They have two (possibly spheroidal) mouths that are connected by a throat, which could be straight or winding. You can image a wormhole as a tunnel that has two ends, both going to different points in spacetime. These points can lead to different locations, different points in time or a combination of both.

Stability

A wormhole is also called an Einstein-Rosen bridge or an Einstein-Rosen wormhole. However, recent research suggests that a wormhole containing "exotic" matter could remain open and unchanged for longer periods.

Exotic matter

Exotic matter contains negative energy density and huge negative pressure. If a wormhole contained adequate exotic matter, it could be used as a means of sending information or travellers through space.

Time travel

A wormhole could also connect two different universes. Some scientists speculate that if one mouth of a wormhole is positioned in a certain manner, time travel would become possible. There is a possibility that the addition of "regular" matter could destabilise the wormhole as well.

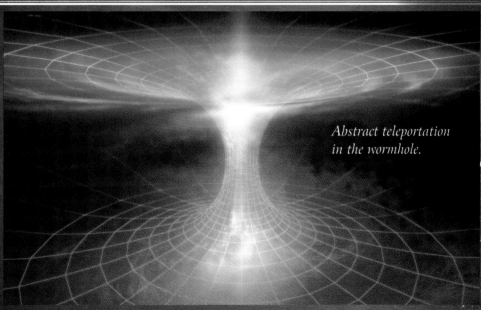

Abstract teleportation in the wormhole.

Too small for time travel

Wormholes such as these might prove to be too small and brief for human time travel.

Wormholes and the Theory of General Relativity

Physicists Albert Einstein and Nathan Rosen used the Theory of General Relativity in 1935 to suggest that "bridges" connecting two different points in space and time may exist, reducing the travelling time and distance.

Speedy travel

Wormholes could allow superluminal or faster-than-light travel. If two points are connected by a wormhole, then the time taken to cross it would be less than the time taken by a light beam to travel through space outside the wormhole.

A tunnel in space

In space, masses that place pressure on different parts of the universe could eventually combine to create a kind of tunnel. This tunnel would, in theory, join two separate times and allow passage between them.

OBSERVING SPACE

The observation of space and the theories related to celestial objects and their behaviour fall under the umbrella of Astronomy.

An artist's representation of the night sky as observed by a satellite.

Hubble Space Telescope

Hubble Space Telescope takes extremely high-resolution images with almost no background light. As a result, it has recorded some of the most detailed visible-light images. Many have led to breakthroughs in astrophysics, such as accurately determining the rate of expansion of the universe.

Amateur Astronomy

Amateur astronomers use the unaided eye, binoculars or telescopes to view the moon, planets, stars, comets, meteor showers, star clusters, galaxies and nebulae.

An amateur skygazer looks through a basic, manual telescope. This needs to be pointed and focussed by hand.

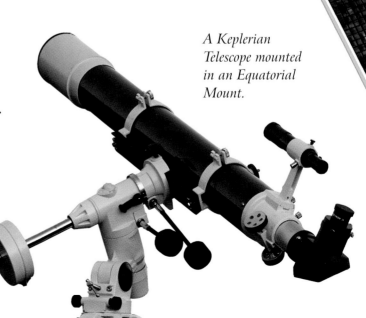

Telescopes

A telescope is an instrument that aids in the observation of remote objects by enhancing images. The simplest telescope has just two lenses. A telescope mount supports the mass of the telescope and allows for accurate pointing of the instrument. The Arecibo requires only a few minutes of observation to collect adequate energy for analysis.

A Keplerian Telescope mounted in an Equatorial Mount.

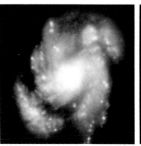 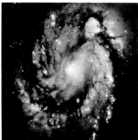

The spiral galaxy M100, shot with HST before and after corrective optics.

Observatories

An observatory consists of telescopes and supporting instruments through which you can observe celestial objects. Every observatory focuses on different aspects of space such as the Sun moon and stars.

The IAU 26th General Assembly, Prague

IAU

The International Astronomical Union is the internationally recognised authority for assigning designations to celestial bodies such as stars, planets, asteroids, etc. It classified Pluto as a dwarf planet, thereby reducing the number of planets in the solar system to eight.

The Hubble being deployed from Space Shuttle Discovery in 1990.

SETI

The search for extra-terrestrial intelligence or SETI is the collective name for numerous activities undertaken search for intelligent, extra-terrestrial life. Electromagnetic radiation is monitored for signs of transmissions from civilisations on other worlds.

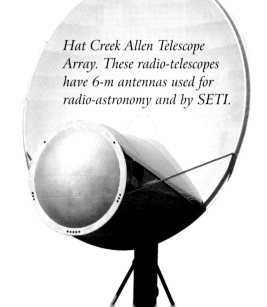

Hat Creek Allen Telescope Array. These radio-telescopes have 6-m antennas used for radio-astronomy and by SETI.

ROCKETS

Rockets are vehicles used to send manned spacecraft, unmanned space probes and satellites into space. The force of exhaust gases from the rear of the rocket, produced by the combustion of the fuel in its engine, leads to pressure called "thrust" which pushes the rocket in the opposite direction of the exhaust flow.

Energy requirement

Rockets need energy in the form of fuel to propel into space. The fuel that is used to power rockets can be divided into two major categories: liquid and solid.

A rocket designed for space flight

Stages of launch and design

The first stage's function is to impart the initial thrust needed to overcome Earth's gravity and to lift the entire weight of the vehicle, and its payload, off of Earth. At the second stage, the rocket engines and propellants continue to speed up the vehicle.

The fuel is at a high pressure and when it combusts, it bursts out of the exhaust at the bottom of the rocket, that enables it to liftoff into Earth's orbit or beyond.

1. **Liquid fuels**: These fuels range from an easily available one such as kerosene, used upwards of ground temperature, to liquid hydrogen ("cryogenic" fuel), which must be maintained at the extremely low temperature of minus 253 Celsius. Another liquid fuel, hypergolic, immediately lights upon contact with an oxidiser. These fuels are tremendously lethal and thus difficult to manage.

2. Solid fuels: These are simple in design, like big fireworks. They have a casing filled with a rubbery mixture of solid compounds that burn quickly once ignited. Solid rocket motors burn their fuel until it is exhausted. The exhaust from the fuel burning comes out through a nozzle at the bottom of the rocket casing and provides a forward thrust.

An extremely high amount of heat and pressure is built up under the rocket pushing it off the ground. Once the fuel has been used up, the tank separates from the rocket and becomes space debris.

The two rocket launchers strapped to the spacecraft to enable the launch.

HUMANS IN SPACE

Human spaceflight is space travel with a crew aboard the spacecraft. Humanity has been been able to leave Earth's atmosphere and enter space.

Space Launch

Space launch is the earliest part of any lift-off which is the first phase of space flight.

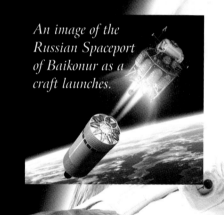

An image of the Russian Spaceport of Baikonur as a craft launches.

Current flight capabilities

China's Chang'e 4 lander and Yutu 2 rover made an epic landing on January 3rd at the Von Kármán crater on the far side of the moon. The mission marks the first time that any spacecraft has soft-landed on the moon's far side. It's was a challenging feat because the moon blocks signals to our planet, so the vehicles require supplemental satellite relays to stay in touch with Earth.

Commercial spaceflight

History was made as Virgin Galactic's SpaceShipTwo, VSS Unity, landed from her maiden spaceflight to cheers from Richard Branson and the Virgin Galactic teams and The Spaceship Company on December 13th, 2018.

Not only was this the first human spaceflight to be launched from American soil since the final Space Shuttle mission in 2011, but the very first time that a crewed vehicle built for commercial, passenger service, reached space.

Pictured here is Astronaut Bruce McCandless floating free in space with the help of a space suit and Manned Manoeuvring Unit.

An astronaut using a space simulation capsule to get used to the loss of gravity.

Effects of spaceflight on humans

Spaceflight has many negative effects on the body. The environment of space is lethal without appropriate protection.

The vacuum of space

The vacuum of space results in the removal of all gases, including oxygen, from the bloodstream. After nine to 12 seconds, deoxygenated blood reaches the brain and results in a loss of consciousness. Death would gradually follow after two minutes of exposure.

The effects of weightlessness

Weightlessness has harmful effects on human health. It can cause muscle atrophy. In the absence of gravity, fluids tend to build up in the upper half of the body. This causes balance disorders, distorted vision and a lossof taste a nd smell.

Increased radiation levels

Without the protection of Earth's atmosphere and magnetosphere, astronauts are exposed to high levels of radiation. This can damage lymphocytes, the cells involved in maintaining the immune system, leading to lower immunity. Solar flare events, while rare, can administer a fatal dose of radiation.

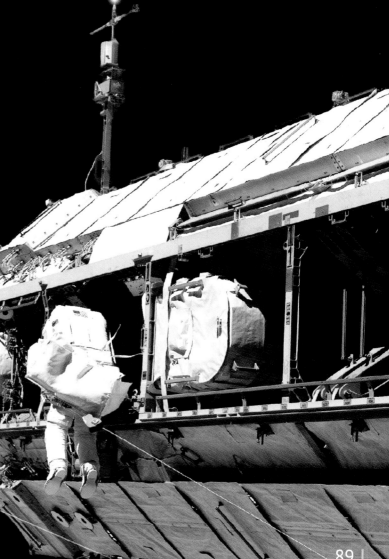

Astronaut in outer space photographed against the backdrop of Earth.

SPACE DEBRIS

Space debris is the collection of defunct objects in orbit around Earth. It is also popularly known as orbital debris, space junk and space waste. Space debris include spent rocket stages, old satellites and fragments from disintegration, erosion and collisions. As orbits overlap with new spacecrafts, debris may collide with operational spacecrafts and pose a significant hazard.

There are estimated to be over 128 million pieces of debris smaller than 1 cm (0.39 in) as of January 2019. There are approximately 900,000 pieces from one to ten cm. The current count of large debris (defined as 10 cm across or larger) is 34,000. There are over 300,000 pieces larger than one centimetres that are estimated to exist below the 2000 kilometres altitude. For a standard of comparison, the International Space Station orbits in the 300–400 kilometres range.

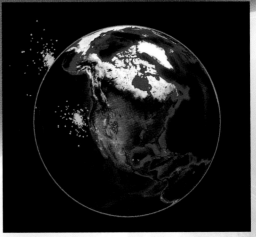

Space debris in Earth's orbit

Most space debris are smaller than one cm. They include the following:

- dust from solid rocket motors
- products of surface degradation, such as paint flakes
- frozen coolant droplets that are released from RORSAT nuclear-powered satellites

A comparatively big piece of space debris, measuring about five centimetres.

Hazards posed

Impacts of debris particles cause erosive damage. Damage can be reduced by the addition of ballistic shielding to the spacecraft. An example is a "whipple shield", which is used to protect some parts of the International Space Station. The number of objects in space influence the chance of collision.

Kessler syndrome

A chain reaction known as the "Kessler syndrome" would rapidly increase the number of debris objects in orbit. It would greatly increase the risk of operating satellites. The cost of space missions would increase greatly. Hence, measurement, growth mitigation and removal of debris are activities that are taken seriously within the space industry today.

An artist's conception of an orbital band of garbage and junk circling Earth.

SATELLITES

A satellite is an artificial object that has been intentionally placed into orbit, unlike natural satellites like the moon. The world's first artificial satellite, Sputnik 1, was launched by the Soviet Union in 1957.

Launch and functioning

Satellites are propelled by rockets that launch from land. Some satellites are launched at sea, while others can be launched from planes.

Current status

A few hundred satellites are currently operational. Space probes have been placed around the Moon, Mercury, Venus, Mars, Jupiter, Saturn, Vesta, Eros and the Sun, becoming their artificial satellites.

Uses

Common satellite classifications include military and civilian Earth observation satellites, communications satellites, navigation satellites, weather satellites and research satellites. Space stations and human spacecraft in orbit also fall under the category of satellites.

The first artificial satellite displayed in the exhibition in GUM, 2011, at the State Central Museum of Contemporary History of Russia.

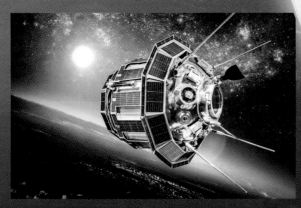

Space satellite orbiting Earth with the Sun in the background.

Communications Satellites

A communications satellite is an artificial satellite for the purpose of telecommunications. It is used for communications to ships, vehicles, planes, as well as for TV and radio broadcasting.

This satellite, called the AEHF, is used for secure radio communications

Pictured here is a full-size model of Earth observation satellite ERS 2.

Satellite telephones

Telephone calls from landline telephones are relayed to an Earth station. From here, they are transmitted to a geostationary satellite. Satellite communications provide connections to Antarctica, rigs at sea, aeroplanes, and serve as a backup for hospitals.

Television

Television requires simultaneous geosynchronous satellites to deliver relatively few signals of large bandwidth to many receivers, a requirement of televisions.

Internet

Satellite communication technology is used to connect to the Internet via broadband data connections. This is very useful for users located in remote areas who cannot access a cable-based broadband connection, or for those who require high availability of services.

A life-size, cut-away model of a Venera type Venus communication lander on display.

Radio

A satellite radio is a digital radio signal that is broadcast by a communications satellite. It covers a much wider geographical range than terrestrial radio signals.

93

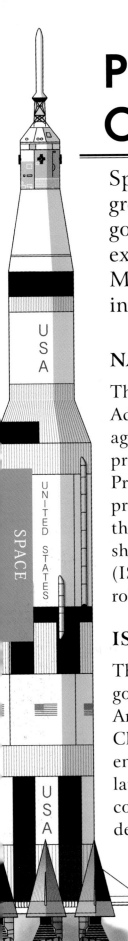

PROMINENT SPACE ORGANISATIONS

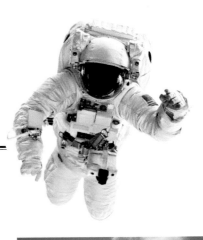

Space exploration requires a great amount of resources. Thus, governmental agencies co-ordinate and execute space exploration programmes. Multiple private space agencies are also interested in spaceflight.

NASA's motto is "for the benefit of all". Depicted here is its seal

NASA

The National Aeronautics and Space Administration (NASA) is the government agency of the USA responsible for the civilian space programme, and aeronautics and aerospace research. President Eisenhower established NASA in 1958. Their programmes include the Apollo moon-landing missions, the Skylab space station and the invention of the space shuttle. It supports the International Space Station (ISS). It focuses on exploring bodies with advanced robotic missions.

The ISRO logo.

ISRO

The Indian Space Research Organisation(ISRO), India's government space agency, built India's first satellite, Aryabhata. ISRO sent its first mission to the moon, Chandrayaan-1, in 2008. The Mars Orbiter Mission entered the Mars orbit in 2014. On 22 July 2019, India launched its second moon mission, Chandrayaan-2. It lost contact with the Vikram lander and its rover. The ISRO declared in August 20020 that, 'Though the soft-landing attempt (of the lander carrying the rover) was not successful, the orbiter, which was equipped with eight scientific instruments, was successfully placed in the lunar orbit. The orbiter completed more than 4,400 orbits around the Moon and all the instruments are currently performing well.'

Chandrayaan-2

ESA

European Space Agency

The European Space Agency(ESA) is an intergovernmental organisation with 20 member states. Its headquarters are in Paris, France. ESA is responsible for setting a unified space and related industrial policy, recommending space objectives to the member states and integrating national programmes for satellite development, into the European programmes as much as possible.

SpaceX, a company run by Elon Musk, launched the world's most powerful reusable rocket for the first time in history in 2013. This was the first time that a space rocket operated by a private company took off, carrying with it a very expensive sports car!

The Roscosmos logo. Roscosmos is headquartered at Shchepkin Street 42, Moscow.

POCKOCMOC

RFSA

The Russian Federal Space Agency (RFSA) is responsible for the Russian space programme and aerospace research. It is headquartered in Moscow. It contributed to the ISS and continued to fly additional Soyuz missions. Some future projects are the Soyuz successor and scientific robotic missions to one of the Mars moons.

Japan Aerospace Exploration Agency's logo

Japan Aerospace Exploration Agency (JAXA)

JAXA is Japan's national aerospace agency. Established in 2003 it is headquartered in Tokyo. JAXA's projects include, the Advanced Land Observation Satellite, carbon dioxide monitoring and rainfall observation. JAXA is also developing technology for supersonic transport.

The Soyuz TMA-9 spacecraft launches from the Baikonur Cosmodrome in Kazakhstan on 18th September 2006 carrying a new crew to the International Space Station.

The science museum at Nagoya displaying a rocket outside.

MOON LANDING

A moon landing is the arrival of a spacecraft on the surface of the moon. Moon landings include both manned and unmanned or robotic missions. The first human-made object to reach the surface of the moon was the Soviet Union's Luna 2 mission on 13 September 1959.

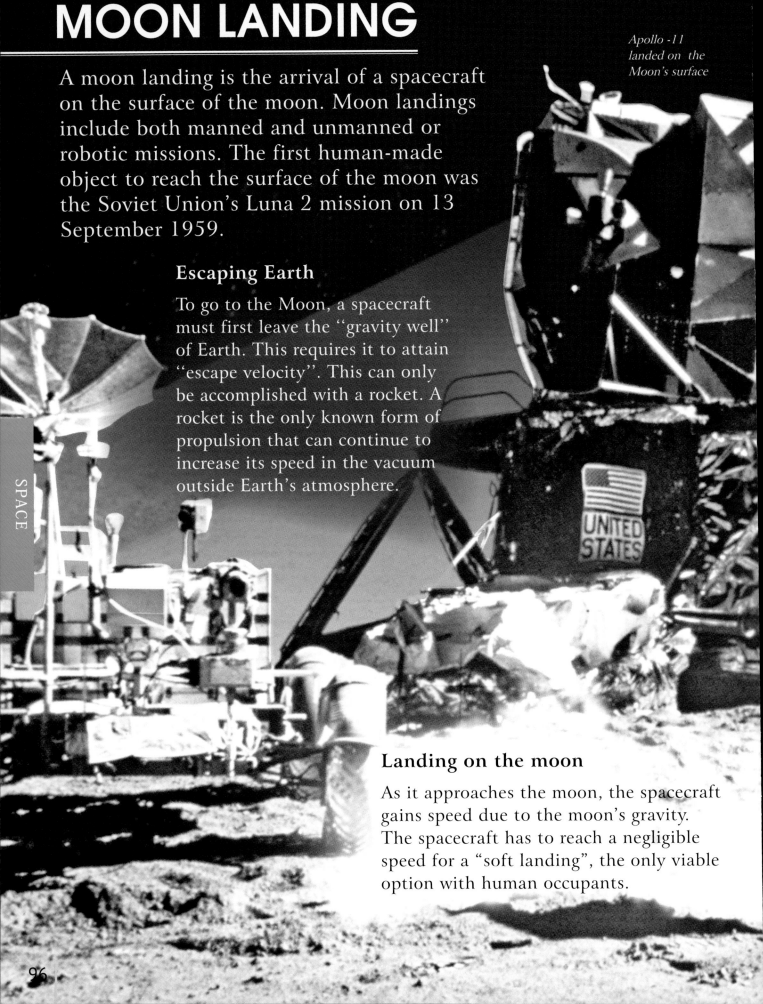

Apollo -11 landed on the Moon's surface

Escaping Earth

To go to the Moon, a spacecraft must first leave the "gravity well" of Earth. This requires it to attain "escape velocity". This can only be accomplished with a rocket. A rocket is the only known form of propulsion that can continue to increase its speed in the vacuum outside Earth's atmosphere.

Landing on the moon

As it approaches the moon, the spacecraft gains speed due to the moon's gravity. The spacecraft has to reach a negligible speed for a "soft landing", the only viable option with human occupants.

Technical difficulties

A moon departure rocket must be carried to the moon's surface by a moon-landing rocket. The moon departure rocket, and larger moon landing rocket, must be lifted by the original launch vehicle. This greatly increases the size of the original launch vehicle and makes moon missions expensive and difficult.

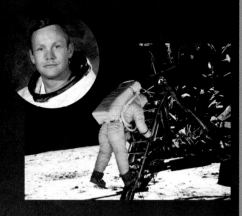

Luna 2

Luna 2 became the first spacecraft to reach the surface of the moon and also the first artificial object to land on another celestial body. The Luna 2 had external boosters instead of propulsion systems.

Apollo 11

Apollo 11 was the spaceflight that landed the first humans on the moon. Americans Neil Armstrong and Buzz Aldrin landed on the surface of the moon on 20 July 1969. The third member of the mission, astronaut Michael Collins, piloted the command spacecraft alone in lunar orbit until Armstrong and Aldrin returned to it for the trip back to Earth.

ASTRONAUT

Human spaceflight requires extensive screening and testing of candidates. Those accepted to become astronauts in the US, report to the Johnson Space Center (JSC) in Houston, NASA's primary astronaut training facility.

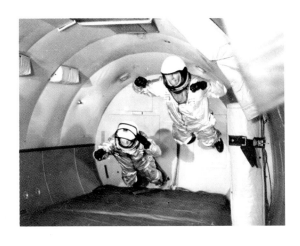

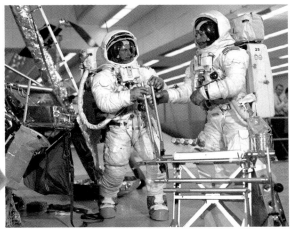

The Apollo 12 lunar Extravehicular Activity (EVA) crew members, Pete Conrad and Al Bean, conduct a simulation of the lunar surface activity.

Selection process

Spaceflight began with the selection of military fighters and test pilots in the 1960s with considerable focus on physical capability. It has now evolved into a search for aptitude in engineering, sciences, life sciences and mathematics.

Astronauts pictured during water egress training in a large indoor pool at Ellington Air Force Base, Texas.

Training in space

The Space Station Mockup and Training Facility is a complete imitation of the ISS, providing conditions to match those experienced upon the orbiting space station. The Virtual Reality Laboratory prepares astronauts for spacewalks and robotic arm operations. In a simulated microgravity environment generated by powerful computers, astronauts learn how to orient themselves in outer space.

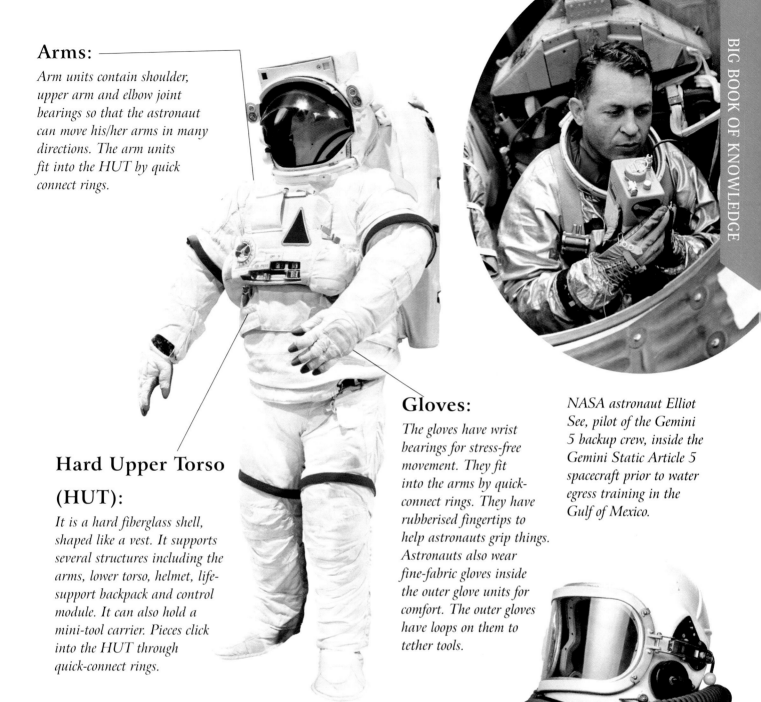

Arms:

Arm units contain shoulder, upper arm and elbow joint bearings so that the astronaut can move his/her arms in many directions. The arm units fit into the HUT by quick connect rings.

Hard Upper Torso (HUT):

It is a hard fiberglass shell, shaped like a vest. It supports several structures including the arms, lower torso, helmet, life-support backpack and control module. It can also hold a mini-tool carrier. Pieces click into the HUT through quick-connect rings.

Gloves:

The gloves have wrist bearings for stress-free movement. They fit into the arms by quick-connect rings. They have rubberised fingertips to help astronauts grip things. Astronauts also wear fine-fabric gloves inside the outer glove units for comfort. The outer gloves have loops on them to tether tools.

NASA astronaut Elliot See, pilot of the Gemini 5 backup crew, inside the Gemini Static Article 5 spacecraft prior to water egress training in the Gulf of Mexico.

Spacesuits

Spacesuits protect people from getting very hot or cold. They provide oxygen to breathe, hold water to drink and prevent astronauts from being harmed by space dust. The suits have special gold-lined visors to protect the eyes from bright sunlight. On the back, there is a backpack which holds oxygen for breathing. It eliminates the carbon dioxide that is breathed out. The back of the suit also holds several small thruster jets. If an astronaut drifts away from the space station, he or she could use them to fly back. Space suits have radio transmitters/receivers so that spacewalking astronauts can talk with ground controllers and/or other astronauts.

IN SPACE

Astronauts on space missions have 12-hour working shifts. Since water is not available in space, astronauts use a cloth dipped in soapy water to clean themselves. They conduct experiments and make observations. Regular maintenance has to be carried out at the space station or shuttle. A part of their time is spent doing daily household chores.

Food

Since the amount of food an astronaut can carry is limited, space food needs to be compact and crammed with all the nutrients required for a balanced diet.

Exercise

Due to the weightlessness in space, astronauts do not use their muscles sufficiently. If an astronaut spends a long time in space, his/ her muscles will degenerate unless exercised rigorously.

During an almost eight-hour spacewalk, Walheim and astronaut Stanley Love (out of frame), mission specialist, installed a grapple fixture on the Columbus laboratory and prepared electrical and data connections on the module while it rested inside Space Shuttle Atlantis' payload bay. The crew members also began work to replace a large nitrogen tank used for pressurising the station's ammonia cooling system.

The Expedition Four and STS-110 crewmembers share a meal in the Zvezda Service Module on the ISS. In zero-gravity, Everyday meals taste like paper.

Spaceflight accidents

There have been many accidents during space missions. There have been over 20 astronaut and cosmonaut fatalities till date.

Soyuz 1, 24 April 1967

The Soyuz 1's parachute did not open properly after atmospheric re-entry. Vladimir Komarov was killed when the capsule hit the ground at high speed while landing.

Soyuz 11, 30 June 1971

The crew of Soyuz 11 were killed after a cabin vent valve accidentally opened at service module separation, leading to decompression.

Challenger, 28 January 1986

The Space Shuttle Challenger was destroyed as it disintegrated on launch. All seven crew members died including Christa McAuliffe, the first civilian educator designated to teach from space.

Columbia, 1 February 2003

The spacecraft broke apart during re-entry into Earth's atmosphere, leading to the death of Rick D. Husband, William McCool, Michael P. Anderson, David M. Brown, Kalpana Chawla, Laurel B. Clark and Ilan Ramon.

An artist's representation of what an accident in outer space could be like.

Other activities

Astronauts read or watch the TV in their leisure time. Occasionally, robotic activities and space walks take place.

Space shuttle Challenger disaster. Space shuttle exhaust plumes entwined around a ball of gas after a few seconds after the explosion caused by ruptured O-rings. Jan. 28, 1986.

FAMOUS ASTRONAUTS

The idea of humans in space refers to human spaceflight. Human spaceflight saw a lot of competition and created the "space race" of the Cold War. As a result, many astronauts achieved great fame.

The Vostok 1 capsule on display at the RKK Energiya museum.

Yuri Gagarin–First Man in Space

Yuri Gagarin was a Russian- Soviet pilot and cosmonaut. Gagarin became the first human to journey into outer space and the first to orbit Earth when his Vostok spacecraft completed an orbit of Earth on 12 April 1961.

Valentina Tereshkova

The first woman in space was Soviet Valentina Tereshkova. She was on board the Vostok 6 which was launched on 16 June 1963, and orbited Earth for almost three days.

Valentina Tereshkova

On 27th March, 1968, Gagarin died in a MiG-15 UTI crash near the town of Kirzhach.

Alan Shepard

Alan Shepard

He was the first American and second person in space. He was launched on 5 May 1961, on a 15-minute sub-orbital flight.

Alexei Lenov

Sally Ride

Sally Ride

She was the first American woman in space during the Space Shuttle Challenger's mission STS-7, on 18 June 1983.

Pham Tuan

He was the first Asian (Vietnamese) in space, aboard Soyuz 37 on 23 July 1980.

Alexei Leonov

He was the first person to conduct an extravehicular activity (EVA), on 18 March 1965, on the Soviet Union's Voskhod 2 mission.

Neil Armstrong

He was the first human to walk on the moon in 1969.

Pham Tuan

Dennis Tito

He was the first self-funded space tourist on board the Russian spacecraft Soyuz TM-3 on 28 April 2001.

Dennis Tito

Neil Armstrong

Buzz Aldrin

He was the second human to walk on the moon in 1969.

Buzz Aldrin

Yang Liwei

Yang Liwei

He was the first person sent into space by China.

EXPLORING SPACE

Space exploration has reached unprecedented levels. The "Kármán" line, starting at an altitude of 100 kilometres above sea level, is the starting point of outer space.

Space Mining

Gold, iron, nickel and platinum mined from Earth's crust, originally came from the asteroids that hit Earth. Earth might run out of phosphorus, antimony, zinc, tin, silver, lead, indium, gold and copper in as little as 60 years. Minerals could be mined from an asteroid, then taken back to Earth or used in space for construction materials. This includes iron, nickel and titanium. A mine can be dug into the asteroid and the material extracted through the shaft. For volatile materials in extinct comets, heat can be used to melt and vaporise the matrix, and then extract the resulting vapour.

The RepRap 1.0 "Darwin" is a self-replicating machine. It is theorised that these could be used for space mining as they can create their own components themselves.

Space Manufacturing

Space manufacturing is the production of manufactured goods outside a planetary atmosphere. Potentially hazardous processes can be performed in space with minimal risk to the environment of Earth or other planets. Items that are too large to launch on a rocket can be assembled in orbit for use. Space vacuum allows the creation of extremely pure materials by using vapour deposition. Space can provide readily available extremes of heat and cold due to the lack of an atmosphere.

This painting shows an asteroid mining mission to an Earth-approaching asteroid. Asteroids contain many of the major elements, which could provide the basis for industry and life on Earth.

A NASA image of insulin crystal growth in outer space (left) as opposed to on Earth. Microgravity allows crystal formation of a better quality.

The future of space tourism as digitally rendered by an artist.

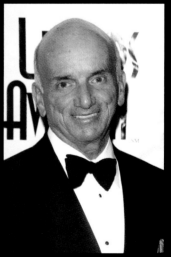

Dennis Tito, pictured above, is the world's first space tourist.

Space Tourism

Space tourism refers to recreational space travel. It can be either on government-owned vehicles or on private vehicles. American businessman Dennis Tito was the world's first space tourist on 28 April 2001, and spent seven days on board the ISS. He was followed by South African computer millionaire Mark Shuttleworth (2002) and American businessman Gregory Olsen (2005). Iranian-born American entrepreneur Anousheh Ansari became the first female fee-paying space traveller and visited the ISS in September 2006.

SPACE AND MILITARY

The USA and the USSR used space exploration to demonstrate technologies with potential for military application. Outer space has been used for imaging and communications satellites. Some ballistic missiles pass through outer space during their flight. Spy satellites are used by militaries to take accurate pictures of their rivals' military installations.

An aerial view of Osama bin Laden's compound in the Pakistani city of Abbottabad released by the CIA. Satellite surveillance played a critical role in the operation that resulted in Osama's capture.

Spy Satellites

Spy satellites are formally referred to as reconnaissance (recon) satellites. Early warning satellites warn of an attack by detecting ballistic missile launches. Nuclear explosion detection satellites identify and characterise nuclear explosions in space. Photo surveillance satellites provide imaging of Earth from space. Electronic-reconnaissance satellites intercept stray radio waves and decrypt encoded ones for intelligence. Radar imaging satellites can be used during the nights or through cloud cover.

Space Expo Resurs Spy Satellite: apparently Russian built, was displayed at the Space Expo in Noordwijk, the Netherlands in July 2015.

An artist's concept of the interception and destruction of nuclear-armed re-entry vehicles by a space-based electromagnetic railgun. The LTV Aerospace and Defense Co. has demonstrated hypervelocity launch technology in the laboratory that is applicable to a ballistic missile defence system.

Space Warfare

Space warfare refers to combat that occurs in outer space. This includes ground-to-space warfare, such as attacking satellites from Earth, and space-to-space warfare, such as satellites attacking satellites or spacecrafts attacking each other. In 2008, the USA used a SM-3 missile to destroy a spy satellite, while it was 247 kilometres above the Pacific Ocean.

An artists's representation of the future of the USA Space Command in 2020.

An image created to show a missile destroying a satellite in space

- **Ballistic Warfare** — Systems proposed for ballistic warfare range from ground and space-based anti-missiles to rail guns, space-based lasers, orbital mines and other futuristic weaponry.

- **Electronic Warfare** – Since spacecraft and satellite rely very heavily on electronics, these systems are designed to jam, sabotage and outright destroy enemy electronics.

- **Kinetic bombardment** — The energy gained while falling from orbit would rival powerful explosives.

- **Directed-energy weapons** —Rail guns and lasers work in space, but the batteries in space aren't big enough to power them.

Futuristic anti satellite weapon (ASAT) that will apparently destroy other artificial satellites by the process of "circular saw".

Military communications

Communication satellites are used to co-ordinate military action and receive intelligence. A soldier in the battle zone can access satellite imagery of enemy positions. He can e-mail the coordinates to a bomber hovering overhead.

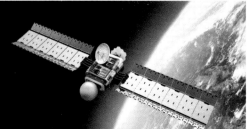

A file photo of a military satellite taken by another in space.

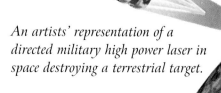

An artists' representation of a directed military high power laser in space destroying a terrestrial target.

SPACE COLONISATION

Space or extra-terrestrial colonisation is permanent human habitation off planet Earth. The reasons for its popularity is the survival of human civilisation and the biosphere in case of a planetary-scale disaster, and vast resources in space for expansion of human society and the possibilities of development and evolution.

A digitally created image of what space settlements would look like

Space colonies

Space settlements have to provide for the material needs of thousands of humans; something extremely difficult in an environment hostile to human life. Technologies such as controlled ecological life support systems have yet to be developed properly. The cost of sending anything from Earth's surface into orbit would roughly cost US $20,000 per kg, making a space colony an extremely expensive project.

Goldman Award winner and noted environmentalist Terri Swearingen famously said, "We are living on this planet like we have another one to go to". Her comment highlights the fact that Earth is rapidly running out of resources.

Terraforming

Terraforming or "earth shaping" is the theoretical process of deliberately modifying a planet's, moon's or any other body's atmosphere, temperature, surface topography or ecology to make it habitable for Earth-like life. Mars is usually considered to be the most likely candidate for terraforming. Several potential methods of altering the climate of Mars may fall within humanity's technological capabilities.

Moons of certain gas giants satisfy the criteria to be habitable. This is more likely since moons are more numerous than planets.

An artist's conception of what Mars would look like during various stages of terraforming.

Planetary Habitability

Planetary habitability is the measure of a planet or a natural satellite's potential to develop and sustain life. Stars should be sufficiently big to the necessary temperature, but small enough to have an adequately long life span to sustain life. The stars fluctuating brightness should be sufficiently low so that the planet does not experience any extreme conditions of heat or cold. The planet's mass should be large to hold an atmosphere, but small enough to have significant landmasses. Seasons must occur regularly and not be extreme so that they won't be hostile to life. The planet must have sufficient should amounts of heavier elements for life to evolve and sustain. The environment on the planet should contain diverse micro pockets to encourage evolution of life.

SPACE LAW

There are laws that protect space, as well as humans in space. The conduct in the area above Earth as well as the lower atmosphere is regulated by the space law.

Peaceful exploration

All countries have permission to peacefully explore space, but unexplored space territory cannot be claimed by any country. The Outer Space Committee, formed in 1959, signed a treaty to prohibit nuclear tests in space. The Nuclear Test Ban Treaty was signed in 1963.

Outer Space Treaty

The Outer Space Treaty is agreed to by most countries. The Legal Subcommittee of the United Nations General Assembly (UNGA) originally formed it in 1966. The Outer Space Treaty only bans nuclear weapons and weapons of mass destruction in space. Thus, in 2006, the UN General Assembly proposed Space Preservation Treaty against all the weapons.

An artists' representation of Earth and the space in future.

The principles of the Outer Space Treaty are given below

- The exploration and use of outer space shall be carried out for the benefit and interests of all countries.

- Outer space shall be free for exploration and use by all states.

- Outer space is not subject to national appropriation by claim of sovereignty, by means of use or occupation or by any other means.

- States shall not place nuclear weapons or other weapons of mass destruction in orbit or on celestial bodies or station them in outer space in any other manner.

- The moon and other celestial bodies shall be used exclusively for peaceful and non-military purposes.

- Astronauts shall be regarded as the envoys of humankind.

- States shall be responsible for national space activities whether carried out by governmental or non-governmental activities.

- States shall be liable for damage caused by their space objects.

- States shall avoid harmful contamination of space and celestial bodies.

Science is a way for us to gain knowledge about how and why things happen the way they do. This is done by using our senses to observe the world and by conducting experiments to investigate how it works.

SCIENCE TODAY

The rapid progress in science and technology during the late nineteenth and early twentieth centuries resulted in rapid economic advancement. Therefore, the twentieth century is called the "century of science". Science has made path-breaking success in the last few decades, be it in fields of genetics, nanotechnology or particle physics.

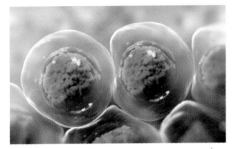

The human embryonic cell.

Human embryonic stem cells

Human embryonic stem cells can alter themselves into any tissue in the body. However, human embryos are destroyed during the process of cell extraction. In 2007, two teams of researchers used genetic modification to transform ordinary skin cells into cells that appear to function like embryonic stem cells.

Contribution of life science

The advances in life sciences have helped in the development of effective methods of diagnosis, treatment and prevention of several diseases.

Advances in technology have led to several pathbreaking discoveries.

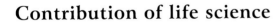

Nanotechnology

Nanotechnology involves working with any substance on the atomic or molecular scale. At the nano (10–9 mm) level, the material properties change drastically, which can be used to develop many products and processes. Nanotechnology can create many new materials and devices in the fields of medicine, electronics, biomaterials, energy producing materials, etc.

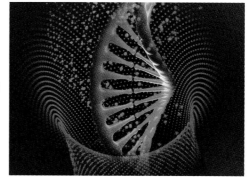

Nanotechnology is the study and application of very small things and can be used across all other science fields.

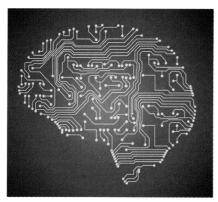

Human brain as an engineering processing machine signifying artificial intelligence

Neural network

Neural network refers to a computer modelled system that closely resembles the human brain and nervous system. Artificial neural networks are processing devices whose function is similar to that of the human neuronal system. They are widely used in biomedical research. They also have applications in the fields of diagnostics, robotics, business and medicine, where pattern recognition is required.

Artificial intelligence

In 2020, artificial intelligence (AI) is moving to practical usage and value stage. On the positive side, AI trends include energy-efficient AI, quantum neural networks and the role of natural language processing in understanding proteins.

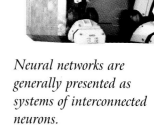

Neural networks are generally presented as systems of interconnected neurons.

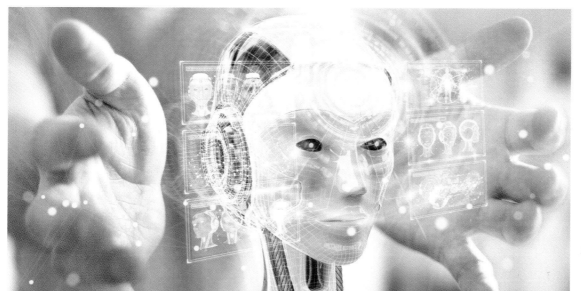

Businessman on blurred background using digital artificial intelligence.

115

SCIENTISTS

A scientist has expertise in areas of science and engages in a systematic study to acquire knowledge. From a light bulb to laptops, everything we use is a result of scientific inventions. When a question arises in a scientist's mind, he starts doing experiments and gaining more information. The moment they find the result, a new invention is born or discovery is made.

Famous Physicists

1. Sir Isaac Newton:
Newton (1642–1727) was an English scientist, mathematician and physicist. He developed his theories of gravitation and the Newton's Laws of Motion.

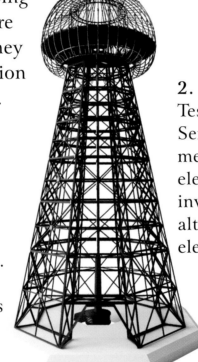

2. Nikola Tesla:
Nikola Tesla was an American-Serbian futurist, physicist, mechanical engineer, electrical engineer and inventor. He designed the alternating current (AC) electricity supply system.

A magnifying transmitter or Wardenclyffe tower was invented by Nikola Tesla.

A Newtonia reflector or telescope was invented by Newton

3. Niels Bohr:
A Danish physicist, he developed the Bohr Atomic Model in which he stated that the energy levels of electrons are specific and electrons revolve around the atomic nucleus in stable orbits.

The atomic model was designed by Bohr

4. Albert Einstein: Albert Einstein was a German theoretical physicist. He is known for the Theory of Relativity, and for his equivalence formula of mass-energy that is, $E = mc2$.

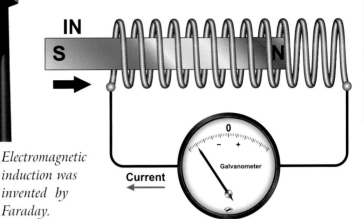

The solar panel is an invention based on Einstein's mass-energy theory

2. Michael Faraday: He helped electricity to be easily utilised. He discovered electromagnetic induction and electrolysis.

Electromagnetic induction was invented by Faraday.

5. C.V. Raman: Sir Chandrasekhara Venkata Raman was an Indian physicist. He is known for the Raman Scattering, an occurrence where when light traverses a transparent material the deflected light's wavelength gets affected.

Light passes through a prism and breaks into rainbow colours due to change in wavelength.

3. George Washington Carver: Carver is known for his innovation in the field of crop management, agriculture and the utilisation of various agricultural products for manufacturing and industrial purposes.

Crop management and agriculture advanced due to Carver's studies.

Famous Chemists

1. Sir Humphry Davy: He invented the Davy Lamp, which helped miners in mines, despite the presence of flammable gases. He also found that chlorine was an element.

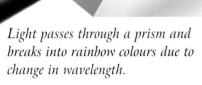

The miners safety-lamp was invented by Humphry Davy.

4. Marie Curie: Polish chemists, Marie and her husband, discovered polonium and radium. She introduced the use of X-ray technology and radium in medicine.

The X-ray is a technology based on Madame Curie's research

Famous Ecologists

1. Leonty Ramensky: Ramensky was a plant ecologist. Ramensky believed that biotic communities comprise species behaving individualistically.

2. Emma Lucy Braun: Braun's research focussed on vascular and deciduous forests. She was the first woman president of the Ecological Society of America. She fought for the conservation of natural areas and set up various natural reserves.

3. John Thomas Curtis: He contributed towards creating numerical procedures in the field of ecology. He and 39 of his Ph.D. students authored,

The Vegetation of Wisconsin – An Ordination of Plant Communities, which is a significant contribution to the domain of plant ecology.

Curtis compared the ecological systems of two places that were geographically apart.

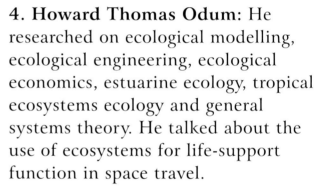

4. Howard Thomas Odum: He researched on ecological modelling, ecological engineering, ecological economics, estuarine ecology, tropical ecosystems ecology and general systems theory. He talked about the use of ecosystems for life-support function in space travel.

Odum studied the effects of the law of thermodynamics on ecological systems

5. Howard Thomas Odum: He researched on ecological modelling, ecological engineering, ecological economics, estuarine ecology, tropical ecosystems ecology and general systems theory. He talked about the use of ecosystems for life-support function in space travel.

The subject of James Brown's research was harvester ants.

Famous Biologists

1. Antonie van Leeuwenhoek: Leeuwenhoek was the first to observe bacteria underneath a microscope. It is believed that Leeuwenhoek built over 200 microscopes that had various magnifications.

2. Edward Jenner: Jenner is known for the discovery of the world's first vaccine – the smallpox vaccine.

A vaccine is used not only to cure a disease but also to protect a person from acquiring it.

3. Robert Brown: Brown was one of the first biologist to explain what cell nucleus was. He also made contributions in paleo-botany, the study of prehistoric plant life.

Cell nucleus

4. Charles Darwin: His writings introduced the idea of evolution into mainstream science. He collected various scientific evidences, which supported his theory of Natural Selection.

5. Louis Pasteur: The concept of vaccination against diseases was put forward by Pasteur. He developed the vaccines for anthrax and rabies. He is known for pasteurisation, the process utilised to treat wine and milk, so that they are not contaminated by bacteria.

Pasteurised milk is created by a process invented by Pasteur.

6. Gregor Mendel: Mendel created the science of genetics. His first heredity law states that genes exist in pairs and the paired gene becomes divided when the cell is divided.

Mendel formulated his law by studying the hybrid of green and yellow peas.

119

BUILDING BLOCKS

Molecules are the building blocks of all the materials around us. Molecules are made up of atoms. A molecule may contain a few, a hundred or even a million atoms.

Structure of atom with respect to the position of electrons, neutrons and protons.

Atoms

An atom comprises a nucleus that is made up of protons and neutrons and surrounded by electrons. Atoms are composed of three subatomic particles called electrons, protons and neutrons. Among them, electrons are the smallest and are found in shells or orbits that surround an atom's nucleus.

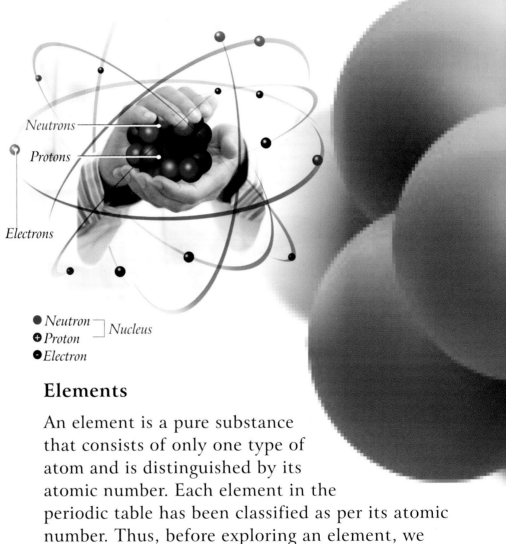

Neutrons

Protons

Electrons

● *Neutron* ⎤ *Nucleus*
⊕ *Proton* ⎦
⊖ *Electron*

Molecules

A molecule is a group of two or more atoms that bond together. If we think of atoms as letters, then molecules are the words that the letters form. Therefore, a molecule is the smallest unit of a substance that has all the properties of that substance.

Elements

An element is a pure substance that consists of only one type of atom and is distinguished by its atomic number. Each element in the periodic table has been classified as per its atomic number. Thus, before exploring an element, we should know what is meant by an atomic number.

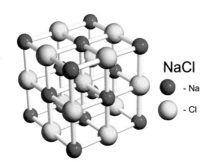

NaCl

● - Na

○ - Cl

Electrons

The atomic number of an element is defined as the total number of protons present within the nucleus of an atom of that element. For example, one atom of carbon contains six protons; thus, the atomic number of carbon is six. Every element has a unique atomic number.

Strong chemical bonds hold the atoms in a molecule together. The bonds are formed when atoms share particles called electrons. Electrons are found either alone or in pairs in the outer part of atoms. When two atoms with unpaired electrons approach each other, the unpaired electrons may form a pair. Both atoms then share the pair. This holds the atoms together.

A beam of electrons deflected in a circle by a magnetic field.

Electric current is the flow of electrons. In electric circuits, this charge is carried by moving electrons in a wire.

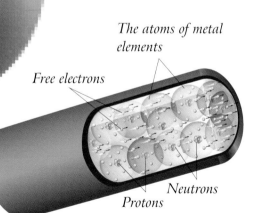

The atoms of metal elements

Free electrons

Protons

Neutrons

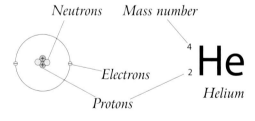

Neutrons   Mass number

Electrons

Protons

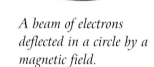

$$^{4}_{2}\text{He}$$

Helium

Atomic and mass number depiction

Mass number

Mass number is defined as the total number of protons and neutrons present within the nucleus of an atom. Mass number = number of protons + number of neutrons.

Mass and location of electrons

Electrons possess minuscule mass, such that they exhibit properties of both particles and waves. It is impossible to learn the precise locations of electrons within a molecule. Despite such a limitation, there are regions around an atom where electrons have a high probability of being found. These regions are atomic orbits.

MATTER

Matter is anything that occupies space and has mass. It is composed of atoms. Matter includes all physical objects.

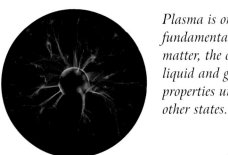

Plasma is one of the four fundamental states of matter, the others being solid, liquid and gas. Plasma has properties unlike those of the other states.

States of Matter

Matter can exist in three phases- solid, liquid and gas. The state or phase of matter depends mainly upon pressure and temperature.

Solids

The atoms and molecules of a solid are tightly packed together in a regular arrangement. Therefore, they have a definite shape; for example, a round ball and a square book. Solids have a definite volume and a fixed shape.

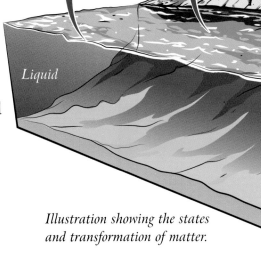

Plasma

Gas

Liquid

Illustration showing the states and transformation of matter.

Solids   Liquids   Gases   Plasma

Liquids

The molecules of a liquid are very close to each other but can slip over each other to change their position. Liquids have a definite volume but they do not have a definite shape.

Gases

The molecules of a gas are not close to each other, and can move easily and quickly.

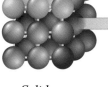

Properties of Matter

All substances have a varied array of different characteristics called properties.

Hardness

This property determines how easy or difficult it is to shape or scratch a substance.

A diamond has a hardness rating of 10 on the Mohs scale of mineral hardness.

Solid

Flexibility and elasticity

Flexibility refers to the ability of some materials to twist or bend, whereas elasticity refers to the ability of a material to stretch in different directions before returning to its original position.

Mass and density

Density refers to the weight of a substance in relation to its size. Dense materials such as brass and lead are used for weights, whereas materials with low density (such as wood) float on water.

A graduated cylinder containing various coloured liquids with different densities.

Conduction of electricity

Materials, such as metals, that are good electric conductors enable an electric current to pass through them with ease.

Solubility

Solubility refers to the ability of a substance to dissolve in water.

CHEMICAL REACTIONS

A group of atoms is called a molecule. Transformation of molecules from one form to another is called a chemical reaction. The forces that bind two atoms are broken and new bonding forces are created, resulting in the formation of a whole new compound having totally different properties as compared to the substances with which it was originally made up.

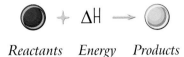

Reactants   Energy   Products

Endothermic Reaction

The reactions that absorb heat or energy from their surroundings are called endothermic reactions. When they absorb heat from the surrounding, the surrounding temperature decreases.

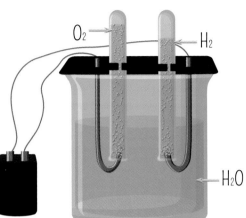

$$2H_2O + \Delta H \rightarrow 2H_2 + O_2$$

Endothermic Reaction

Melting of ice

Reactants   Products   Energy

Exothermic Reaction

When a chemical reaction between two substances occurs, energy is released in the form of light, heat, sound or electricity. Such reactions are called exothermic reactions. As exothermic reactions release heat, they raise the temperature of the surroundings around them.

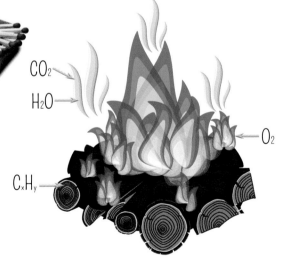

$$C_xH_y + O_2 \rightarrow CO_2 + H_2O + \Delta H$$

Exothermic Reaction

Rusting nails.

124

SCIENCE

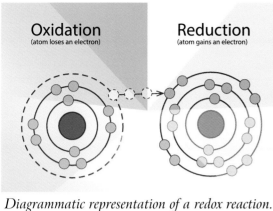

Diagrammatic representation of a redox reaction.

Redox Reaction

Redox is a combination of oxidation and reduction process. Here, gain as well as loss of electrons occurs within substances. Oxidising agents are those substances, which gain electrons and reducing agents are those substances, which lose electrons.

Since reduction means the gain of electrons, the major application of reduction reaction is found in the battery industry. The purpose of a battery is to create electricity, it works mainly by the transfer of electrons from one place to another.

Rusted iron, oxidation of iron

Redox pairs

Oxidation-reduction reactions are similar to acid-base reactions. Oxidising agents are those substances, which gain electrons and reducing agents are those substances, which lose electrons. Both oxidising and reducing agents form redox pairs.

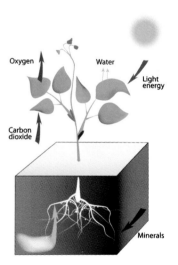

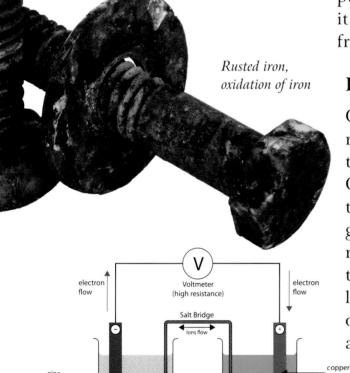

Sodium reduces silver ions to form silver.

Reversible Reaction

Reactions in which we are able to reverse the process and get the reactants back from the products are called reversible reactions. In order to break the bonding forces between atoms, heat energy, pressure and other changes are introduced in the chemical reaction. This causes the molecules of the product to become unstable and break into the molecules of the reactants.

METALS AND NON-METALS

The core of Earth containing iron

Metals are minerals found in rock. They can be separated from the rocks using heat. Metals are known for conducting electricity and heat well. Many metals are strong, shiny, and hard. They are also often malleable, meaning they can be shaped without breaking or cracking. Non-metals are poor conductors of heat and electricity, and are amorphous, non-malleable and highly volatile.

Iron

Iron is highly valued for its strength and its ability to provide much stronger alloys, such as steel. It is the most common element on Earth It is used in manufacturing and industries. Steel, an alloy of iron, is valued for its strength.

Stainless steel kitchenware.

Alloy

Many metals that we use today are alloys. Alloys are metals that combine two or more elements. They could also be called metallic compounds. Often alloys are stronger and harder than pure metal.

Steel is a very strong type of alloy. There are a variety of steel alloys. A common one is made out of iron combined with small amounts of carbon. Stainless steel that we use for utensils and kitchen appliances is steel with chromium. Steel is used in much of the world's industries.

Cutting process of hard alloys

Superalloys

Superalloys are high-performance alloys with brilliant mechanical strength; they do not distort under influence of extreme temperatures and are corrosion, rust or oxidation resistant. They are primarily utilised in engines in the aerospace and marine industries and weapons manufacturing. Inconel, Hestelloy, TMS alloy and RB199 are some examples.

Jet plane engine

Light Alloys

Light alloys are based on aluminium, titanium, beryllium and magnesium and have great mechanical strength. Tablets and smartphones are crafted from these alloys as they make the devices lighter and portable. Aluminium alloys are used in the construction of aeroplanes because this alloy is light, economical and a bad conductor of electricity.

Process of controlling the manufacture of microcircuits on a wafer of silicon.

Silicon

Earth's crust is made of 28 per cent silicon. Silicon is a major component of glass. Glass is a part of modern architecture; most scientific apparatus and items of daily use. Every electronic device relies on silicon for functionality. Silicon is also used to make solar cells.

The body of a metal flashlight is made from light alloys.

MACHINES

A machine is a system that makes human life easy. Machines require energy to work; be it thermal, mechanical or electrical. Simple machines like the wheel don't require much energy as compared to complex machines like the computer. If a machine is efficient, it will make use of minimum energy to give maximum output.

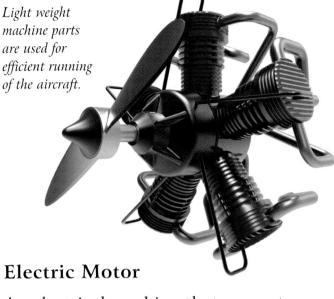

Light weight machine parts are used for efficient running of the aircraft.

Altimeters can be seen in the cockpit of an aircraft.

Electric Motor

An electrical machine that converts electrical energy into mechanical energy is called an electric motor. The present day electric motor was invented in 1886 by American inventor Frank Julian Sprague. They are used in water pumps, refrigerators, vacuum cleaners, cars, fans and so on.

Barometer

A barometer is an instrument to measure atmospheric pressure. It was invented in 1643 by Italian physicist and mathematician Evangelista Torricelli. The barometer is a glass tube that is open at one end and sealed at the other. This tube is filled with mercury and placed inverted in a container known as a reservoir.

An old barometer

Steam Engine

Steam engines convert heat energy into mechanical energy. The steam engine was improvised and started being used for generation of electricity. Steam engines are used in railways, ships and industries.

Microwave Oven

Microwave ovens cook food by means of high-frequency electromagnetic waves(microwaves), instead of any sort of flame or heat.

Satellite

A satellite moves around Earth. Meteorological departments forecast using weather satellites. Telephone, and radio work due to communication satellites.

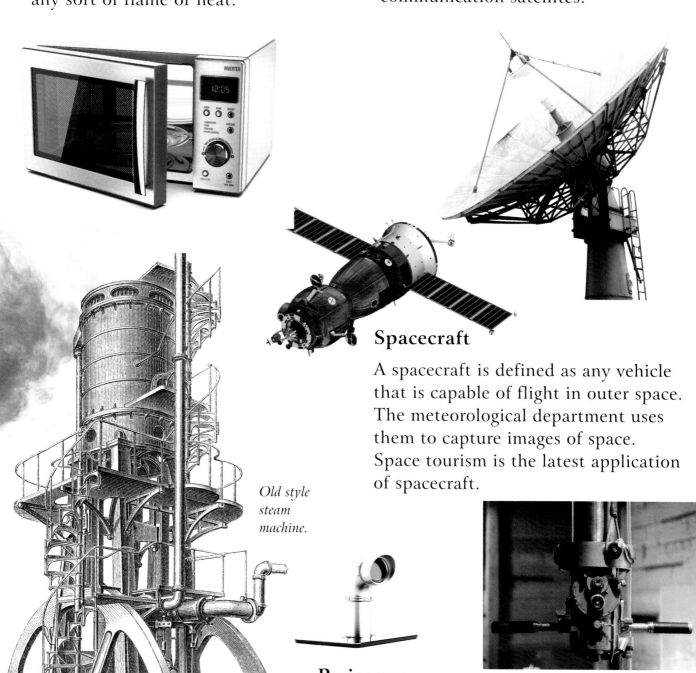

Old style steam machine.

Spacecraft

A spacecraft is defined as any vehicle that is capable of flight in outer space. The meteorological department uses them to capture images of space. Space tourism is the latest application of spacecraft.

Periscope

The periscope is an optical instrument, that helps one to see objects above or below their eye level. The periscope is used in naval wars when there is low visibility.

FORCE

Force is something that causes the motion of an object. Force helps objects to slow down or accelerate. All physical activity uses force. Force are of many types.

Girl doing elastic rope exercise.

The more the weight, the higher the pressure

Stretch and Pull

Elasticity is the ability of a distorted material body to return to its original shape and size. A balloon will retain its original shape when deflated.

Torque force is applied to change the tyre with a wheel wrench

Pressure

Pressure is expressed as the force exerted per unit area. If you push your thumb against the wall, the wall will not be damaged. However, if you push a board pin with the same amount of force, it might penetrate the wall.

Torque

Torque can be defined as a force used to rotate or turn things. A crowbar, used to open boxes that have been nailed shut, works on the principles of torque.

Turning Force

When a body is rotated, it moves in the direction in which the force is applied, like the force applied to a door knob to open it.

Electromagnetic Forces

Electromagnetic force is the force exerted by the electromagnetic interaction of electrically charged or magnetically polarised particles or bodies.

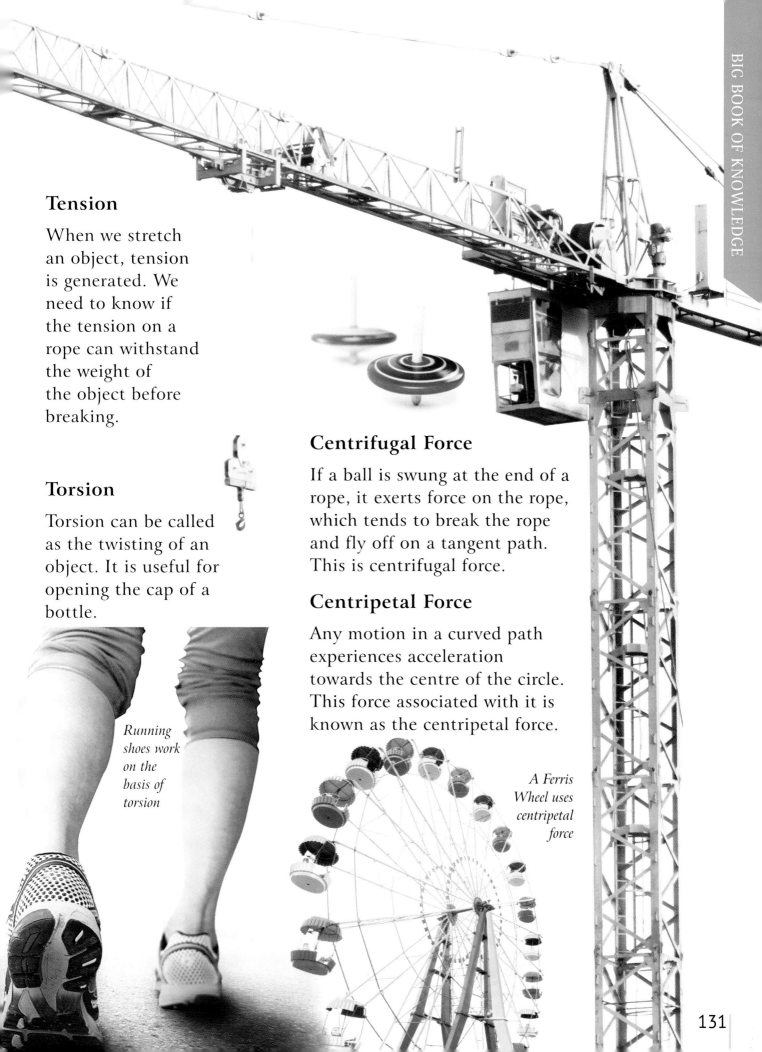

Tension

When we stretch an object, tension is generated. We need to know if the tension on a rope can withstand the weight of the object before breaking.

Torsion

Torsion can be called as the twisting of an object. It is useful for opening the cap of a bottle.

Running shoes work on the basis of torsion

Centrifugal Force

If a ball is swung at the end of a rope, it exerts force on the rope, which tends to break the rope and fly off on a tangent path. This is centrifugal force.

Centripetal Force

Any motion in a curved path experiences acceleration towards the centre of the circle. This force associated with it is known as the centripetal force.

A Ferris Wheel uses centripetal force

131

ENERGY

Energy is the capacity to perform a task. Energy can be converted from one form to another, but never destroyed. The sum total of energy in the universe is always constant, which is a property called the conservation of energy.

Potential Energy

Potential energy is the energy that a body has because of its position or configuration in a force field. For example, the higher an object is elevated, the greater is the gravitational potential energy.

An object at a height has potential energy as gravity is acting on it and can cause the object to fall.

Kinetic Energy

Kinetic energy is the energy that a body possesses by virtue of its motion; a body at rest has zero kinetic energy. The motion may be along a path, rotational on an axis or any combination of motions.

A falling object has kinetic energy as it is in motion.

Electrical Energy

Electrical energy is a kind of kinetic energy that is formed because of the movement of electric charges. For lighting, operation of electronic equipment, automotive engines, entertainment applications and a variety of other uses, electric energy has no rival.

Food and Chemical Energy

In animals, energy is provided by consumption of plants or other animals. Plants are the only living organisms capable of creating energy from the sun, the rest of the living organisms have to depend upon them for their energy requirements.

Nuclear Energy

Nuclear energy can be harvested from two types of reactions – fission and fusion. While nuclear fission is used as a source of energy, there are certain problems associated with it – mainly due to the highly toxic, radioactive nature of the waste produced which can cause severe environmental degradation, and number of diseases in animals and humans.

Nuclear explosion

Windmills and solar panels; sources of renewable energy

Renewable Energy

Renewable energy is made from sources that are infinite. Renewable energy makes use of the energies of the Sun, wind, tides, flowing water and so on. Solar energy is used to heat water and electricity generation is mainly generated through solar cells or photovoltaic cells.

ELECTRICITY

Electricity is the set of physical occurrences related to the flow and presence of electrical charge. It is only during the second half of the nineteenth century, that electricity's practical applications came into being.

A cellphone being charged.

Electricity Production

Generation of electricity uses the conversion of movement or mechanical energy into electricity. The process includes turbines that are rotated using various sources of energy like wind, water, gas and steam. It lights a spark that gets collected by a generator and distributed as usable electricity.

Solar and photovoltaic energy

Solar thermal panels utilise the Sun's energy to heat water that can be used in washing and heating. Photovoltaic panels utilise the photovoltaic effect to turn the Sun's energy directly into electricity.

Solar panels convert solar energy to electricity.

A man starting a generator.

Hydroelectricity

Hydroelectricity is harnessed from the kinetic energy in moving water; the water moves with adequate speed and volume to spin a turbine, which in turn rotates a generator.

Dams are used to harness water and create electricity.

Wind power

Wind turns the blades of the windmills, which spin a shaft, which is connected to a generator that generates electricity. These turbines convert kinetic energy in the wind into mechanical energy.

Windmills are used to generate electricity.

Electromagnetism

Electromagnetism is a type of physical interaction that occurs between electrically charged particles. Electromagnetic force manifests itself through forces between the charges and magnetic force. Electromagnetism manifests as both electric fields and magnetic fields. A changing electric field generates a magnetic field; conversely, a changing magnetic field generates an electric field. The principle of electromagnetism is the basis of the operation of electrical generators, motors and transformers. It is used in MRI machines in hospitals.

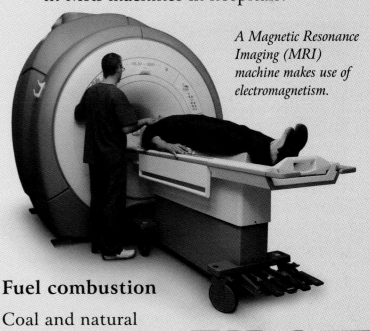

A Magnetic Resonance Imaging (MRI) machine makes use of electromagnetism.

Fuel combustion

Coal and natural gas are used to heat water and generate steam, which rotates the turbine and generates electricity.

Electricity is collected and generated from power houses.

LIGHT

Light is a form of energy that is produced from a specific source. Millions of fast travelling photons make up this light. Light travels in the form of a wave.

A prism dispersing colours of different wavelengths.

Visible Light

White light, visible to us, is composed of seven colours. They are violet, indigo, blue, green, yellow, orange and red.

Wavelength of Light

If we were to measure light on a scale, it would quite literally be like a wave. The distance between the two highest points on the wave is the same as the distance between the two lowest points. This distance is called a wavelength.

Dispersal of white light into various colours by a diamond.

Different wavelengths of colours

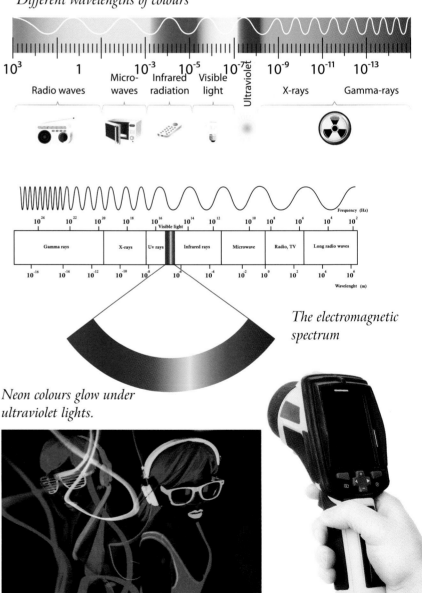

| 10³ | 1 | 10⁻³ | 10⁻⁵ | 10⁻⁷ | 10⁻⁹ | 10⁻¹¹ | 10⁻¹³ |
| Radio waves | | Micro-waves | Infrared radiation | Visible light | Ultraviolet | X-rays | Gamma-rays |

The electromagnetic spectrum

Infrared/ Ultraviolet

The invisible energy of electromagnetic radiation with wavelengths longer than visible light are known as infrared; the wavelengths shorter than visible light are known as ultraviolet rays. Infrared light is used to make night vision goggles that enable one to see objects in the dark. Our bodies need ultraviolet light to create Vitamin D.

Neon colours glow under ultraviolet lights.

Intensity

Intensity is the brightness measure of light. It is measured at a rate at which light energy can be delivered to a given unit of surface area. For example, a bulb with higher watts usage will provide more intensity of light or will be able to brighten a larger area in the house.

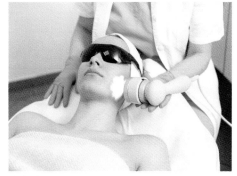
A light meter.

Photon

A photon is a mass-less, charge-less, stable quantum of light. The intensity is a function of the number of photons striking a given surface area per unit time.

A camera works on the principles of optics.

Photoelectric effect

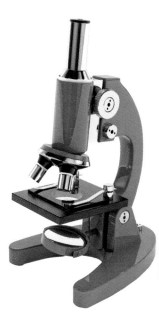
A microscope working on the basic principles of quantum optics.

Optics

Optics is the study of the science of light. The human eye contains photoreceptor cells, which act as natural optical devices. Magnifying glasses, photographic lenses, rear-view mirrors, microscopes and telescopes are all applications of optical phenomena and principles.

GRAVITY

Force that attracts two things towards each other is called gravity. Any free-falling object is under the influence of gravity. The measure of force of gravity for any given body is the weight of that body. Our weight is a measurement of the force of Earth's gravity acting upon us.

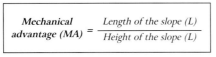

Normal force

Force of friction

L

H

Acceleration

90°

Gravity

θ

$$\text{Mechanical advantage (MA)} = \frac{\text{Length of the slope (L)}}{\text{Height of the slope (L)}}$$

Ball falling down due to gravitational force.

What is acceleration due to gravity?

Gravity is experienced by us in everyday life. The reason behind objects falling on the ground is the inherent property of Earth exerting a force of attraction on objects. This force is the force of gravity and the acceleration generated on these objects because of this force is acceleration due to gravity. In this case, force is better known as the weight of objects.

$$F_g = G\frac{m_1 m_2}{r^2}$$

Newton's Law of Universal Gravitation

This law states that any two bodies in the universe attract one another with a certain amount of force. Newton put forward that the amount of gravitational force on an object depends on its distance along with its mass. The further you move from the object, the lesser the gravitational force one will feel.

Newton discovered gravity after observing an apple falling from a tree.

How does Newton's law affect Earth?

The force of gravity that an object with mass exerts on another object weakens as the distance between the two object increases. The Moon exerts gravity on Earth, which causes ocean tides on Earth. When the tides are high, we know that the Moon is very close to us. The mass of the Sun is much larger than that of Earth and so Earth rotates around the Sun.

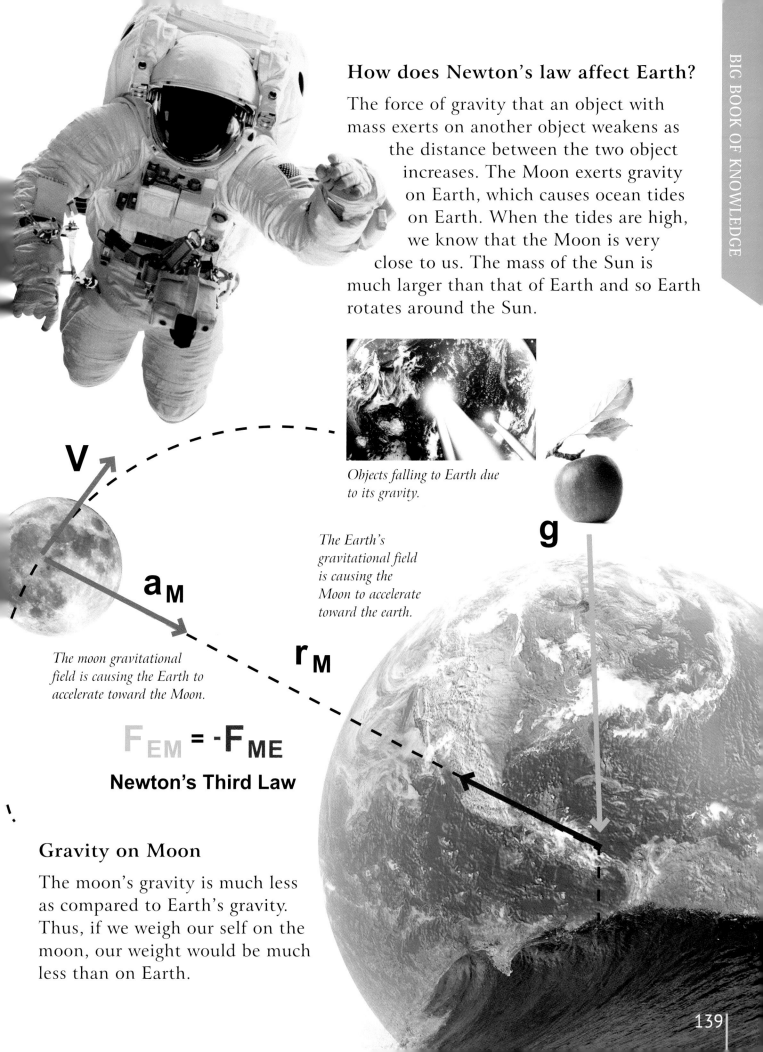

Objects falling to Earth due to its gravity.

The Earth's gravitational field is causing the Moon to accelerate toward the earth.

V

a_M

r_M

g

The moon gravitational field is causing the Earth to accelerate toward the Moon.

$$F_{EM} = -F_{ME}$$

Newton's Third Law

Gravity on Moon

The moon's gravity is much less as compared to Earth's gravity. Thus, if we weigh our self on the moon, our weight would be much less than on Earth.

LAWS

Scientific laws are the description of an observed phenomenon. They may be explained in words or mathematical equations. While the laws are fundamental, they refer to flawless systems, which are hard to obtain in the real world.

Archimedes' Law

Archimedes' principle is a scientific law that explains why objects sink or float. It is used in shipbuilding, air and water travel, and as a safety and measuring tool.

The boat float because the amount of water it displaces is equal to the weight of the boat.

This law was discovered by an mathematician and inventor, Archimedes, who was from ancient Greece. One night as he was getting into the tub, he noticed that the further down he sank, the higher the water would rise and the more bathwater spilled out. This led him to develop a scientific law called Archimedes' principle. According to this law, when an object is dropped into water, some of that water is displaced. At the same time, buoyancy is pushing up on the object, which changes its weight. If the weight of the object is heavier than the amount of water it displaces, the object will sink. If the amount of water displaced is equal to the weight of the object, it will float.

Hair charged by the same polarity repel each other.

Coulomb's Law

Coulomb's Law is one of the basic ideas of electricity in physics. The law looks at the forces created between two charged objects. As distance increases, the forces and electric fields decrease. This simple idea was converted into a relatively simple formula. The force between the objects can be positive or negative depending on whether the objects are attracted to each other or repelled.

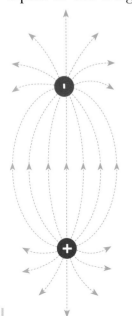

Force lines between two unlikely charged particles

Joule's Law

When current flows through a wire, heat is generated. The household iron makes use of this law. In an electric bulb, a thin filament of metal wire exists. When electricity is passed through this wire, heat is generated and the heated wire filament glows.

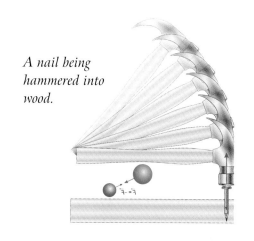

A nail being hammered into wood.

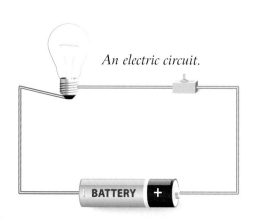

An electric circuit.

Newton's Laws of Motion

According to Newton's First law of Motion, every object in a state of uniform motion tends to remain in that state unless an external force is applied to it. Newton's second law states that when a force acts on an object, that object will accelerate in the same direction as the force. The third law postulated that for every action, there is an equal and opposite reaction.

Ohm's Law

Ohm's law states that the current flowing through a conductor is directly proportional to the potential difference across its two points.

Burning fuel releases energy that lifts off a rocket.

The circuit shows the relationship between current, voltage and the resistance, following the Ohm's law

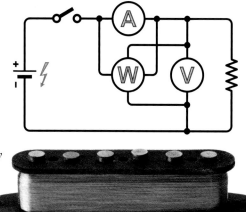

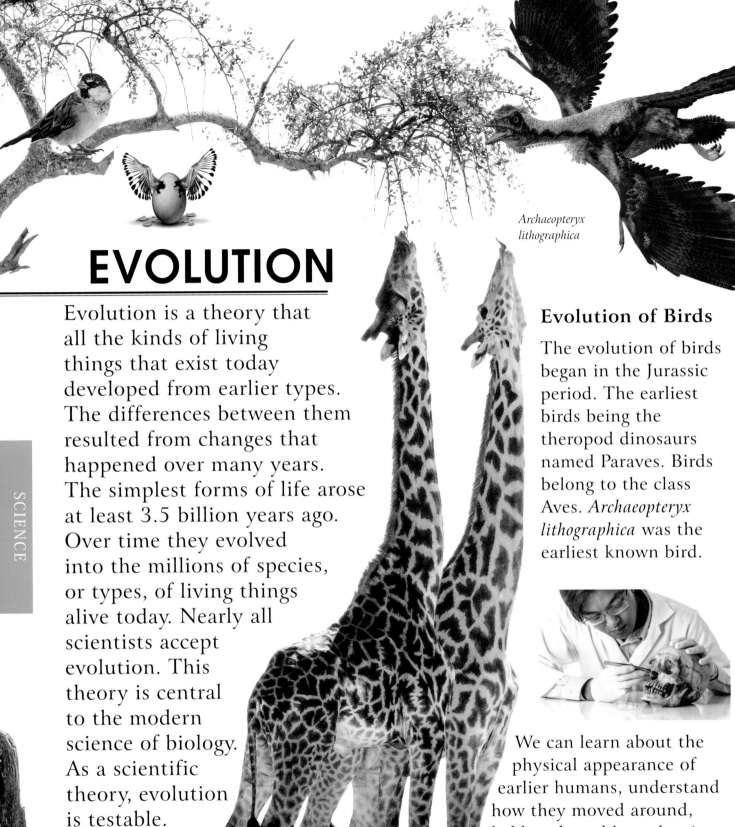

EVOLUTION

Evolution is a theory that all the kinds of living things that exist today developed from earlier types. The differences between them resulted from changes that happened over many years. The simplest forms of life arose at least 3.5 billion years ago. Over time they evolved into the millions of species, or types, of living things alive today. Nearly all scientists accept evolution. This theory is central to the modern science of biology. As a scientific theory, evolution is testable.

Archaeopteryx lithographica

Evolution of Birds

The evolution of birds began in the Jurassic period. The earliest birds being the theropod dinosaurs named Paraves. Birds belong to the class Aves. *Archaeopteryx lithographica* was the earliest known bird.

We can learn about the physical appearance of earlier humans, understand how they moved around, held tools and how the size of their brains changed over a long time by examining the bone size, shape and markings left on the bones by their muscles.

Long neck of a giraffe developed through adaptation.

Evolution of birds from dinosaurs

As birds are considered to have evolved from theropod dinosaurs, some of their properties seem to have changed in the process. For example, Compsognathus was the first species to have feathers. They had short hair-like feathers which provided them with insulation and protection. It is not proved why they were of different colour and sizes.

Evolution of wings

Another point of study is the change in the digits of dinosaurs. The first theropod dinosaurs had hands with small digits and one long digit. Slowly, these digits were lost.

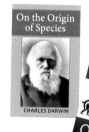

Creative representation of the prehistoric man

Model of Tarbosaurus Tyrannosaurid theropod dinosaur with hands at a theme park.

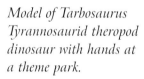

Homo sapiens *Homo neanderthalensis* *Homo Erectus* *Australopithecus africanus* *Sahelanthropus tchadensis*

Charles Darwin

The exact nature of our evolution has been the subject of debate and investigation since the great British naturalist Charles Darwin published his monumental books *On the Origin of Species* (1859) and *The Descent of Man* (1871).

Human evolution

Humans are Homo sapiens, a culture-bearing, upright-walking species that live on the ground and evolved from extinct primates in Africa between 100,000 and 200,000 years ago. The extinct hominins are related to us and so are the apes (both living and extinct).

BIRTH OF NEW SPECIES

The process by which a new species forms from an existing species is called speciation. In nature, speciation occurs by allopatric, peripatric, parametric and sympatric ways.

Peripatric

In this type of process, natural selection is the dominant factor, which causes only a particular type of species to survive.

Allopatric

This occurs when two populations of the same species separate geographically from one other. They adapt differently according to their environments. They face different mutations and genetic drifts, and become completely different species unable to reproduce with one other.

Parapatric

In this type of process of speciation, a small group of organisms gets separated from the rest of the population and slowly evolves into a different species than the main population, because of the genetic drift.

	Allopatric	Peripatric	Parapatric	Sympatric
Original population				
Initial step of speciation	Barrier formation	New niche entered	New niche entered	Genetic polymorphism
Evolution of reproductive isolation	In isolation	In isolated niche	In adjacent niche	Within the population
New distinct species after equilibration of new ranges				

Sympatric

This is a process in which two or more types of species evolve from the same ancestor without any geographical barrier and both types of species are able to survive.

Cospeciation

Cospeciation is the process where one population speciates in response with another and is a result of the associate's dependence on its host for its survival.

The tick surviving on the body of a dog comes close to cospeciation except that the dog's body doesn't provide an environment long enough for the ticks to evolve.

The tick surviving on the body of a dog comes close to cospeciation except that the dog's body doesn't provide an environment long enough for the ticks to evolve.

The cat family

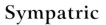

CELLS

A cell is the smallest unit of life. Cells make up the structure of the body, absorb nutrients from food, convert these nutrients into energy and perform specialised functions. Cells reproduce to form new cells, thereby explaining how organisms reproduce and grow.

Cell structure

All cells are composed of some common building blocks, regardless of whether they are plant cells or animal cells and whether they have different functions or location. These building blocks are called "biomolecules".

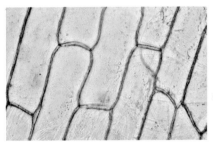

Microscopic view of what a plant cell looks like from the inside (Plant Cell Anatomy).

Smooth endoplasmic reticulum

Central vacuole

Cytoplasm

Golgi apparatus

Mitochondria

Peroxisome

Carbohydrates

Carbohydrates are the main source of energy in our body. The most common carbohydrate is sugar. Carbohydrates provide structure and help in the defence mechanism of cells. They also help in communication and adhesion.

Lipids

A range of fats, oils, waxes and steroid hormones come under lipids that form cells. Fats also serve as a source of energy and form the cell membrane. These materials provide protection against microbes. Lipids in the form of steroid hormones regulate cell activity.

Proteins

Different amino acids join together and form different types of proteins. Protein is a body building constituent. Proteins are useful in cell transport, maintaining cell contact and controlling its activity.

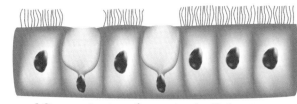

Microscopic view of an animal cell showing anatomical structures.

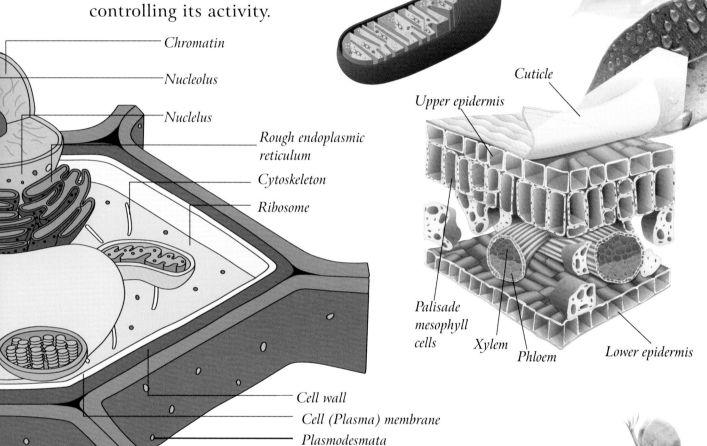

Chromatin

Nucleolus

Nuclelus

Rough endoplasmic reticulum

Cytoskeleton

Ribosome

Cuticle

Upper epidermis

Palisade mesophyll cells

Xylem

Phloem

Lower epidermis

Cell wall

Cell (Plasma) membrane

Plasmodesmata

Adjacent cell wall

Cells divide and re-divide to help a plant grow.

Nucleic acids

There are two types of nucleic acids found in our body. They are RNA and DNA. DNA is found in the nucleus and it carries genetic information, whereas RNA helps in protein synthesis.

Unicellular organisms

While plants and animals are made up of millions of cells, a unicellular organism is made up of only one cell. There are three main types of unicellular organisms which exist in all biomes: bacteria, yeast and protozoa.

Bacteria

Bacteria cannot be seen without a microscope. Bacterial cells do not possess a nucleus. They may or may not contain a flagellum, which is used for movement. Every bacterial cell has a membrane, a cell well; as well as the chromosomal DNA.

Yeast

Yeast is a type of fungi which is made up of just one cell. Yeast is used to convert sugar into alcohol. It has plant-like cells and cell walls.

Protozoa

Protozoa like to live in moist places, and largely live in water. Protozoa have pseudopodia which takes food into the cell. The contractile vacuoles in the cell allow for waste removal. Protozoa also use pseudopodia to move.

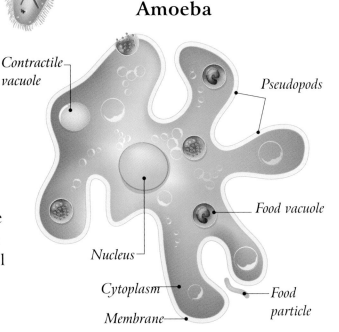

An aloe vera leaf made of parenchyma cells.

Amoeba

Contractile vacuole

Pseudopods

Food vacuole

Nucleus

Cytoplasm

Food particle

Membrane

Multicellular organisms

These organisms are made up of many cells which might exist independently or in integrated groups. Here, different cells or groups of cells are assigned different tasks. Some of these are called specialized cells. Many multicellular organisms also form tissues and organs.

SCIENCE

Plant cells

Plant cells are covered by a thick cell wall to give them rigidity. A plant cell can also produce its own food.

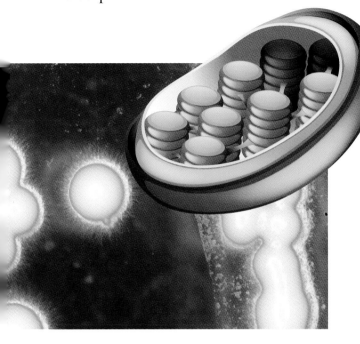

Types of plant cells

Parenchyma cells
Collenchyma cells
Sclerenchyma cells

Leaf surface showing plant cells

1. These cells have a large vacuole filled with water and other materials; and are surrounded by a membrane called tonoplast.
2. These cells are covered with a thick cell wall made up of cellulose.
3. They have plasmodesmata, which are the pores in the cell membrane.
4. Plastids like chloroplast, amyloplast, chromoplast and elaioplast are present. Chloroplast contains a green pigment called chlorophyll that absorbs sunlight and water, and helps in making food for the plant. This process is called photosynthesis.
5. Cell division occurs in the presence of phragmoplast.

Animal cell

Animal cells are eukaryotic cells; or cells with a membrane-bound nucleus. DNA in animal cells is situated within the nucleus. Animal cells have various sizes and irregular shapes. They are visible to the human eye only with the help of a microscope.

EARLIEST ORGANISMS

The first living organisms were called "prokaryotes". With the help of photosynthesis, the single-celled prokaryotes released enough oxygen into the atmosphere to change the gases present in it. The atmosphere now contained oxygen and other gases which could support life. This in turn helped develop organisms with complex structures.

Photosynthesis

Bacteria is a developed and modern prokaryotic cell.

Cell

Simple cells gradually developed into more advanced cells. DNA was contained within the nucleus of these cells and different parts were used for different tasks. These cells were called "eukaryotic cells" and could convert food into energy.

Endoplasmic reticulum

Building blocks of life

Elements such as carbon, hydrogen, oxygen, nitrogen, sulphur and phosphorous combine to form carbohydrates, proteins, lipids and nucleic acids— the building blocks of life.

Carbon molecules

Animal cell

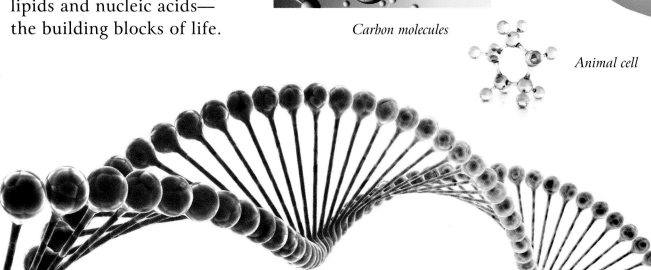

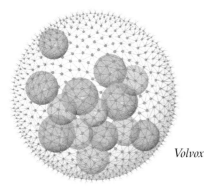

Volvox

Soon, many eukaryotic cells came together to form multicellular organisms such as the ancient Volvox, which was an aquatic organism.

The earliest multicellular organisms had soft bodies and lived in the sea. Most of them slowly began to resemble the modern-day jellyfish.

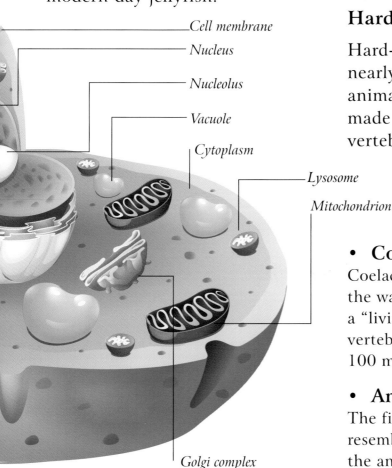

Cell membrane

Nucleus

Nucleolus

Vacuole

Cytoplasm

Lysosome

Mitochondrion

Golgi complex

Hard-bodied animals

Hard-bodied animals appeared on Earth nearly 500 million years ago. These animals had skeletons. Their bodies were made hard and strong by the presence of vertebrae.

- ### Coelacanth

Coelacanth is a type of fish that is found in the waters surrounding Africa. It is called a "living fossil". It resembles the earliest vertebrates, which came into existence nearly 100 million years ago.

- ### Amphibians

The first amphibians developed from fish that resemble the coelacanth of today. They are the ancestors of today's mammals, birds and reptiles. The first four-legged animal came into existence more than 350 million years ago. The first human beings came into existence only four million years ago.

An example of the Coelacanth

LIFE OF A PLANT

Plants make their own food through a process known as photosynthesis. Roots absorb water. Leaves take in carbon dioxide from the air and absorb sunlight with the help of chlorophyll in the leaves. This process produces carbohydrates and oxygen. Carbohydrates are stored in the leaves as starch and oxygen is released into the atmosphere through the stomata.

The growing stem and leaves of the seedling have emerged from below the ground.

Rafflesia or the corpse flower is a parasitic plant.

Heterotrophic nutrition

Some plants latch onto other plants and organisms for their nutrition. This mode of nutrition is called heterotrophic nutrition. Heterotrophic nutrition occurs in two types of plants: parasitic and saprophytic.

Growing into a plant

Plant cycle begins from seeds or spores. Non-flowering plants have spores on them. Spores are microscopic reproductive cells. Flowering plants give seeds. These seeds sprout into seedlings underground if they receive sufficient nutrients, water and sunlight.

Process of photosynthesis

The roots of a plant begin to grow from the seedling and spread into the soil. The stem appears above the soil. Leaves and flower buds then grow on the stem. Over time, the flower buds open to show the flower.

Production of seeds

Flowering plants produce their own seeds. Usually, pollen grains are carried to other flowers by wind. This is called "pollination". Some insects also help carry out the process of pollination. Honeybees sit on flowers to take the nectar from it. As they do this, the pollen in the flower sticks to their bodies. As they travel, they carry pollen grains with them. When they sit on another flower, they transfer the pollen to it.

Pollen grains are stuck to the legs of the honeybee.

Plant Reproduction

The reproductive system of a plant can be sexual or asexual. Flowers are a necessary part of sexual reproduction. All non-flowering plants carry out asexual reproduction.

Male and female parts of the flower

Stamens, the male part of the flower, produce pollen grains. Pollen grains contain two sperm cells. Carpels contain egg cells which fuse with these sperm cells to fertilise the egg and produce the embryo of the seed. This seed can then germinate into a new plant.

Spreading Seeds

Seeds spread to different parts of a landform as they cannot grow near the parent plant. They might not get enough sunlight and water. There are different methods of dispersal.

The seeds of the dandelion are separated from the flower.

SCIENCE

Water

These seeds are waterproof. They might be hollow or fluffy to enable them to float in water.

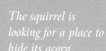

The seeds of the lotus plant are also dispersed through water.

The squirrel is looking for a place to hide its acorn.

Animals

Some seeds are contained in fruits which animals eat. After eating the fruit, the animals might spit or excrete these seeds. Squirrels like to store acorns for winter. Some squirrels might forget where they have hidden the acorn. These acorns might grow into trees.

Wind

Some seeds are very small and light. They might have wings or fluffy bits. Such seeds can easily be carried away by the wind.

Burdock seeds with hook-like structures

Hitch-hiking seeds

Some seeds are sticky while some seeds have hook-like structures. When an animal interacts with the plant, these seeds stick to the hair or fur on the animal's body. They go where the animals go. Later, they might drop from the animal on a suitable part of land and grow.

LIFE OF ANIMALS

The life cycle of a living organism is the sequence of developmental stages that it passes through towards adulthood. In some species, it is a very slow and gradual process, whereas in others, it is fast. For example, the life cycle of some insects is only of a few weeks, whereas the life cycle of sea urchins lasts for many years.

Reproduction

Sexual reproduction is found in animals with separate male and female genders. Animals like slugs, snails and barnacles can reproduce asexually. Mammals give birth to young ones–whereas like dogs, giraffes and elephants, birds, fish and reptiles lay eggs. In some animals like sharks, eggs are incubated inside the body, before birthing the young.

The caterpillar attaches itself to a twig and sheds its outer skin, and within hours, changes into a pupa.

As tadpoles change into frogs, they slowly develop legs and their tail starts shrinking.

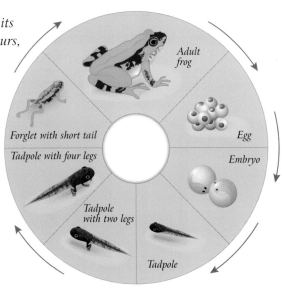

Adult frog

Egg

Embryo

Forglet with short tail

Tadpole with four legs

Tadpole with two legs

Tadpole

Different life cycles

Frogs have a very interesting lifecycle. After their birth, baby frogs called tadpoles swim in water with gills. Later, they grow lungs–and can live both on land and water. The lifecycle of an insect is completed in a few stages, namely, egg, larva, pupa and adult.

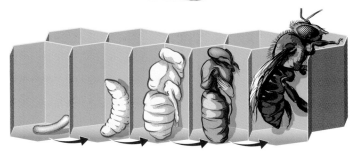

Adaptation

Environmental conditions like water, temperature and light affect the development of an organism. They have to struggle for food, safety and reproduction. Other examples of animals evolving to adapt to their environment is navigating, migrating, camouflaging and hibernation.

Camouflaging and hibernation

A chameleon is the best example of an animal that uses camouflage to protect itself from birds of prey by changing its skin colour to match the background. Bears hibernate for months during and snakes the winters as this helps them conserve their energy and keep warm.

Navigating and migrating

Sandhoppers are small, shrimp-like animals that live on sandy beaches. Every 24 hours, they migrate into the sea. They use the sun to navigate themselves in the direction of the sea, and out of it every day. This helps them survive the heat and cold of the day.

FOOD CHAIN

A food chain is the order of transfer of matter and energy in the form of food from one organism to another. Food chains intertwine locally into a food web because most organisms consume more than one type of animal or plant. Plants that convert solar energy to food through photosynthesis are the primary sources of food.

Tiger attacks a deer that eats plants.

A real life food chain

Consider a grassland. There are various insects that live in it. One of them is a grasshopper that feeds on it. However, this grasshopper is then hunted by rats. Then rats become prey for reptiles like snakes. Snakes are in turn hunted by predator birds like insert eagles and hawks.

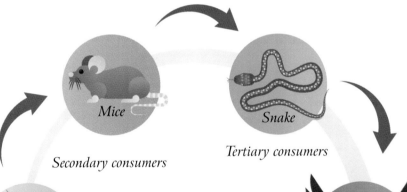

Food Chain

Mice
Secondary consumers

Snake
Tertiary consumers

Hawk
Final consumer

Grasshopper
Primary consumer

Grass
Producer

Fungi
Decomposers

Food chain types

In a predator chain, a plant-eating animal is eaten by a flesh-eating animal. In a parasite chain, a smaller organism consumes a part of a larger host and may itself play host to even smaller organisms. In a saprophytic chain, microorganisms live on dead, organic matter.

The food chain begins from grass and ends with the hawk. If the hawk were to die, it would be fed upon by the microorganisms in the soil, converting it into food for the plants. That is how the loop is closed.

Energy loss

As energy is lost at each step in the form of heat, chains do not normally encompass more than four or five tropic levels. People can increase the total food supply by removing one step in the food chain. Instead of consuming animals that eat plants, people can eat plants directly. As the food chain is made shorter, the total amount of energy available to the final consumers is increased.

159

BIOSPHERE

In the term biosphere, "bio" means life and "sphere" means surrounding. Scientists use the term sphere for describing various parts of Earth where life exists, such as atmosphere, lithosphere, hydrosphere, geosphere, anthrosphere and cryosphere. These spheres constitute the biosphere.

Sun　　*Atmosphere*

Earth

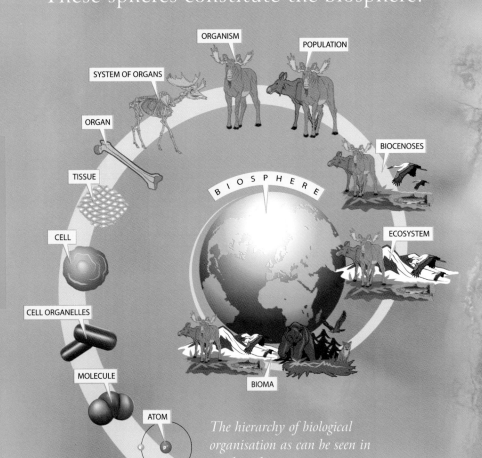

The hierarchy of biological organisation as can be seen in our biosphere.

Biodiversity

Biodiversity or biological diversity is the variation in the life found on Earth along with all the natural processes. Biodiversity includes variations in genes, ecosystems and species.

Balance of life

The number of tigers is decreasing very fast. What will happen if there are no tigers left? Being the carnivorous and dangerous animals that they are, you might want to get rid of them, but they should not disappear as every species is important for life on Earth.

Human action

During the early life of human beings, the number of species living on Earth was very large. But as human beings made progress, the number of species decreased steeply. Because of human behaviour there have been great changes in climate, seasons, atmospheric gases, water and land. These changes, in turn, affect the habitats and behaviours of different species.

As we know, there is a great bonding between living organisms and their surrounding environment; they both depend on each other. By the destruction of any species, the food chain gets disturbed. This affects the ecosystems and, simultaneously, the life of human beings as well.

ECOSYSTEM

Ecosystem is the term used for the community of living organisms that live, stay, feed, reproduce and interact in the same area or environment. An ecosystem is always accompanied by the energy flow and cycling of elements between the biotic and abiotic components present in it.

Aquatic Ecosystem

An ecosystem can be as small as a plant and as large as a desert or an ocean. An ecosystem can be described as the study of the flow of energy and materials through organisms and their environment.

The tallest tree is the canopy

Terrestrial Ecosystem

Trees protected by the canopy.

Broadly, ecosystems are classified into two categories: the aquatic ecosystem and terrestrial ecosystem. Aquatic ecosystem includes marine and freshwater ecosystems while terrestrial ecosystem largely depends upon the type of dominant vegetation. It is further divided into categories like forest, littoral, riparian, urban and desert.

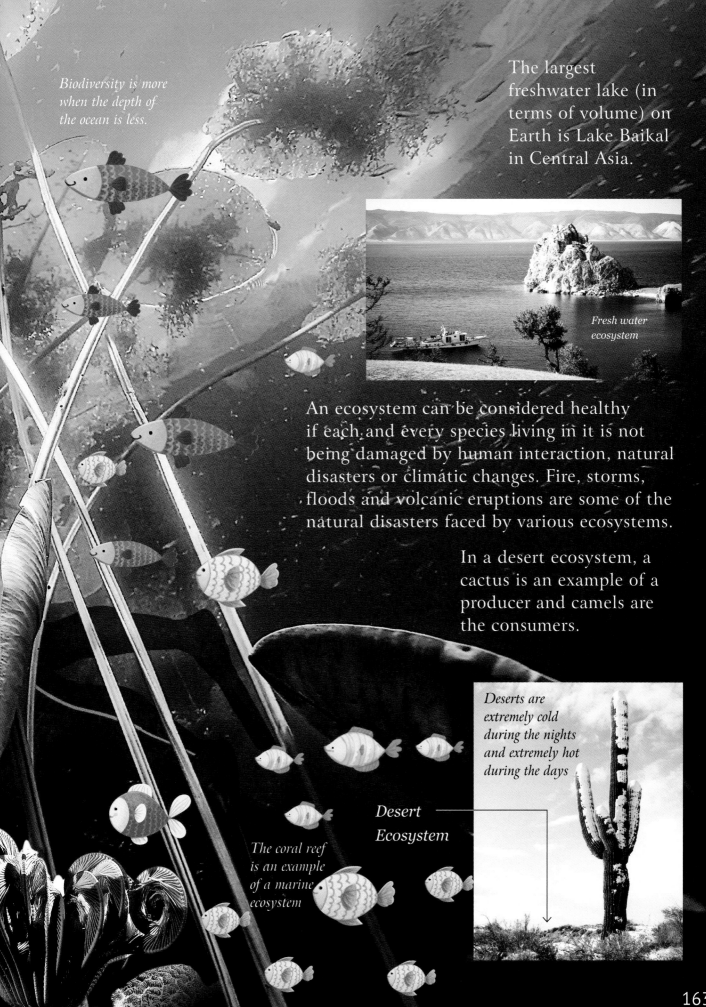

Biodiversity is more when the depth of the ocean is less.

The largest freshwater lake (in terms of volume) on Earth is Lake Baikal in Central Asia.

Fresh water ecosystem

An ecosystem can be considered healthy if each and every species living in it is not being damaged by human interaction, natural disasters or climatic changes. Fire, storms, floods and volcanic eruptions are some of the natural disasters faced by various ecosystems.

In a desert ecosystem, a cactus is an example of a producer and camels are the consumers.

Deserts are extremely cold during the nights and extremely hot during the days

Desert Ecosystem

The coral reef is an example of a marine ecosystem

INTELLIGENT MAMMALS

Mammals are the most intelligent animals. They are animals with hair or fur covering their bodies. The females carry their young ones in their wombs and then give birth to them. The young ones feed on their mother's milk. All mammals are vertebrates, which means that they have backbones.

A mother kangaroo is also called a marsupial as it carries its young one (joey) in a pouch.

The young ones

Most mammal babies stay close to their mothers after birth. A kangaroo baby (called "joey") is as small as a thumb when born. It lives in its mama's pouch. After many weeks it comes outside. At ten months old, it is ready to hop besides its mother.

The koala baby rides its mother's back as she goes hunting for food. The koala mother hunts for food on treetops and the koala baby hangs on tight.

Eating habits

Once mammal babies develop their teeth, they begin to eat solid foods like grass, leaves or meat. For example, the papa wolf hunts for meat, chews it up then spits it out for his babies. The baby wolves first play with the meat and then taste it. They don't go back to milk again.

A cub learning to eat meat.

Mammal babies

Some mammal babies are very weak when they are born. Some are born with their eyes shut. Some are born without the ability to walk. As babies, all mammals feed on their mother's milk. All female mammals have mammary glands which produce milk. Only mammals can produce their own milk. As they grow up, mammal babies learn to eat the food their parents eat.

A time for learning

Baby mammals learn to walk, eat, hunt and play from their parents. When the mama bear eats berries and catches fish, the baby bear watches her and then slowly tries it herself. If the baby elephant tries to leave its mother, she will push it with her big trunk. This teaches the baby elephant to stay with its herd.

COLD-BLOODED REPTILES

Reptiles are animals whose bodies are covered with scales. The young ones hatch from eggs. Being a cold-blooded animal means their body temperature varies with that of the environment. This is different from warm-blooded animals, like mammals, whose body temperatures remain the same.

SCIENCE

It becomes difficult for predators to find the eggs of turtles.

Laying eggs

Turtles, snakes, lizards, alligators and crocodiles are reptiles. All reptiles lay eggs. An alligator lays its eggs and stays close to them for two months until the eggs hatch. Once they do, it leaves. Turtles dig holes in the ground and lay their eggs in the holes. They cover them up with twigs, sticks and mud so that they are hidden. Then, they leave.

The eggs are hatched under the heat of the sun. Baby turtles climb out of the hole in search of food. Parent reptiles do not help their young ones grow up. Some kinds of snakes warm and protect their eggs by rolling their bodies around them. Once they hatch, the snakes leave.

Shedding skin

Reptiles like snakes and lizards shed their skin. As snakes grow, they become too big for their skin. They grow new skin underneath. The old skin becomes loose and wrinkly.

Then, as they crawl between smooth rocks and hard branches, the skin begins to peel off. The skin falls away, leaving the snake with its shiny new skin.

Snake skin

Lizards have legs and tear their old skin off with their mouth. Some even feed on their old skin. Snakes and lizards do not feel pain when they shed their skin. If a lizard's tail breaks off, it simply grows a new one. It does not feel pain upon losing its tail.

Flexible mouths

Snakes feed on rats, lizards, rabbits, eggs and other snakes. Snakes sswallow their food whole; opening their mouths very wide to accommodate their food. The bones in their throats cut and crack their food, and they spit out the remnants.

167

ADAPTIVE AMPHIBIANS

Animals that can live on land and water are called "amphibians". All amphibians are vertebrates, which means that they have a backbone. Historically, it is believed that the first vertebrates on Earth were amphibians. Amphibians are also considered to be the ancestors of mammals and reptiles. Toads, frogs and salamanders are amphibians.

Lower, football-shaped eyes

Can run or hop

Mostly lives on land

Short legs

Stout Body

Toads

Toad's skin is rough and bumpy to touch

Toads and frogs

Frogs and toads have various overlapping characteristics; they have a similar body structure and no tail. Both have eyes on top of their heads. However, a toad is bigger and fatter. Its back legs are smaller and shorter. Its skin has warts and is rough and bumpy to touch. A frog's skin is smooth and shiny. It feels wet to touch.

Life cycle

The female amphibian lays eggs in water. The eggs live in the water as larva. Then comes the "tadpole" stage where the baby frog or toad emerges from the egg with a tail. At this stage, it has gills, allowing them to breathe underwater. As they grow, the larva loses gills and develops lungs. Some amphibians lose their tails and develop front and back legs. Now, amphibians are able to live on land for part of their lives.

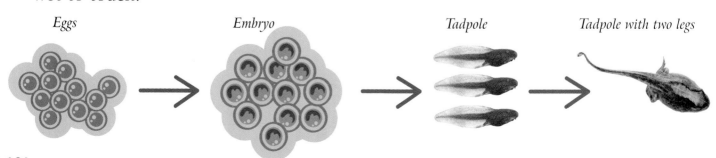

Eggs

Embryo

Tadpole

Tadpole with two legs

SCIENCE

Salamanders

Salamanders and newts have tails. Depending on the species, they vary in size. While some can be tinier than your thumb, others can be larger than an adult human. Salamanders also have thin bodies with four legs. Like reptiles, a salamander is able to grow back its tail and even its legs if it loses them.

Many salamanders are camouflaged, whereas others are boldly patterned or brightly coloured.

Caecilians

Caecilians resemble worms. The larger ones look more like snakes.Caecilians do not have arms or legs.They have thin, elongated bodies. Their skin covers their eyes, which indicates that these animals are partially or completely blind. Caecilians like to remain hidden underground or live in water.

Lays eggs in clusters

Slim body

Higher, bulgier eyes

Can leap or jump

Mostly long-legged creatures

Frog

Mostly lives in water

Smooth and moist skin

Caecilians look like big worms

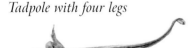

Tadpole with four legs

Young Frog

Adult Frog

169

FEATHERY BIRDS

Birds are warm-blooded animals. Their bodies are covered with feathers that act as insulation. They lay eggs. Birds are bipedal or have two legs that are used for perching, walking and hopping.

Birds have beaks instead of mouths.

Features

Birds are warm-blooded vertebrates. Instead of forelimbs, birds have wings which enable them to fly. All birds have sharp vision which provides them with information about their surroundings. However, their sense of smell and hearing is not as sharp.

Feathers

There are different types of feathers on a bird's body. Feathers only cover some part of a bird's body. Soft feathers or down feathers cover the inner portion of the bird's body. The down feathers keep the bird warm. The other feathers are used to fly.

SCIENCE

Coming out of the egg

Birds lay eggs in order to reproduce. When it is ready, the baby bird uses the tiny tooth on its bill to crack open the egg and push its way out. It loses this tooth a few days later as it no longer needs it.

The peacock is the male bird of this species. It has long, beautiful feathers.

Baby birds

Most baby birds are too weak. They stay in the nest or close to it with their eyes tightly shut. Their bodies do not have feathers and their legs are too weak. The mother bird hunts for food like little worms and feeds it to her babies. However, some birds like baby flamingos, ducks, chickens and geese have wide open eyes and are able to leave their nest a few minutes after they hatch. They follow their mother around for food.

Imprinting

This is a natural biological phenomenon that occurs in newly-born birds and mammals, allowing them to form a bond with their mother as well as providing them with information about their own identity. For birds like ducks, geese and turkeys that start walking as soon as they hatch, the imprint occurs instantly.

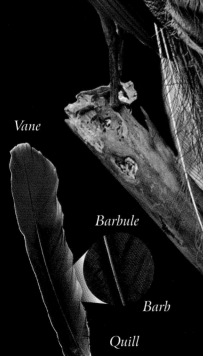

Vane

Barbule

Barb

Quill

AQUATIC FISH

A fish is an aquatic animal that lives in water. However, not all animals that live in water can be called fish. Dolphins and whales are mammals, not fish. The body of a fish is covered with scales. A fish swims with the help of fins and a tail, and has gills to breathe.

Gills

Fish have small slits at the front of their heads. They are placed right behind or next to the mouth. They are gills. Fish take in the oxygen mixed with the water through their gills. They let out carbon dioxide. Aquatic plants use this carbon dioxide to carry out the process of photosynthesis.

All fish more or less have the same number of fins in the same position.

Sticky eggs

Fish lay many eggs at one time. Some fish lay thousands of eggs while some lay millions of eggs. This is because fish eggs are very delicate. Unlike bird or reptile eggs, they do not have hard shells. They are soft and jelly-like. They stick to the ocean floor or a rock. Other fish might eat these eggs. Some eggs might float to the top and dry up. Only a handful of the eggs finally give baby fish.

The shiny, sticky eggs of a clownfish have settled on a surface.

Fins and eyes

Fish have big eyes and no eyelids. Fish swim with the help of their fins. They have one big fin on their back, two smaller ones on their sides, and a broad fin called a tail.

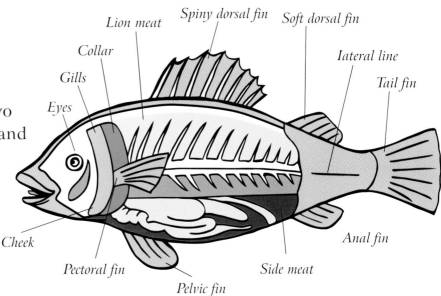

Lion meat
Collar
Gills
Eyes
Spiny dorsal fin
Soft dorsal fin
Iateral line
Tail fin
Cheek
Pectoral fin
Pelvic fin
Side meat
Anal fin

Father fish

Some mother fish, like seahorses, lay their eggs in the mouths and pouches of the father fish. The mother seahorse lays her eggs in the pouch of the father seahorse. Baby seahorses come shooting out of this pouch when they are ready. The father fish guard the nests or spots where the eggs are laid. Once they hatch, father fish teach their babies to swim and feed them food.

MANY-LEGGED ARTHROPODS

Arthropods belong to a class of animals called "Arthropoda". They are classified into insects, arachnids and crustaceans based on how many legs they have. Insects have six legs, arachnids have eight legs and crustaceans have ten legs. There are about a million species of arthropods and billions of each species present on Earth. No matter where you go, you will come across an arthropod.

A grasshopper's organs for taste are located in the mouth, and those for smell are on the antennae.

Six-legged insects

Insects are also called "hexapods" where "hex" means six and "pods" means feet. We can easily differentiate an insect from other types or arthropods by looking at their bodies. An insect has antennae on its head, its eyes and mouth are also present here. The thorax (the part between the head and midsection) of an insect has its six legs and, in the case of adults, its wings. The abdomen has many segments and it contains the organs of reproduction, digestion and excretion.

Crabs have sharp pincers at the ends of their legs.

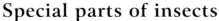

Ladybird

Special parts of insects

Insects taste with their feet. One eye of an insect has hundreds of smaller eyes. These eyes capture only part of the image Insects smell with their antennae or "feelers".

Insects have antennae on their heads.

Eight-legged arachnids

Spiders are classic examples of arachnids. Mites, scorpions and tarantulas are other examples or arachnids. The common feature amongst all of them is that they have eight legs. While some have small, round bodies like mites, others have large, sharp and pointed bodies like scorpions. Some have hair while some do not.

Most arachnids live on land except for some that either live on, or feed on, water. All arachnids are creatures of prey, which means they are parasitic, or completely eat other creatures.

All arachnids have eight legs.

Ten-legged crustaceans

Crustaceans are those arthropods which hav crusts on their skin. Crabs, shrimps and lobsters fall under the category of crustaceans. Unlike other arthropods, most crustaceans are aquatic in nature. Lobsters have a long and lean structure, whereas crabs are round and small. Along with ten legs, crustaceans also have four feelers. Most have gills to help them breathe.

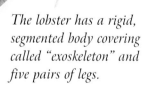

The lobster has a rigid, segmented body covering called "exoskeleton" and five pairs of legs.

HUMAN BODY

The human body is the most intricately working living system. You would be familiar with your body parts, but do you know how many systems are working in your body? The cell is the basic unit of life. Cells combine and form tissue, which in turn form organs, and these organs together form the structure of the body.

Ventral Cavity

Thoracic cavity

Pleural cavity

Mediastinum and pericardial cavity

Abdominopelvic

Abdominal cavity

Pelvic cavity

There are 206 bones in an adult human body. A child has more bones which then fuse as the body grows older.

The human heart beats at a rate of 73 beats per minute. This is the pulse rate that we feel in our wrist.

The human body can be divided into many body cavities like pelvic cavity, thoracic cavity, abdominal cavity and dorsal cavity. Many small cavities are also there, which are called sinuses.

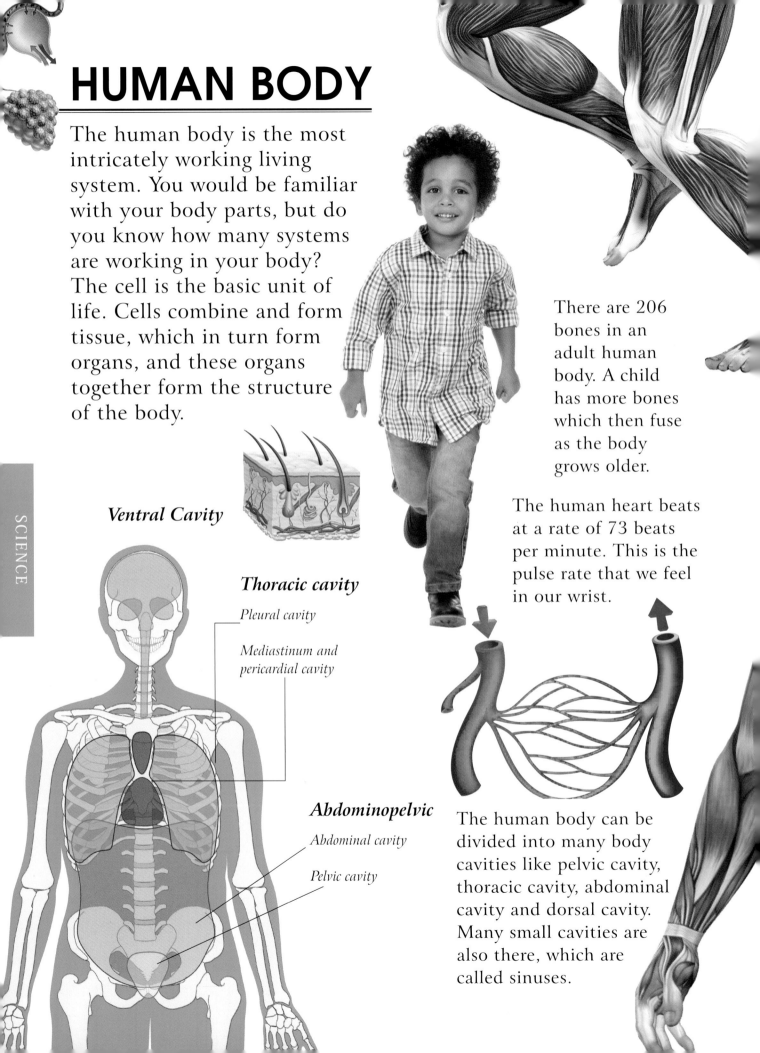

The small intestine found in the abdomen is six metres long.

Copper, zinc, cobalt, calcium, manganese, phosphates, nickel and silicon are found in our body in different forms.

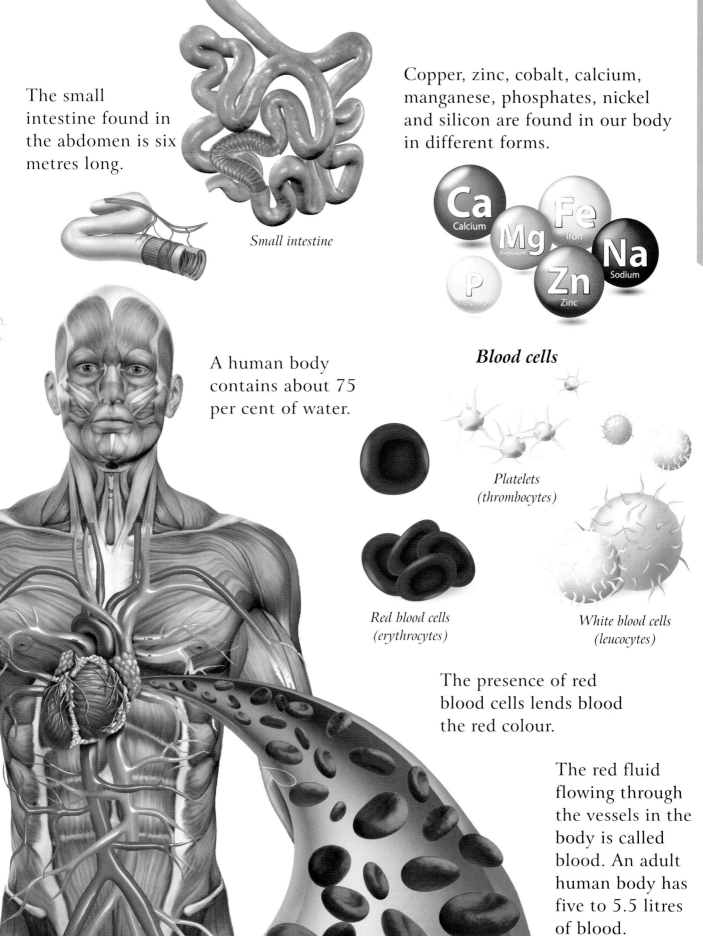

Small intestine

Blood cells

A human body contains about 75 per cent of water.

Platelets
(thrombocytes)

Red blood cells
(erythrocytes)

White blood cells
(leucocytes)

The presence of red blood cells lends blood the red colour.

The red fluid flowing through the vessels in the body is called blood. An adult human body has five to 5.5 litres of blood.

177

BONES

Bones are rigid organs that together constitute the vertebral skeleton. The red and white cells of blood are produced inside these bones. The bones consist of dense connective tissues of cortical and cancellous type. They are light in weight but strong and hard, and store different minerals. The different types of bones are flat, long, short, irregular and sesamoid bones.

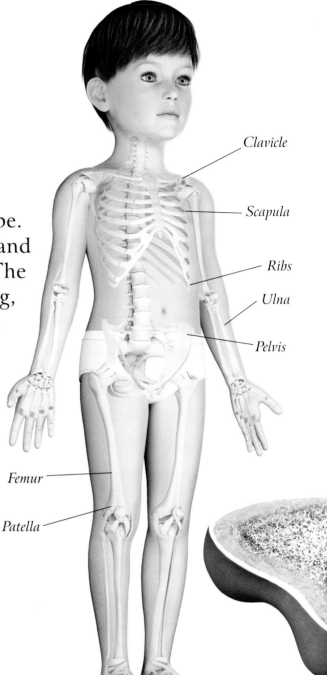

Clavicle

Scapula

Ribs

Ulna

Pelvis

Femur

Patella

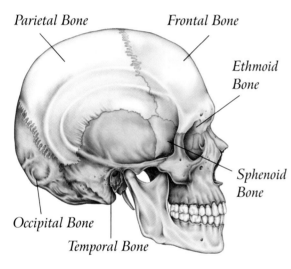

Parietal Bone

Frontal Bone

Ethmoid Bone

Sphenoid Bone

Occipital Bone

Temporal Bone

Skeleton

In our body, the femur (thigh bone) is the longest bone. The stirrup inside the ear is the smallest bone. Each hand has 26 bones.

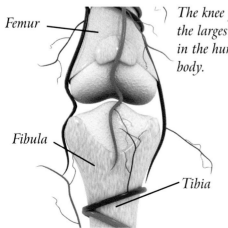

Femur

The knee joint is the largest joint in the human body.

Fibula

Tibia

The elbow joint helps to extend and rotate the forearm and the wrists.

Cartilage

The nose and ears are not made of bone but of cartilage. The cartilage is not as hard as the bone and is made out of flexible bone tissue. This is the reason why we can squish our nose and bend our ears without breaking them.

Bone injury

There are basically three types of fractures. The first is a hair-line fracture. This type of fracture happens when the impact on the bone is not too high and is a minor crack. The second type of fracture is called a complete fracture. This ranges from a gap between the crack in the bone to a completely snapped bone. Third type is when, the bone slips out of its position. This is known as a dislocation. This can occur at any of the joints.

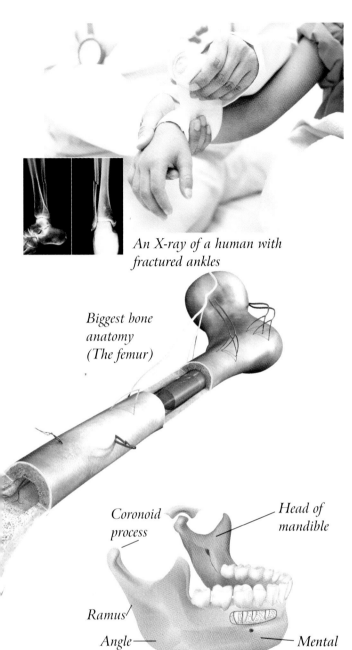

An X-ray of a human with fractured ankles

Biggest bone anatomy (The femur)

Coronoid process

Head of mandible

Ramus

Angle

Mental foramen

Joints

Joints, also known as bony articulations, are the strongest point of meeting of two or more bones; also attach teeth and cartilage in the body with one another. Think what would have happened, if our body would have been composed of a single, rigid bone. We would have been strong, but without any locomotion or movement. That is why joints are vital in our body.

Structure of a joint

A joint is covered by a tough, fibrous capsule, which restricts its motion, and a fluid called synovium present inside the joint capsule, which provides lubrication and prevents friction. Ligaments are muscles that give strength to the joints and avoid dislocation. Tendons are muscles that attach the bones to other muscles. Thus, joints are parts of the body that make bending, stretching, twisting and turning activities possible.

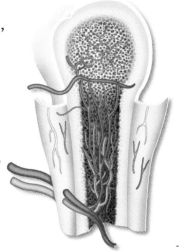

The upper bone is called a femur and the lower two bones are the tibia and fibulla.

179

MUSCLES AND MOVEMENT

A total of 650 muscles constitute the muscular system of the human body. . Our daily life activities like walking, sitting, standing, bending, drinking and eating are all controlled by muscles. There are many other functions of the muscles like pumping of the heart and breathing with lungs.

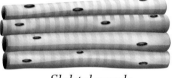

Skeletal muscle

Cardiac muscle

Smooth muscle

Types of muscles
Skeletal muscles

Skeletal muscles are the striated, voluntary muscles of our body. They control all the consciously performed activities.

Smooth muscles

Smooth muscles are also known as involuntary muscles as these are controlled by the unconscious part of the brain. These muscles are spindle-shaped muscles found in the visceral organs of the body. Their wave-like actions generate peristalsis movement and help in passing food, blood, urine, and air from one organ to another.

Skeletal muscle

Cardiac muscles

Cardiac muscles are the striated involuntary muscles found in the heart. These types of muscles can generate electrical impulses, which produce rhythmic contractions in the heart.

The human body has to make use of multiple and many muscles while running.

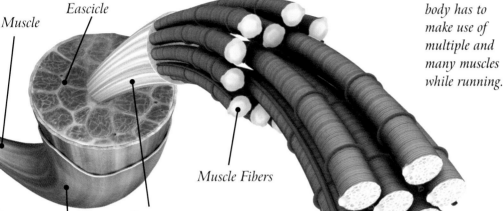

Muscle

Eascicle

Muscle Fibers

Perimysium

Epimysium

Nucleus

How muscles get fatigued

Our muscles get fatigued when we work excessively. This is because our muscles use energy from one or the other source of our body to work. During excessive workout, the muscles lack this energy, causing waste products like lactic acid to get accumulated, thereby making us feel tired.

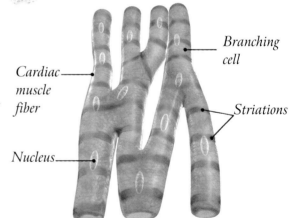

Cardiac muscle

Branching cell

Cardiac muscle fiber

Striations

Nucleus

Functions of the muscles

Muscles are the only part of the body possessing the ability to contract. That is why they are necessary for locomotion or movement. Muscles maintain the posture of the body and are also responsible for generating body heat.

We use the muscles of our back and stomach to bend over and touch our toes.

NERVES

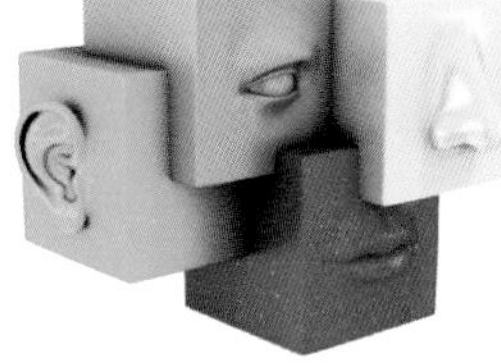

A nerve is a specialised cell or cord-like bundle of fibres that transmits nerve impulses in the form of electrochemical signals from different organs to the brain and from the brain to different organs and body parts. The term used for diseases related to nerves is neuropathy.

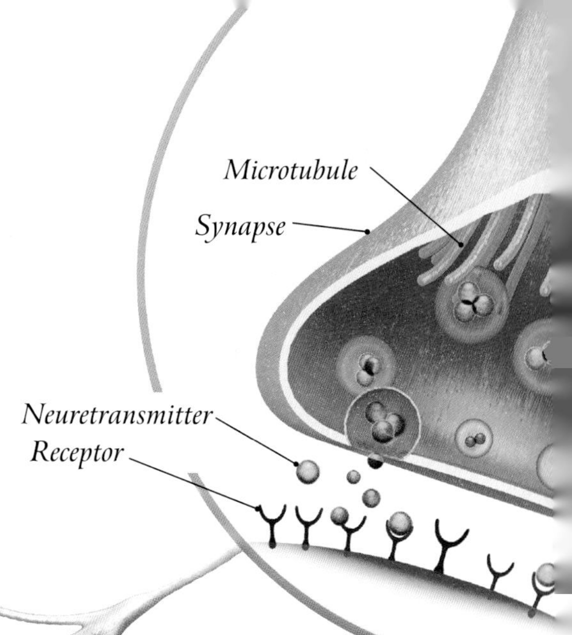

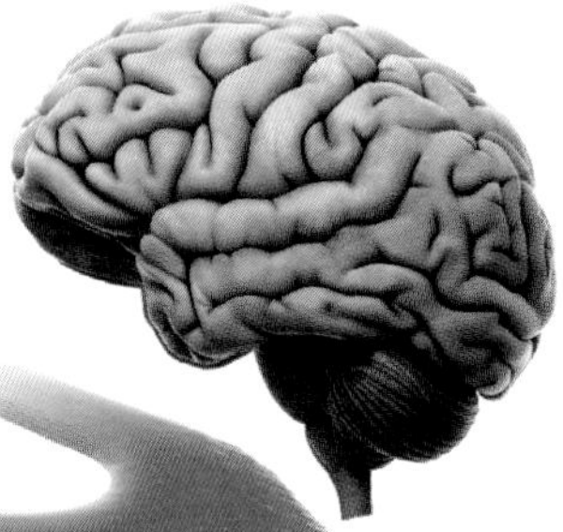

The brain is the headquarter of our nervous system.

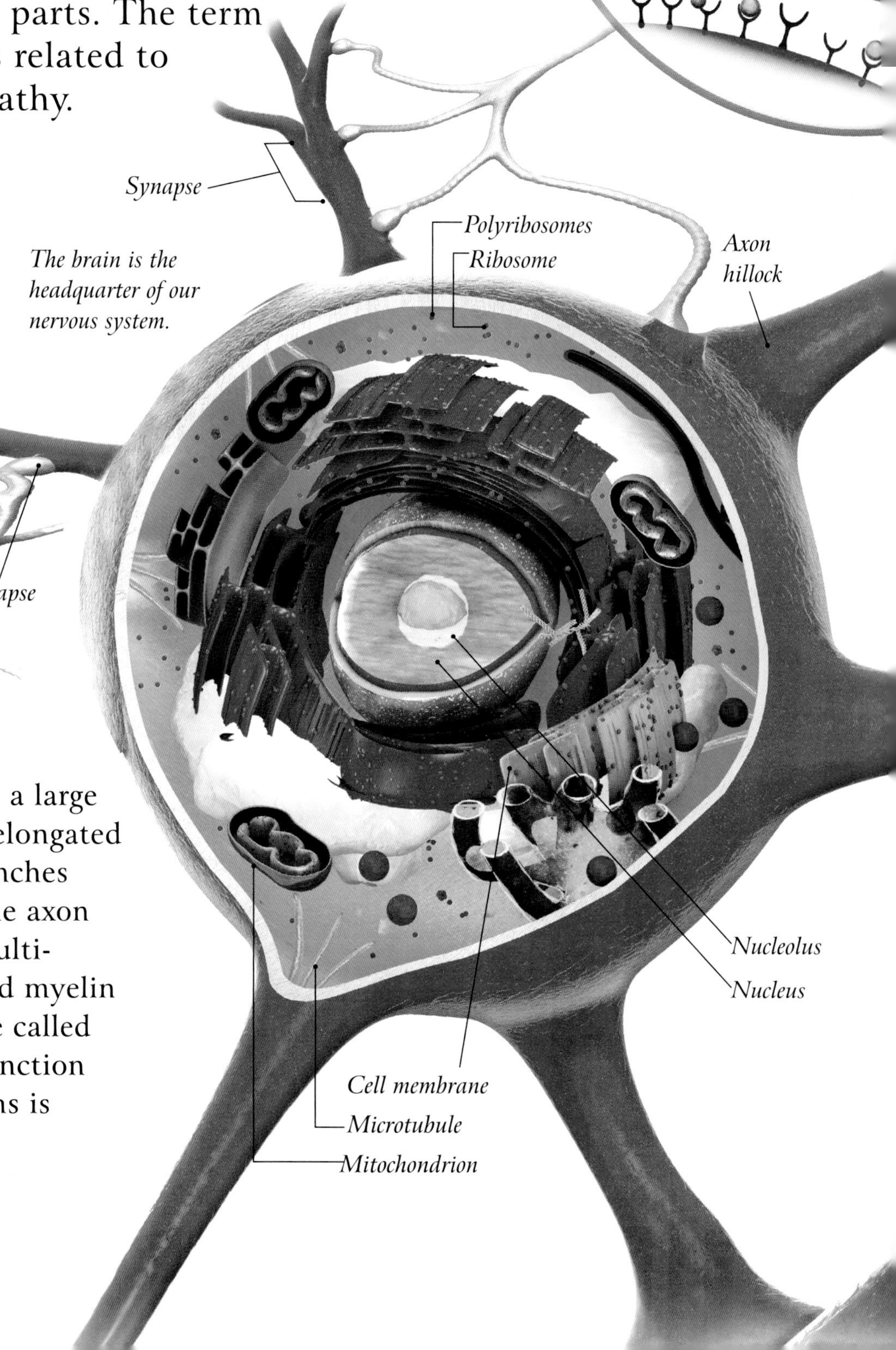

Microtubule

Synapse

Neuretransmitter

Receptor

Synapse

Polyribosomes

Ribosome

Axon hillock

Synapse

Nucleolus

Nucleus

Cell membrane

Microtubule

Mitochondrion

Structure

A neuron comprises a large cell body with one elongated axon and many branches called dendrites. The axon is surrounded by multi-layered sheath called myelin and/ or a membrane called neurilemma. The junction between two neurons is called the synapse.

Types

There are three types of nerves based on the direction of the electrical signals they carry.

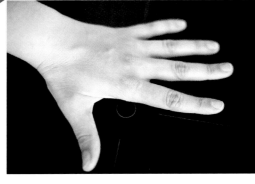

Node of Ranvier

Sensory nerves: These nerves transmit impulses from the sensory organs to the brain. For example, when we touch a hot utensil by mistake, the sensory nerves from the skin of our hands send signals to our brain.

Myelin sheeath

Nucleus

Microtubule

Microfilaments

Motor nerves: These nerves transmit impulses from the brain to organs, glands and muscles. For example, on getting a message from our hand, the brain signals the hand to move it back and we retract our hand.

Autonomic nerves: These nerves control involuntary actions of the body like temperature regulation, digestion, blood pressure and heart rate. For example, our heart beats faster to pump more blood when we are active.

183

SENSES

Aristotle mentioned five sense organs present in the human body. Sense is the physiological capacity of an organism to react to some external stimuli. The five senses that a human body has are smell, sight, sound, taste and touch.

Seeing: A human being possesses a pair of eyes for visual perception. Each eye remains connected to the brain by the optic nerve, which gives electrical impulses to the brain for detecting and forming images. Different parts of the eye include lens, conjunctiva, retina, pupil, cornea, iris and fovea. Rods and cones are the two photoreceptor cells present in the eye.

Smell: The nose is an organ that detects smell or olfaction. It has hundreds of small olfactory receptors which are responsible for the detection of odorants (i.e., compounds that have an odour) which give rise to the sense of smell. Our brain can store memories with respect to different smells. This is why we can recognise smells.

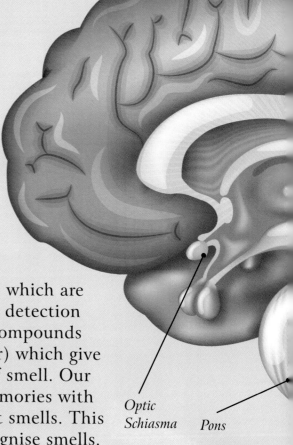

Optic Schiasma   Pons

Taste: Tongue is the sense organ of taste that has taste buds present on it for differentiating between various tastes like bitter, sour, sweet and salty. We taste these different tastes at different parts of the tongue.

SCIENCE

Sound: Ears are the sense organs for hearing. The tympanic membrane in the ear vibrates on hearing a sound. These vibrations reach the small bones of the internal ear that sends signals to our brain and enables us to hear.

Limbic Lobe

Parietal Lobe

The five sensory organs that enable us to survive.

Occipital Lobe

Touch: This is a perception that results from the excitation of the minute hair and various nerve endings present all over the body that communicate with the brain.

Pineal Gland

Cerebellum

More than five
Besides these five senses, there are many other senses by which a human body can react to many changes in the environment, like temperature, pain, balance, vibration, time, thirst, hunger and many other internal stimuli.

Brain has the capacity for perceiving, interpreting and organising the data received by sense organs. Sensing initially occurs at the cellular level, which then goes to the brain by the nervous system.

BLOOD AND CIRCULATION

The circulatory system of the body includes the heart, lungs, arteries, veins, capillaries, coronary vessels and blood. This system facilitates the movement of nutrients, gases, blood as well as hormones.

Constitution of blood

Blood constitutes 55 per cent plasma and 45 per cent blood cells. Different types of blood cells are produced in the bone marrow of human beings.

Plasma

The plasma is a liquid containing water, proteins, glucose and nutrients. It performs the function of transportation.

Platelets

Platelets help in clot formation, thus preventing bleeding.

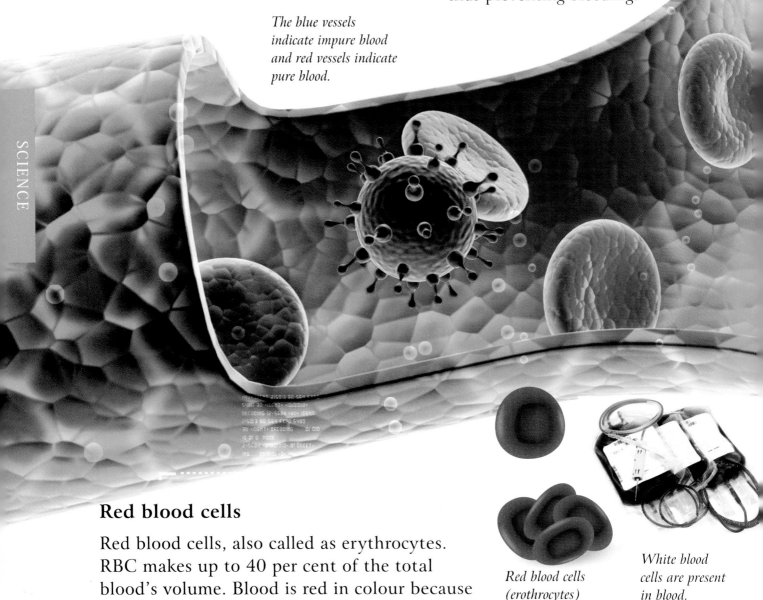

The blue vessels indicate impure blood and red vessels indicate pure blood.

Red blood cells (erothrocytes)

White blood cells are present in blood.

Red blood cells

Red blood cells, also called as erythrocytes. RBC makes up to 40 per cent of the total blood's volume. Blood is red in colour because of the presence of a protein called haemoglobin.

White blood cells

White blood cells, also known as leukocytes, constitute only one per cent of the blood. Based on the presence or absence of cytoplasmic granules, they are classified into two groups: granulocytes and agranulocytes.

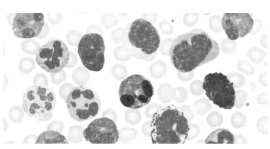

White blood cells

Functions

They are our bodyguards as they fight infections. They produce a special protein called antibodies for fighting various foreign elements.

White blood cells (lymphocytes)

Functions

Red blood cells carry oxygen from our lungs to the rest of our bodies. Then they make the return trip, taking carbon dioxide back to our lungs to be exhaled.

TGM 254
GR 2 N25.4

25.34
54.57
20   JH

RESPIRATION

Most cell activity requires chemical energy. Respiration is the cellular process of releasing energy from food. Cells require energy for activities such as growth and cell division. In animals, muscle cells require energy for contracting and nerve cells require energy for transmitting nerve impulses.

Organ system

The organs involved in respiration are nose, trachea, bronchi, bronchioles, lungs and diaphragm.

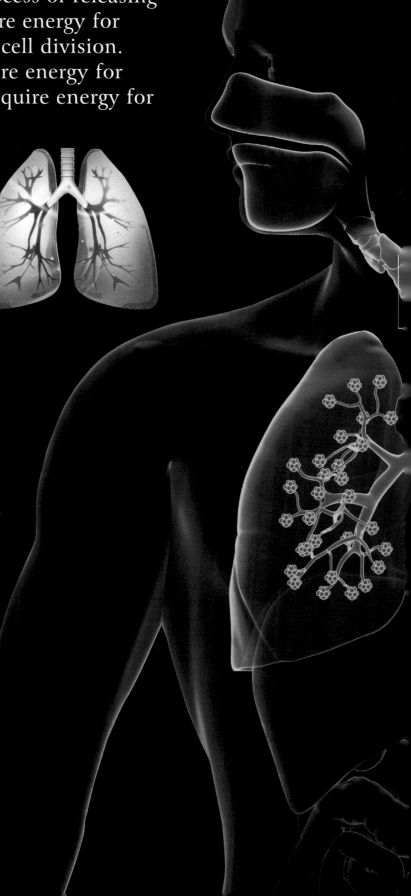

Factors affecting respiration

The main food used by cells for respiration is glucose.If oxygen is present then animal, plant and yeast cells can carry out aerobic respiration.

If oxygen is absent then respiration can still take place. Animal, plant and yeast cells complete the breakdown of food by carrying out fermentation. 15 times more energy is released per molecule of glucose when oxygen is present and aerobic respiration occurs.

The process of respiration is controlled by specific enzymes so is affected by the temperature of the cell environment.

As the human body has a large volume, ventilation is required, which affects the process of respiration. The transport pigment called the haemoglobin also plays an important role in the process of respiration. For example, when your body is doing a heavy workout, blood is pumped faster and hence the rate of respiration also increases.

Respiration

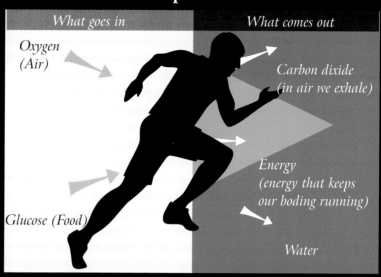

What goes in	What comes out
Oxygen (Air)	Carbon dixide (in air we exhale)
	Energy (energy that keeps our boding running)
Glucose (Food)	
	Water

Process of respiration

There are two lungs present in the chest cavity. Different types of muscles like pectoral muscles, external intercostal muscles and accessory muscles aid in the process of respiration. Nostrils have small hair that act as a filter and remove the dust and dirt from the air that is breathed in.

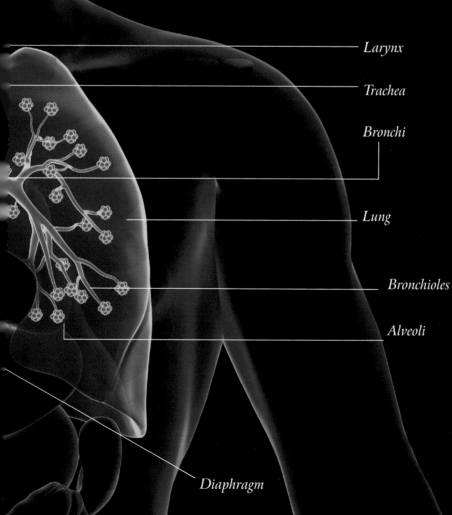

Larynx

Trachea

Bronchi

Lung

Bronchioles

Alveoli

Diaphragm

A man inhaling fresh air through his nose.

DIGESTION

The digestive system is one of the vital organ systems of our body. It is surprising how digestion actually occurs within the body and how we get energy from food. Food is the essential source of a body to obtain energy, vitamins and minerals. Digestion is the process that changes food into a simpler form, which our cells can absorb.

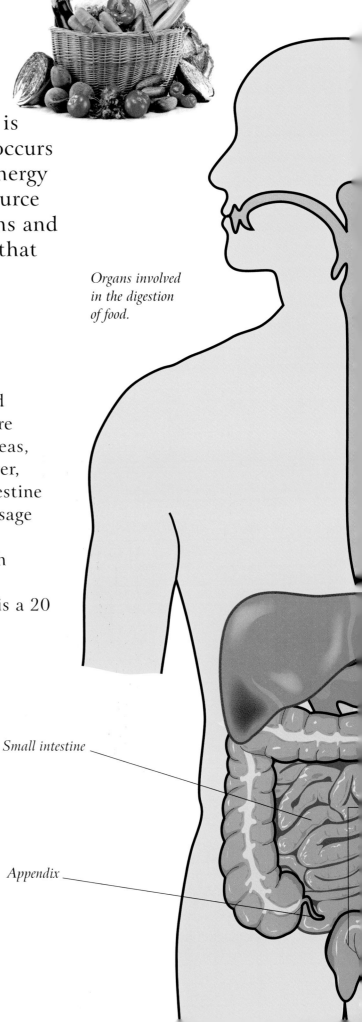

Organs involved in the digestion of food.

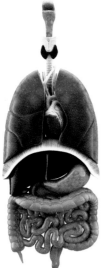

SCIENCE

Organ system

Different organs involved in the digestive system are teeth, oesophagus, pancreas, stomach, gall bladder, liver, small intestine, large intestine and anus. The entire passage through which the food journeys, from the mouth to the anus, is called the gastrointestinal tract. It is a 20 to 30-feet-long tube.

Passage of food

Mastication or chewing: The whole process of digestion starts from the mouth, where the teeth crush and chew food. This process is called the mastication of food. The saliva from the salivary glands mixes with food, forming a semi-liquid mass called bolus. The starch digests at this stage.

Small intestine

Appendix

Swallowing:

This bolus then passes through the oesophagus. In this stage, no digestion occurs and food passes through this pipe by peristalsis movement into the stomach.

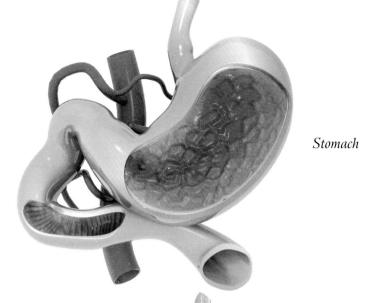

Stomach

Stomach:

As food comes to the stomach, it gets mixed with gastric juice, which is mainly composed of pepsin and hydrochloric acid. At this stage, protein digestion occurs.

Small intestine

Small intestine:

The food leaving the stomach is called chyme. Chyme enters the duodenum, the first part of the small intestine and mixes with the digestive enzymes coming from the pancreas and liver. At this stage, the remaining digestion occurs.

Large intestine:

The food then enters the cecum, colon and rectum. Water and minerals are re-absorbed by the colon, and the waste material goes out of the body through the rectum and a small opening called the anus.

 *Oesophagus*

Stomach

Large intestine

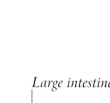

 Rectum

DNA

DNA, or deoxyribonucleic acid, is the hereditary material in humans and almost all other organisms. Nearly every cell in a person's body has the same DNA. An important property of DNA is that it can replicate, or make copies of itself. Each strand of DNA in the double helix can serve as a pattern for duplicating the sequence of bases. This is critical when cells divide because each new cell needs to have an exact copy of the DNA present in the old cell.

Nucleus of the eukaryotic cell

Discovery of DNA

English molecular biologists Francis Crick and American molecular biologists James Watson got the Nobel Prize in 1953 for the discovery of three-dimensional, double helical structure of DNA.

Analysing DNA samples

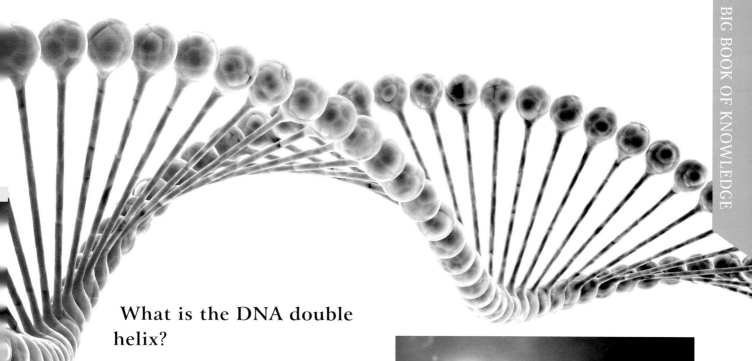

What is the DNA double helix?

The term "double helix" describes the DNA's two-stranded chemical structure. The shape gives DNA the power to pass along biological instructions with great precision. DNA's double helix's sides of the ladder has strands of alternating sugar and phosphate groups. These strands run in opposite directions. Each "rung" of the ladder is composed of two nitrogen bases paired together by hydrogen bonds. DNA's unique structure enables the molecules to copy itself during cell division.

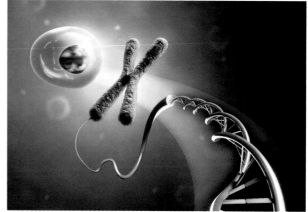

Formation of an animal cell from DNA

DNA location

In eukaryotes, DNA is present inside a cell in the nucleus. As the cell is very small and organisms have many DNA molecules per cell, each DNA molecule must be tightly packaged. This packaged form of DNA is called a chromosome. An organism's complete set of nuclear DNA is called its genome. Humans and other complex organisms have a small amount of DNA called mitochondria in their cell structure. Mitochondria generates the energy that the cell requires to function properly.

Scientist studying DNA Helix

KNOW YOUR GENE

The gene is a basic physical and functional unit of heredity that is transferred from an organism to its offspring and gives specific characteristics to the offspring. All organisms have genes related to their traits, from the eye colour to the many biochemical processes of life.

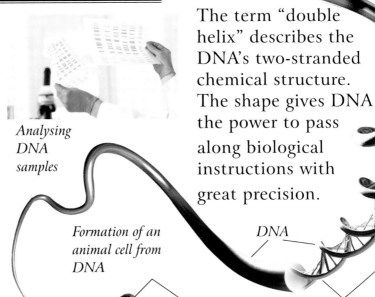

Analysing DNA samples

The term "double helix" describes the DNA's two-stranded chemical structure. The shape gives DNA the power to pass along biological instructions with great precision.

Formation of an animal cell from DNA

DNA

Gene

P arm

Cell

Nucleus

Chromosome

Mung bean is genetically modified

Nucleus of the eukaryotic cell.

Function of gene

A gene is the basic physical and functional unit of heredity. Genes are made up of DNA. Some genes act as instructions to make molecules called proteins. However, many genes do not code for proteins. In humans, genes vary in size from a few hundred DNA bases to more than 2 million bases. Every person has two copies of each gene, one inherited from each parent. Most genes are the same in all people, but a small number of genes (less than 1 percent of the total) are slightly different between people. Alleles are forms of the same gene with small differences in their sequence of DNA bases. These small differences contribute to each person's unique physical features.

RNA

RNA is short for ribonucleic acid. The nucleic acid that is used in key metabolic processes for all steps of protein synthesis in all living cells and carries the genetic information of many viruses. Unlike double-stranded DNA, RNA consists of a single strand of nucleotides, and it occurs in a variety of lengths and shapes.

The transmission of genes enables the child to have the characteristics of its parents.

194

Variation

Changes in the physical appearance of organisms are caused due to differences in their genes and the effect of their surroundings. Natural selection can be the cause of evolution if the offspring have a lot of genetic variation.

Few examples of different types of mutation of fruits and vegetables.

Exotic mutation in a pineapple making it look different from others

Kiwi in apple

Unusual mutation of carrot

Selection, mutation, migration and genetic drift were the processes that cause variations in genes.

Genetic disorder in a sheep caused by mutation.

Analysing DNA samples

Scientists keep track of genes by giving them unique names. Because gene names can be long, genes are also assigned symbols, which are short combinations of letters (and sometimes numbers) that represent an abbreviated version of the gene name. For example, a gene on chromosome 7 that has been associated with cystic fibrosis is called the cystic fibrosis transmembrane conductance regulator. Its symbol is CFTR.

What is a mutation?

Nucleotides, the building blocks of DNA, and their mutations change the observable traits of an organism. Mutations are also called errors in the genes.

Scientist studying DNA Helix

195

ENDANGERED SPECIES

A great biodiversity is found among animals on Earth, but due to gradually changing conditions like climate changes, diseases, hunting by human beings and habitat loss, many animal species are now either extinct or on the edge of extinction.

Mandarin duck

Over-hunting and over-fishing

These are some practices that create problems for a species to thrive. Animals are often hunted for food, medicine, leather products and providing a safe environment to other domestic animals and people.

Endangered Species

Of the 44,838 species assessed worldwide using the IUCN Red List criteria, 905 are extinct and 16,928 are listed as threatened to be extinct. Millions of species still need to be assessed to know their status. Palaeontologists suggest that about a third of amphibians, a quarter of mammals and every one out of eight birds are under the category of endangered species.

Siberian tiger

Bobcat

Dodo bird

Loggerhead turtle

SCIENCE

White tailed eagle

Loss of habitat

Humans are rapidly clearing forests to meet the demand for wood products. There is a growing need of land for agriculture, housing, transport and many other purposes. In this process, we deprive animals of their natural home.

Jackass penguin

Climate change

Due to global warming, there is drought, melting of glaciers and extreme temperatures. Animals cannot quickly adapt to these conditions. Polar bears are diminishing because of the rapid melting of the ice in polar regions.

Invasive species

Introduction of a new species to an area can make the native species endangered. This happens due to additional competition for food, shelter and reproduction for which the native species are not adapted.

Bactrian camel

Orangutans

Habitat preservation

This one of the approaches used to stop deforestation and preserve the natural habitat of animals. More national parks, sanctuaries and marine protected areas should be developed.

Pollution

We are polluting the environment by making air, water and soil unfit and unhealthy to use. Some industries dump their waste into rivers. This destroys the aquatic life and poisons the animals that drink from it. Garbage, plastics, oil spills, introduction of heavy metals and chemicals have harmed species to a great extent.

African wild dog

The logo of WWF(World Wildlife Fund) is a giant panda; the animal, which is on top of the list of endangered species.

Panda

Restoration of habitats

Sometimes, restoration of degraded habitats is possible by maintaining the land and environment, removal of invasive species and the reintroduction of the native species.

Captive breeding

This is the process of providing breeding environment to animals in fully controlled and restricted settings. For example, many types of snakes, like Boa Constrictors, are bred in captivity.

A plant grown in a controlled, artificial environment

Anti-poaching measures and laws

The government should make laws and apply strict punishment for the hunting of endangered species or selling any item that is made from the skin, bones and teeth of these endangered animals.

Government initiative to save Rhino in Nepal

Tibetan antelope

Remove fragmentation barriers

We should closely watch the barriers that we make by building roads, farms and cities through the forests. These activities create hurdles in the lives of the animals.

Control pollution

By stopping pollution and global warming, nature can once again become a safe haven for animals.

THE EXTINCTION OF SPECIES

The causes of extinction were prehistorically dominated by natural processes such as geological transformation of Earth's crust and major climatic oscillations, as well as species interactions. Since the ascent of man, the causes of extinction have been dominated by the activities of humans.

SCIENCE

Extinct species

Thylacine, also known as the Tasmanian tiger, became extinct in 1936 as it was hunted to protect the sheep and small farm animals.

Passenger Pigeons

went extinct as recently as 1914. They were hunted on a large scale for their meat.

The Woolly Mammoth is an extinct species of elephant.

As per scientists, long lasting natural calamities are the major cause for extinction.

Quagga is an extinct animal.

Dodo birds became extinct around the 1670s. They were known to have been hunted by sailors on a large scale as they were so easy to catch. Also, the pets of these sailors had developed a taste for Dodo eggs.

Quaggas became extinct in 1883 due to being hunted indiscriminately for their meat and leather.

Mass extinctions are periodic elevations in the extinction rate. Such extinctions are caused due to catastrophes. These events were geologically rapid, occurred worldwide, had a large number of species going extinct at the same time period and spread across all the world's ecosystems.

POPULATION EXPLOSION

The term "population explosion" is used to indicate the rapid growth rate of human beings in a short period in an area. This gives rise to many other problems like shortage of food, place, jobs and every natural resource on Earth.

Population density of Sao Paulo is 9000 people per square kilometres.

Over crowded Earth.

Future estimate

In demographics, which is the study of populations, the world population is the total number of humans currently living, and was estimated to have reached 7,800,000,000 people as of March 2020. It took over 200,000 years of human history for the world's population to reach 1 billion, and only 200 years more to reach 7 billion.

There is progressive advancement in the field of science, daily. We are stressing more on hygiene, sanitation, nutrition and proper growth requirements. All these factors increase the birth rate and decrease the death rate, giving a longer life to human beings. This is one of the reasons for overpopulation.

A colour coded map of the world denoting the densely and the sparsely populated continents.

Birth rate

With the advancement in the fields of science and technology, many medicines, vaccines and treatments were discovered, which increased the survival rate of the infants.

Controlling measures

The government spreads awareness about the various birth control measures available in the market. As it is not possible to increase the death rate, we can only control the birth rate.

Death rate

Overpopulation cannot stop advancement in the field of science. Humans have won over many deadly diseases and discovered various treatments. As of 2020, it is estimated that the U.S. crude death rate will be 8.3 per 1,000, while the global rate will be 7.7 per 1,000. It was reported by United Nations in in 2019 that the world population was growing at a slower pace.

Poverty

This is also one of the reasons for the increasing birth rate. People produce more children for having more earning hands in the family. Also, people under the poverty line have no means to get contraception.

Immigration

POLLUTION

Pollution is the contamination of the natural environment with foreign substances or naturally occurring contaminants. Pollution affects the whole ecosystem: the air we breathe, the water we drink or the land on which we build our homes. There are different types of pollution: air, water, noise and soil pollution.

Heavy smoke from industries leads to polluted air.

A graphical representation of how air gets polluted.

Air pollution

Air pollution is the contamination of air. The main causes of air pollution are fossil fuel burning, industries, and mining. Air pollution causes respiratory infections, heart diseases, strokes, lung cancer, asthma and also affects the central nervous system.

Main household pollutants are particulate matter, new paint, cooking smoke and tobacco, fumes formed by smoking.

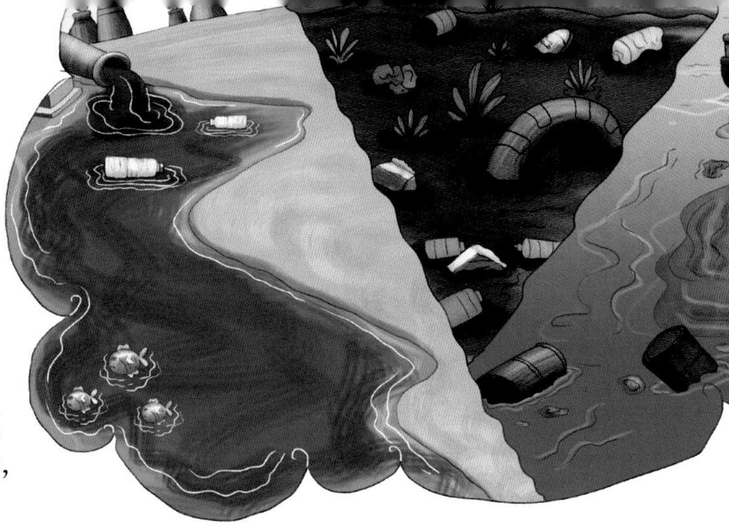

Water pollution

Water pollution is the contamination of water bodies like rivers and lakes by chemicals, pathogens, and microbes. The main cause of water pollution is dumping untreated waste in rivers and lakes. Sewage waste, industrial waste, radioactive waste, plastic all contribute to water pollution.

Oil spill near the beach.

Soil pollution

Household dumping, littering, sewage spills, oil spills, radiation spills, industrial wastes, and extensive use of chemicals in agriculture to increase productivity are some of the sources of soil pollution.

Mining destroys land and soil, and imbalances the ecosystem.

205

Noise pollution

People generally use loudspeakers when they are celebrating. Even on the road, we can hear a lot of horns and other loud sounds. All these noises not only affect the hearing ability of human beings but also of the animals living nearby.

River Ganga in Varanasi

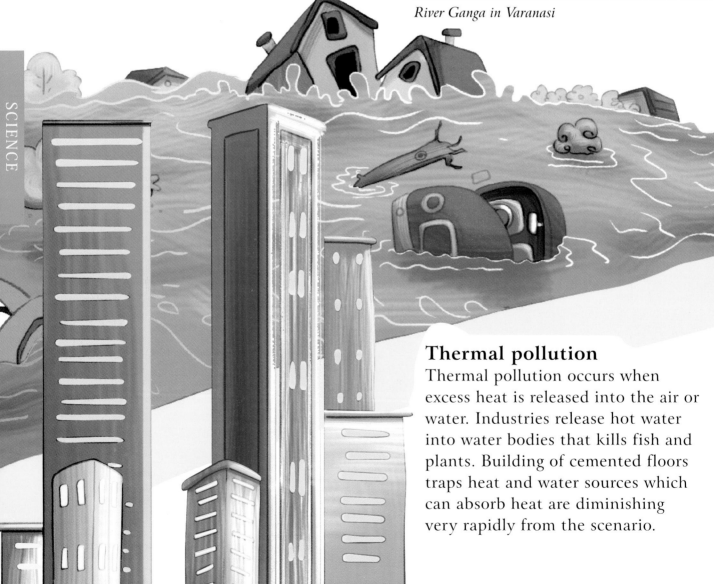

Recording heat generated at the chimney with infrared thermal cameras.

Thermal pollution

Thermal pollution occurs when excess heat is released into the air or water. Industries release hot water into water bodies that kills fish and plants. Building of cemented floors traps heat and water sources which can absorb heat are diminishing very rapidly from the scenario.

Light pollution

Excessive use of artificial lights on the roads and at home is termed as light pollution. It affects the sleep cycle and is responsible for hormonal changes in the bodies of organisms.

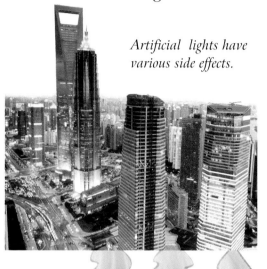

Artificial lights have various side effects.

Nuclear bomb attacks had severe side effects on cities.

Radioactive pollution

Radioactive pollution occurs due to accidents of nuclear power plants and improper disposal of radioactive waste. USA attacked Hiroshima and Nagasaki with nuclear bombs, killing millions of people and infecting the survivors along with their future generations, with deadly diseases.

Pollution has adverse effects on the environment. It is necessary to control it. Many countries have laws to control pollution. We too can help in this initiative by some practices like recycling, reusing, waste minimisation, checking our vehicles regularly for pollution, not littering anywhere, etc. Thus, we are the ones who can make our Earth clean and green.

GLOBAL WARMING

Global warming is the rise in temperature of the whole surface of Earth, including oceans, land area and the lower layers of the atmosphere. Global warming is the reason for the changes in Earth's climate. Scientists have proven by many facts that the temperature of Earth has risen approximately 0.4–0.8 in the past 100 years.

The effect of global warming on the water bodies of Earth

Burning fossil fuels, coal, petroleum, oil, deforestation, and increasing use of land for agriculture and building purposes have contributed to increasing the quantity of greenhouse gases tremendously. CO_2 is the gas that can remain in the atmosphere for a very long period of time and have adverse effects on the atmosphere.

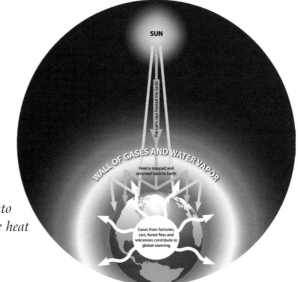

Gases and water vapour rise into the atmosphere and trap all the heat released by the Sun.

Effects

Global warming can result in changes in the ecosystems, causing some species to move away from their ecosystems and evolve and multiply, while others that cannot move and might become extinct.

Solutions

Forests absorb large quantity of emissions, thus growing more plants, using recycling bags and paper, buying used furniture and goods, are practices that we should adapt. We should not waste paper and reduce air travel.

Promote plantation

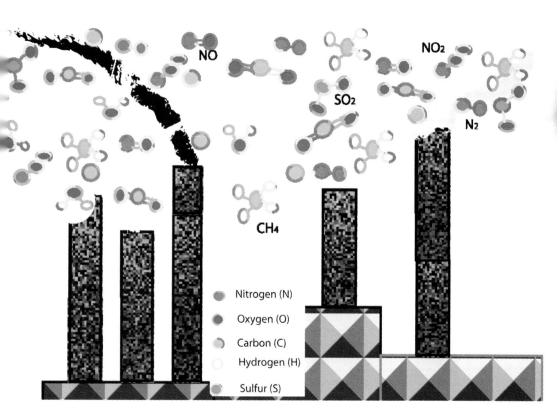

NO

NO_2

SO_2

N_2

CH_4

Nitrogen (N)
Oxygen (O)
Carbon (C)
Hydrogen (H)
Sulfur (S)

A lot of gases produced by the factories get released into the atmosphere

Some ways of saving electricity are:

- Use CFL or LED lighting
- Use thermostats
- Electrical appliances with more energy stars should be purchased
- Regularly clean the filters in air conditioners and furnaces, and defrost the freezer.
- Electrical appliances should not be left on standby mode.
- Use sunlight to dry clothes instead of using the dryer every time.

STOP GLOBAL WARMING

Use of renewable sources of energy

We can use solar energy for cooking, heating, and power supply. Currently, energy can be produced by the Sun, wind, and by burning biomass. The shift towards the use of renewable sources of energy can save money and reduce the emission of harmful gases.

Mass bike ride in Thailand to reduce fuel consumption and global warming.

Recycled products

Conserve water

It requires a lot of power to draw water to tanks and purify it. So, by conserving water, we can save energy as well.

Green transportation/public transport

Drive less and walk more. Plan car pooling or use public transport for travelling instead of using your own vehicle. Instead of using gas guzzling cars, electric cars, smart cars and cars that run on vegetable oil or some other renewable source of or use a bicycle instead of a car; it is not only healthy for the body but also for the environment.

Be prepared

There are some consequences of global warming that are inevitable, like the sea level rising, extreme temperatures, growing wildfires and severe heat waves. Thus, we should be prepared for them.

Eat more local food

A lot of fuel gets used in the production, packaging and transportation of food that is grown far away from you.

CLIMATE CHANGE

Climate is the weather condition of a place, which stays the same for a long period of time. It depends on various factors like the amount of sunlight received, proximity to oceans and altitude, plate tectonics, volcanic eruptions and biotic processes. If the factors influencing climate are imbalanced, it will result in a change of climate. Climate change is the change in temperature, precipitation, winds and other factors for a prolonged time. Extremely hot summers are an example of climate change. The reason can be that either too much heat is entering Earth or not enough amount of heat is going out.

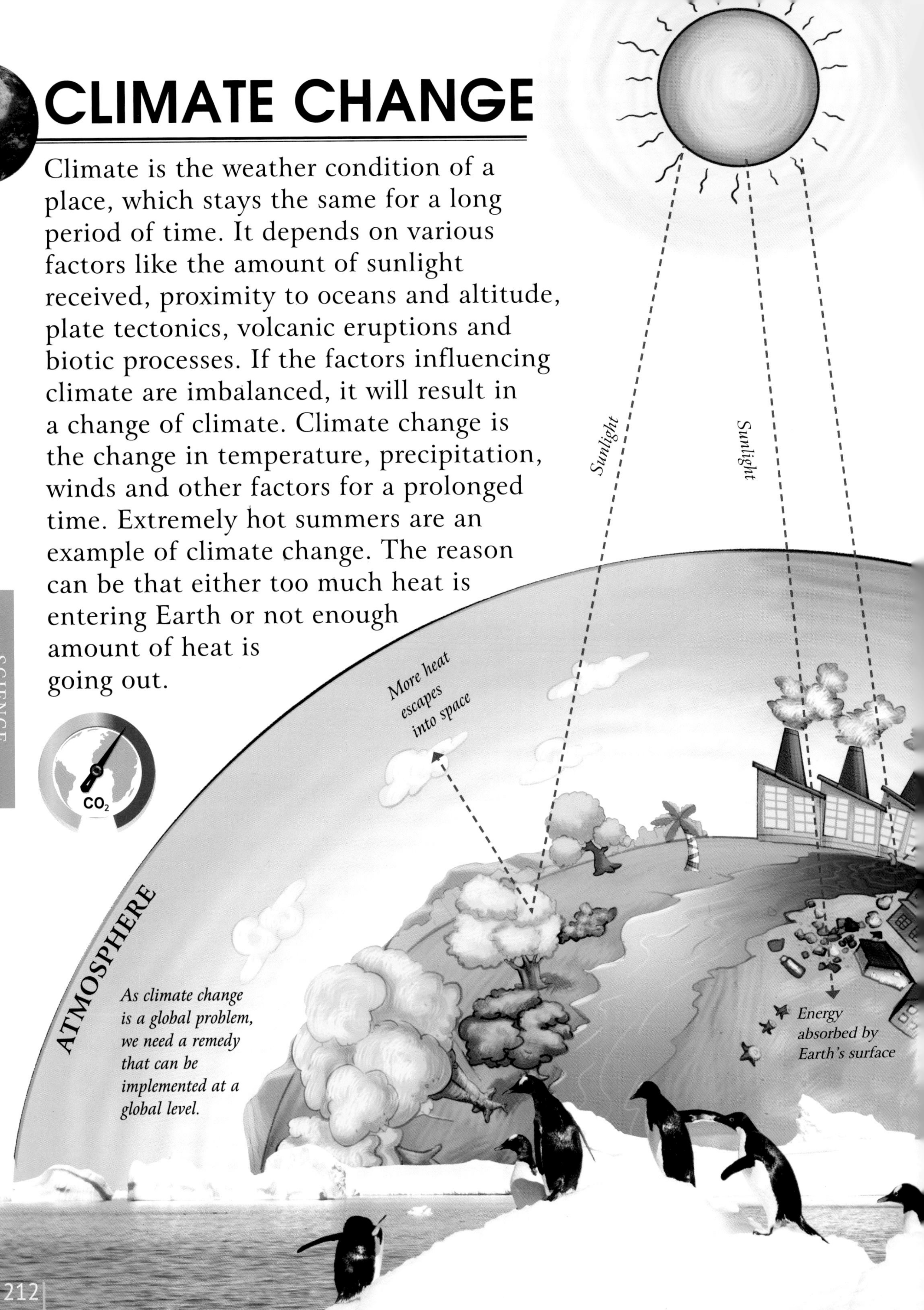

CO_2

Sunlight

Sunlight

ATMOSPHERE

More heat escapes into space

As climate change is a global problem, we need a remedy that can be implemented at a global level.

Energy absorbed by Earth's surface

Over 100 people participated in the global warming attention march in New York City

Before   *After*

Greenhouse gases trap heat in the atmosphere so less heat escapes into space.

Causes of climate change

• Continental drift

Approximately 200 million years ago, all continents were a part of a large land mass. Subsequently, they got separated and moved apart forming different continents with variations in climates. Scientists believe that this drift has not stopped and continues to take place even today.

• Volcanic eruptions

Studies have shown that the large volume of gases released by volcanic eruptions can stay for long in the atmosphere and influence the climate.

• Earth's axis

Earth revolves around the Sun in an orbit. Its axis of revolution is not fixed; there is always some gradual change in the direction of the axis. This change in axis can be a reason for climate change.

• Ocean currents

Ocean currents can transfer heat across the planet. Oceans cover three-fourth of Earth's surface and can absorb double the amount of heat as compared to land. These currents are responsible for climate changes in many parts of the world.

High temperatures are causing the ice which is the polar bear's habitat to melt.

The quantity of greenhouse gases like water vapour, carbon dioxide, methane, nitrous oxide and chlorofluorocarbons has increased largely due to burning fossil fuels like coal, oil and natural gas. Cutting down trees has reduced forests, which have the capacity of absorbing carbon dioxide to a great extent.

As the concentration of these gases is increasing, they are absorbing more heat and making the surface warm. Carbon dioxide is responsible for 64 per cent of global warming.

Many ecosystems are at a risk of collapsing due to the change in weather. Coral reefs are deteriorating. As ice melts on the polar regions, animals like polar bears and walruses will lose their habitat. The number of endangered species is increasing day by day.

Trees are killed by acid rain that is produced by emissions of sulphur dioxide and nitrogen dioxide.

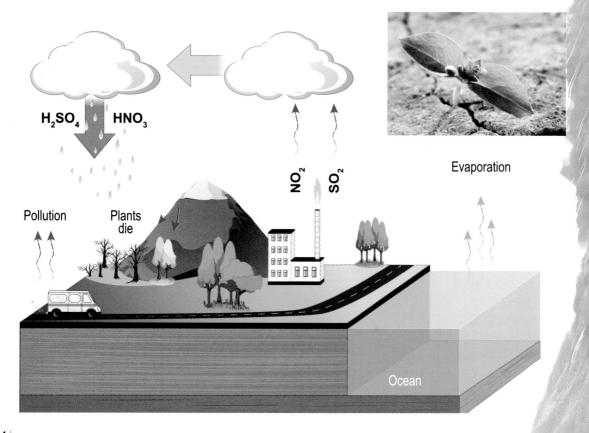

H_2SO_4 HNO_3

NO_2 SO_2

Evaporation

Pollution   Plants die

Ocean

Consequences

Weather is becoming more extreme. Increased temperature leads to storms and hurricanes. Chances of flooding, wildfires and drought conditions have gone up.

The ice on the Arctic Sea has decreased greatly; alpine glaciers are melting and the ice cover of the Northern parts is greatly reducing.

Approximately 90 per cent of the heat released in the atmosphere is absorbed by oceans. This causes the acidification of ocean water. Many aquatic species are endangered due to these climatic changes. Flood and droughts are common.

Soil cracked with weed that resulted in barren land

Dead fish due to floods

Wild animals migrating for better living conditions

Food security

A major concern is to find new sources of food, in case of uncertain rainfall and unexpected attacks of weeds, diseases and pests. Transportation is affected by flooding that causes scarcity of many commodities.

In the future, there will be a conflict for the basic needs of all living organisms, including human beings, They will all need to migrate in search of a better place.

WASTE AND RECYCLING

With the onset of industrialisation and urban growth, big dumps of waste have covered a large area of land. Waste is all the things that we throw away. This not only affects hygiene but also harms the lives of animals, birds, and trees found in that area. There are many methods of waste disposal.

The three Rs – reduce, reuse and recycle, can help in waste management.

Landfill

Landfills are the most popularly used method of waste disposal that focus on burying the waste in land. There is a process used that eliminates the odours and the dangers of the waste before it is placed into the ground.

Birds flocking over a landfill

Incineration

Incineration or combustion is another disposal method in which municipal solid wastes are burned at high temperatures. This converts them into residue and gaseous products. It can reduce the volume of solid waste to 20–30 per cent of its original volume, along with the space they take up and the stress they put on the landfills.

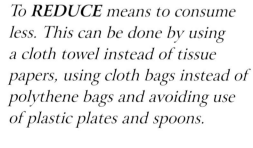

To **REDUCE** means to consume less. This can be done by using a cloth towel instead of tissue papers, using cloth bags instead of polythene bags and avoiding use of plastic plates and spoons.

Plastic bottles can be easily recycled into new plastic products

SCIENCE

Recycling

Recycling is the process of transforming waste material into new products to prevent the consumption of fresh materials. Many things that we throw in the dustbin are recyclable like cans, newspapers, boxes, cardboard, plastic bottles, envelopes, glass bottles, jars and clothes. Different types of wastes are treated differently and recycled into consumable products.

*To **REUSE** means to make a habit of reusing old items. We can reuse things like old furniture, packages, boxes in creative ways or give them to the needy.*

RECYCLING *is the process of taking old discarded materials and making new products from them. This way we can reduce the amount of energy and raw materials used in the production of fresh material. We can also control pollution at a personal level by reducing waste.*

The production of paper bags requires less energy and they are also easier to recycle than plastic bags.

Nuclear energy should be created in an eco-friendly way

Following are a few ways of recycling:

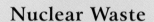

- Reuse plastic bags
- Batteries are filled with toxic materials, so go green by buying batteries that you can recharge. If your laptop or phones have stopped working and you plan to discard them, drop them at the electronics recycling depot.
- All biodegradable food-related garbage like egg shells and banana peels can get decomposed and add to the quality of the soil.
- The best way to recycle is to do it every day in your home. Sort newspapers and magazines, plastic containers and bottles and assorted paper while recycling, and urge your friends and family to do the same.

Nuclear Waste

After nuclear fuel is used in a reactor, the remnants are referred to as nuclear waste. This waste is hazardously radioactive and remains in that state for several years.

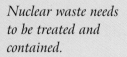

Nuclear waste needs to be treated and contained.

218

How dangerous is nuclear waste?

When nuclear waste is released from the reactor, it is so lethal that by standing unshielded within a few meters of it, a person could receive a lethal radioactive dose within a few seconds and would die of acute radiation sickness. Practically, nuclear waste is never unshielded but is kept underwater for a few years until its radiation decays to levels that can be shielded by concrete in large storage casks.

Recycling nuclear waste

As over 90 per cent of nuclear waste is uranium, it contains 90 per cent usable fuel! This can be chemically processed and placed in advanced fast reactors to close the fuel cycle, which has much less nuclear waste and much more energy extracted from the raw ore. Plutonium and the minor actinides are the longest living nuclides in nuclear waste and can be used as fuel. If these materials are recycled and burnt in fuel, nuclear waste would only remain radioactive for a few hundred years, which would drastically reduce storage concerns. In general, nuclear waste remains radioactive for a few hundred thousand years.

An atomic bomb is essentially a nuclear reaction that creates a lot of nuclear waste.

GEOGRAPHY

Geography is the study of places and the relationships with people and their environment. Geography helps us to understand where things are found, why they are there, and how they develop and change over time.

FORMATION OF THE EARTH

Although planets surround stars in the galaxy, how they form remains a subject of debate. Despite the wealth of information available about our own solar system, scientists still aren't certain how planets are built. But generally it is accepted that the theory of core accretion can be used to describe the formation of Earth.

Earth's atmosphere

Earth's rocky core formed first, with heavy elements colliding and binding together. Dense material sank to the centre, while the lighter material created the crust. The planet's magnetic field probably formed around this time. Gravity captured some of the gases that made up the planet's early atmosphere.

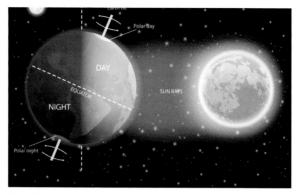

The Sun's light takes eight minutes and 20 seconds to reach Earth.

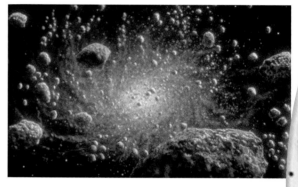

An illustration showing the accretion of Earth.

Earth is the densest planet in the solar system because of its metallic core and rocky mantle.

About 71 per cent of the total surface area of Earth is covered by water and 29 per cent by land.

What happened next?

Collisions from these icy bodies likely deposited much of the Earth's water on its surface. Because the planet is in the Goldilocks zone, the region where liquid water neither freezes nor evaporates but can remain as a liquid, the water remained at the surface, which many scientists think plays a key role in the development of life.

Earth's rotation causes it to bulge at the Equator.

Coming together

Approximately 4.6 billion years ago, the solar system was a cloud of dust and gas known as a solar nebula. Gravity collapsed the material in on itself as it began to spin, forming the Sun in the center of the nebula.

With the rise of the Sun, the remaining material began to clump up. Small particles drew together, bound by the force of gravity, into larger particles. The solar wind swept away lighter elements, such as hydrogen and helium, from the closer regions, leaving only heavy, rocky materials to create smaller terrestrial worlds like Earth.

Early in its evolution, Earth suffered an impact by a large body that catapulted pieces of the young planet's mantle into space. Gravity caused many of these pieces to draw together and form the moon, which took up orbit around its creator.

The flow of the mantle beneath the crust causes plate tectonics, the movement of the large plates of rock on the surface of the Earth. Collisions and friction gave rise to mountains and volcanoes, which began to spew gases into the atmosphere.

STRUCTURE OF EARTH

The shape of Earth approximates an oblate spheroid; a sphere which is flattened along the axis from pole to pole. There is a bulge around the Equator. This bulge results from the rotation of Earth, and causes the diameter at the Equator to be 43 kilometres larger than the pole-to-pole diameter.

Inner Core
It extends another 1,448 km towards the centre of Earth. It is believed that this inner core is a solid ball of mostly iron and nickel.

This illustration shows the movement of two tectonic plates coming together.

Earth's Crust

Earth's crust is a hard and rocky layer. The oceanic crust has greater density than the continental crust. The continental crust is composed of granite rocks. The floor of the ocean is commonly referred to as the "oceanic crust". It is composed of basaltic rocks, gabbros and lava. The oceanic crust is much younger than the continental crust.

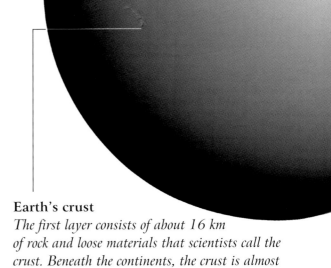

Earth's crust
The first layer consists of about 16 km of rock and loose materials that scientists call the crust. Beneath the continents, the crust is almost three times as thick as it is beneath the oceans.

Continental Crust

Upper Mantle

Lower Mantle

Outer Core

Inner Core

Earth's crust, mantle, inner and outer core

Outer Core
It extends to a depth of around 4,828 km beneath the surface. It is believed that this outer core is made up of super-heated molten lava.

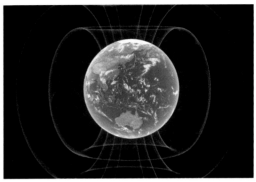

Earth's core is made up of iron, nickel, sulphur and other lighter materials.

An illustration of Earth's magnetic field

The Mantle
It extends to a depth of approximately 2,897 km and is made of a thick, solid, rocky substance that represents about 85 per cent of the total weight and mass of Earth. The first 80 km of the mantle is believed to consist of very hard and rigid rock.

Earth's Mantle

The second layer that makes up Earth's structure is called the mantle. It is about 2,900 kilometres thick. The mantle is in a semi-solid state. The matter at the upper portions of the mantle are hard. As we go lower, the rocks in the mantle get softer.

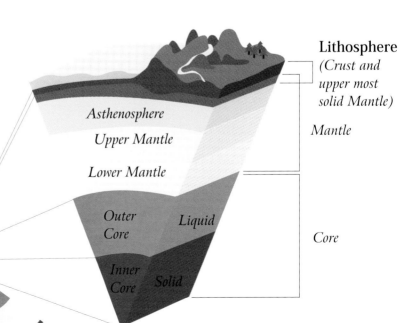

Asthenosphere

Upper Mantle

Lower Mantle

Outer Core

Liquid

Inner Core

Solid

Lithosphere
(Crust and upper most solid Mantle)

Mantle

Core

THE PLATE TECTONICS THEORY

Tectonic plates are large blocks of hard, rocky land. Tectonic plates can be 100–200 kilometres thick. They are composed of hard rocks from Earth's crust and the hard upper part of the mantle (Lithosphere). The heat of the core escapes, and magma rises upwards. Here, it cools, causing the rocks in the mantle to "flow".

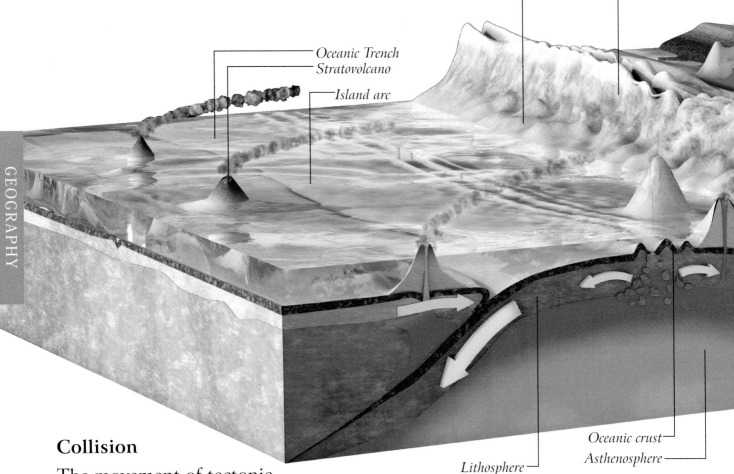

Formation of mid-ocean ridges

Accretionary prism

volcanic arc

Oceanic Trench
Stratovolcano
Island arc

Lithosphere

Oceanic crust
Asthenosphere

Collision

The movement of tectonic plates often leads to collisions.

These collisions are very slow and take place when two tectonic plates come together or "converge". Based on the types of plates that are converging, when two plates collide, one of the plates might be forced below the other. This results in the formation of new matter in the tectonic plate.

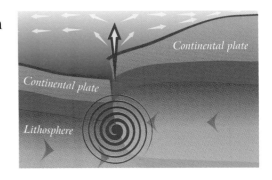

Continental plate

Continental plate

Lithosphere

GEOGRAPHY

Why do tectonic plates move?

As we know, the raging heat of the core escapes into the mantle gradually, causing the magma to rise upwards. Then, it slowly cools, causing the rocks in the mantle to be in motion. This causes the tectonic plates above to move.

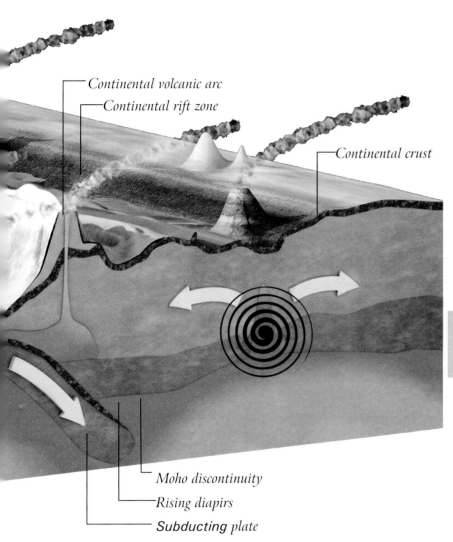

Continental volcanic arc
Continental rift zone
Continental crust
Moho discontinuity
Rising diapirs
Subducting plate

Divergence

When two tectonic plates diverge, the magma and basalt from the mantle rise upwards. Seawater causes the hot magma to cool. This causes the formation of a new oceanic crust. The new oceanic crust pushes the old matter lower and, just as we see in the process of converging plates, the subducted matter melts in the magma.

Three types of plate boundary

Divergernt plate boundary

Transform plate boundary

Convergent plate boundary

Mid-ocean ridges

Mid-ocean ridges are an extensive range of mountains. When two oceanic plates diverge, a new oceanic plate is created. A mid-ocean ridge is formed along its boundary.

*Laurasia,
Gondwana and the
Tethys ocean*

CURIOUS CONTINENTS

Earth's surface is covered with large stretches of land and water. There is no set pattern to the way land and water is divided on Earth's surface. A large, continuous landmass is called a "continent". The land on Earth is divided into seven continents. These are Asia, Africa, North America, South America, Antarctica, Europe and Oceania (in order of size).

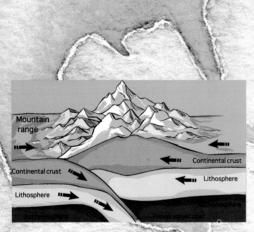

Two continental plates converge

Continental Drift

300 million years ago, Earth's land was joined together as one large supercontinent named "Pangaea". It was surrounded by one large, continuous stretch of ocean named "Panthalassa". Over millions and millions of years, this supercontinent slowly broke apart and wafted away to form the seven continents of today. This is called "continental drift".

225 million years ago

150 million years ago

100 million years ago

Earth today

The four major phases of the Continental Drift Theory

When did Pangaea begin to break apart?

Pangaea began to break into fragments about 200 million years ago. These fragments slowly moved away and settled into their current positions. The landmasses of North America and South America drifted towards the west while Antarctica drifted towards the South Pole.

Pangaea.

Laurasia and Gondwana

Modern world

The Himalayas

Gondwana drifted towards the current continents of Europe and North America. This part was called, "Euramerica". India collided with the part that contained the current continents of Europe and Asia. The Himalayas were said to have been formed due to this collision.

ORES AND MINERALS

Chemical compounds are not found in their pure state in nature due to a large number of adulterating influences present in the natural environment. Instead, they are found in other crystalline naturally occurring inorganic compounds called minerals. These minerals are generally formed by large-scale geological processes rather than through the actions of living organisms.

All about the ores

Ores have a high percentage of a certain element, usually a metal, as one of their constituents.

As such, it is often economically viable to isolate pure elements from particular ores rather than just any mineral that contains the element. For example, while aluminium is present in both clay as well as bauxite, only bauxite is used as an ore of aluminium because it is feasible to extract aluminium from it easily, cheaply and in large quantities.

Therefore, every ore is a mineral, but every mineral is not an ore. Some very important ores are galena for lead, acanthite for silver and magnetite for iron. The process of extracting pure elements from ores is called mining.

*A crane digging at a
mining site for ore.*

Difference between ores and minerals

• Ore comprises minerals; thus all the ores
are minerals, but not all the minerals are ores.

• Ores are mineral deposits, whereas a
mineral is a natural form in which the
metals exist.

• Ores are used to extract metals
economically. Therefore, in ores, a significant
amount of metals are present.

LANDFORMS

Landforms are created by a mix of external and internal forces that continuously act upon them. Landforms are also classified on the basis of how they are created. These are structural landforms, weathering landforms, erosional landforms and depositional landforms.

Volcanoes

Volcanoes look like mountains but are very different from them. The hot magma and molten rocks that are pushed up to Earth's crust sometimes gather beneath a "weak" spot (mostly, the boundary of two tectonic plates). The pressure that pushes them to the crust forces them to break the crust and explode onto the surface.

Tall mountains

Most mountains have steep slopes and a rounded peak. Some are formed by tectonic plate movement. Mountains are also formed by volcanism and the process of erosion.

Violet asters and blazing stars of the temperate grasslands.

A tropical grassland in Africa.

Eroded valleys

Some rivers run along valleys. Over time, sections of these valleys are eroded into broad, flat lands. These are called "erosional plains".

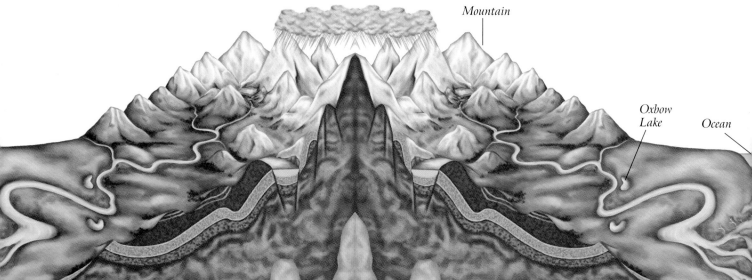

Rain and Snow

Mountain

Oxbow Lake

Ocean

Formation of a plateau

It takes millions of years to form a plateau. The main difference between a plateau and a mountain is that a plateau is completely flat on the top. It is wide, with a greater height than width.

PLATEAU

MOUNTAIN

PLAIN

SEA LEVEL

Weathering landforms

Depositional landforms

Grassslands

Grasslands are found in all continents except Antarctica. They are open and comparatively flat lands. There is an abundance of grass in the grasslands and this is how the plains are easily distinguished as grasslands.

A landscape from the temperate grasslands.

Mesas

Mesas are formed by the erosion of plateaus, hills or mountains by water or wind. Mesas are greater in width than in height. They much smaller than plateaus.

Nature's Table

A plateau is a raised, flat land that has a steep slope on one or more sides.

233

THE WORLD BELOW

The ocean floor is made up of the oceanic crust. On an average, the depth of the ocean is nearly 12,200 feet. It is far from flat. There are tall, rugged mountains on the oceanic crust. There are active and dormant volcanoes, ridges, plateaus, plains and trenches. The life that exists on the surface and even deep inside the ocean is called "marine life".

Continental shelf

Around the continents, there are areas of fairly shallow sea called continental shelves. This is the shallowest part of the ocean floor. Most of the extensive fishing grounds in the world are located on the continental shelf. Different kinds of minerals, petroleum and natural gas can be easily obtained from continental shelves. The Mumbai High in the Arabian Sea is a source of petroleum and natural gas for India.

Salmon is the most commonly caught fish on Indian coasts.

Sea floor sediments

The sea floor is covered with muddy sediment, made up of the remains of tiny plants and animals. They sink to the bottom of the ocean after dying, along with volcanic ash and other materials carried from the land by rivers and winds.

Abyssal plains

The plains on the ocean floor that are located at great depths are called abyssal plains. The plains are located at the base of the continental slopes and stretch over great distances. Different topographic features like sea mounds, mountains and plateaus are formed over these plains.

Oceanic ridges

The submerged mountains on the ocean floor are called oceanic ridges. Sometimes, peaks of the oceanic ridges appear above the ocean surface and are termed as oceanic islands, like the Andamans.

Marine habitats

Marine habitats are classified as open ocean habitats and coastal habitats. Most of the marine habitat lives in the coastal habitats as open ocean habitats are found deepin the ocean.

235

RAINFORESTS OF THE OCEAN

GEOGRAPHY

Corals are a group of invertebrate (lacking a backbone) animals who are extremely small in size. They belong to the phylum Cnidaria (with a silent "c") group of animals. This group also includes other colourful and interesting marine organisms such as jellyfish, sea anemones and hydras.

Corals cannot move and spend most of their lives at one place. They feed on planktonic animals and small fish. They have tentacles on their bodies which they stretch out to grip and catch their prey. Coral reefs sometimes form permanent coral islands which are referred to as "rainforests of the sea". similar to terrestrial rainforests, coral reefs have diverse vegetation and aquatic life.

Polyps

All corals have a common structure called "polyp". This structure is defined by an open end whose mouth has many tentacles coming out of it. It is with these tentacles that they catch their prey. At the end of each tentacle, there are some cells that sting and damage the prey. These cells are called "nematocysts".

Coral polyps with their tentacles extended

Barrier reefs and atolls

Coral reefs sometimes form around extinct volcanoes. These volcanoes are slowly sinking beneath themselves due to their large weights. The coral reefs begin to grow upwards as these volcanoes sink deeper. Such coral reefs are called "barrier reefs". Over time, the original volcanoes become unrecognisable. All that one can see then is a ring of corals that have a surrounding island called "atoll".

Zooxanthellae

The coloured specks are the zooxanthellae.

Corals depend upon zooxanthellae (pronounced as zoeo-zan-the-lee), which are single-celled algae that exist in warm shallow waters which the corals prefer. The zooxanthellae carry out the process of photosynthesis and exchange this food with corals. In return, they take nutrients from the corals. The zooxanthellae allow corals to grow and reproduce faster and form reefs. These single-celled algae also provide corals with their colour.

Threats to existence

If the temperature of the water lowers or increases, then the zooxanthellae begin to get ejected. This results in the corals turning white and dying off. Another threat is crown-of-thorns starfish that feed on the various types of corals. Unfortunately, climate changes, global warming, overfishing and other such factors are putting coral reefs at risk.

DESERTS

Deserts are places whose annual precipitation is less than 25–50 centimetres. This region receives warm air from the equator which falls as cool, dry air as it lost its water vapour over the equator. Deserts occur in certain places due to the lack of moisture in the rain clouds. There are many types of deserts. About one-fifth of Earth's surface is covered by desert regions.

The Gobi Desert

The Gobi Desert is the result of its great distance from the ocean. The moisture present in the cold winds blowing from the Pacific Ocean is lost by the time it reaches this region. Even the little moisture coming from the rain clouds from the Indian Ocean is spent in the Himalayas. As a result, the land-locked Gobi Desert is formed.

Types of Deserts

There are many types of deserts such as subtropical deserts, dry coastal deserts, and polar deserts. Death Valley is the lowest and driest place in the Atacama desert, a coastal desert.

Death Valley deserts

Subtropical deserts

Polar deserts

Camel caravan in Gobi desert in Dunhuang.

Animals of the desert

Most deserts are home to various species of reptiles such as chameleons. They thrive In fact, deserts have the highest species of better in warm deserts than in cold deserts, because the low temperatures would not allow them to develop their life activity. than other landforms. The camel is called the "ship of the desert". It has been domesticated so that it can be used by people for travel.

Vegetation of the desert

As there is very little water, the leaves and stems are short. These plants store water for a very long time. As food is scarce in the desert, these plants have pointy thorns that discourage animals from eating them. Cactus is one of the most common examples of desert vegetation.

Sand dunes

Basically, a sand dune is a large mound of sand. Sand dunes are formed when strong winds blow sand from one place and let it accumulate at another. It is a temporary structure whose size can increase or decrease by the next strong wave of wind.

Aerial view from the dunes and oasis in the desert of Gobi in Southern Mongolia.

A COLD WORLD

Snow is precipitation that falls on Earth's surface in places where the temperature is below 0 °C. Water vapour in the air hardens into crystals of ice, which then form interlaced patterns with other crystals to form snowflakes. If the ground temperature is also below 0 °C, these crystals and flakes of snow can build up and cover the surface in a white blanket of snow.

Where does it snow?

The mountains that have snow have an elevation of about 16,000 feet. Otherwise, snowfall occurs at sea level only between 35° N and 35° S. This mostly takes place at the extreme ends of the Northern and Southern Hemispheres.

Annually, Russia, Greenland, Europe and North America receive the most amount of snow. Antarctica mainly experiences snowfall during the winter. During the winter, the tall mountains of South America and New Zealand receive snow.

Floating Ice

Icebergs are products of glaciers. They are formed by a process called "calving". By this process, chunks of ice break from a moving glacier and drop into the nearby water. The chunks of ice always break at the end or foot of a glacier as this portion is more prone to cracking due to the forward movement of glaciers.

Wild in the Snow

The wildlife of the polar regions (that is the Arctic and the Antarctic) is exposed to one of the harshest climates on Earth. Yet there are many species of animals that live comfortably in this region.

Glaciers

Glaciers are formed when snowfall accumulates and buries the present layer of snow on the surface. The snowflakes harden and compact into solids. These then recrystallise to form the hard ice of a glacier. Due to its weight and gravity, it begins to move on land. They are also called "Ice Rivers". The glaciers present on Earth today can be classified into two types—Alpine glaciers and continental glaciers (ice sheets).

MARINE ENVIRONMENT

As Earth formed, it began to cool. The water in the atmosphere fell to Earth as rainfall and accumulated to form seas. These waters contained ammonia, hydrogen, methane and oxygen which together formed organic compounds whenever they were hit by lightning. Over time, these organisms evolved to form the diverse marine habitat we know of today.

Marine habitats

Marine Organism

The spread of marine organisms is decided by the availability of sunlight, the amount of temperature, salinity, depth and also the amount of nutrients and dissolved oxygen available here. Some marine organisms migrate just as terrestrial organisms do. At night, they travel from the aphotic(without sunlight) zone to the photic(area that receives sunlight) zone in search of food. Some choose to remain in the aphotic zone for their entire lives in order to conserve energy.

Life in the Ocean

There are different habitats in which marine life live. Marine habitats are classified as open ocean habitats and coastal habitats. Most of the marine life lives in the coastal habitats. Open ocean habitats are found deep in the ocean, beyond the continental shelf.

Phytoplankton

Phytoplankton is a type of flora that floats on water. They are single-celled microscopic organisms that are responsible for the process of photosynthesis. They are found on the surface where the water is rich in nutrients. They absorb carbon dioxide and release oxygen into the water. They also convert raw materials into tissues that can be eaten by larger animals. Phytoplankton is active in the epipelagic zone, which is also called "the sunlight zone" as it receives a lot of sunlight.

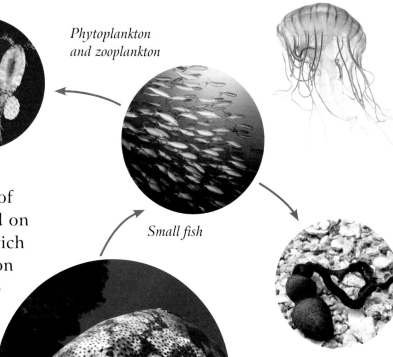

Phytoplankton and zooplankton

Small fish

Benthic organisms

Predator fish

Whale

Epipelagic zone

Tuna, swordfish, dolphinfish, billfish, marlin, mackerels, jacks, flying fish and sailfish also live in the epipelagic zone. Sharks, the deadliest marine creatures known to humans, travel to different zones, including the epipelagic zone, for food. As a wide variety of fish is available here, this zone is deeply connected to marine fishing.

BEACHES

A beach is a stretch of land that lies next to a body of water such as the ocean, sea or river. Beaches are almost always found where water meets land. Most beaches are covered in sand and other sandy particles, pebbles, seashells and rocks.

A beach by the Don river in Russia.

Formation of beaches

Over hundreds of thousands of years, the water and wind that move over the land near a water body, work on the rocks to break them down into pebbles and then into fine particles of sand. Ocean currents, tides and waves carry these sediments far and back again into the water and create a strip of sandy land that is called a "beach".

A sand and shingles beach.

Beaches and seasons

Heavy wind or wind storms that form during the winter carry sand into the air, causing erosion. Over time, it forms a "sandbar". A sandbar is a thin strip of land with exposed sand and sediments. A sandbar might change again in the summer when the waves carry sand from the sandbar back into the beach. As a result, during the winter season, beaches become narrower and steeper. During the summer season, they become wider and have more of a slope.

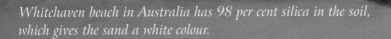

Whitehaven beach in Australia has 98 per cent silica in the soil, which gives the sand a white colour.

GEOGRAPHY

244

Sandy beaches

A sandy beach is formed from the erosion of various types of rocks. The sand type depends upon the type of rocks it is eroded from. Water close to reefs, cliffs and boulders might have white sand.

Beach profile

A beach profile notes the type of beach, vegetation, climate around the beach and quality of the soil. The following beach profiles have been recognised.

A beach having pebbles instead of sand.

Rocky beaches

Some beaches have shingles and pebbles instead of sand. These are called rocky beaches.

Barrier beaches

A barrier beach clearly divides the mainland from the ocean.

Coral beaches

Coral beaches are covered in coral sand. Some coral beaches might have pink or red sand as they are eroded from marine organisms and limestone.

A WORLD OF WATER

Rivers are found in all continents of the world. Almost all types of land can support a river. A river could be as long as a few kilometres or even run across an entire continent. Flowing water is called a "stream". The water from land drains off into a stream. Many such streams flow along their paths and are joined at one point. From this point onwards, the water in various streams flows together as a river.

A flowing river

Current of a river

The movement of the water in rivers is called "current". The maximum current is experienced at the source of a river, especially if the source is followed by a sloping land. Outside factors such as rainfall, precipitation and storms can increase the speed of the current. A strong current can move boulders and weather away mountains.

Lakes

A lake is a landlocked body of water. Just like rivers, there are lakes in all kinds of landforms and in all continents. The world has 307 million lakes, according to calculations made by an international team of scientists. Each lake is different from the other as lakes can differ in size, shape, depth and other features. Unlike rivers, lakes flow very slowly or do not flow at all.

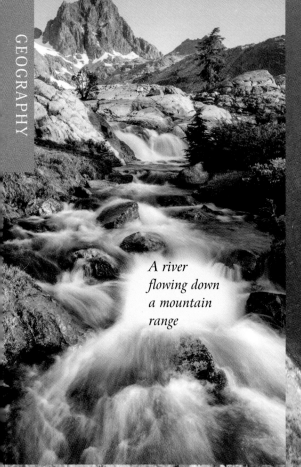
A river flowing down a mountain range

Current of a river

Flow of a river

Flowing rivers have great energy which can shape and carve a landscape. This energy is created by gravity, which pulls the water of the river in the direction in which it moves. The steeper the land, the faster the flow and the more the energy created. A river sometimes branches off into smaller sections.

A natural pond

Iceberg Trail in Glacier Park, Montana, USA

Ponds

Some lakes are very small and only measure a few metres in length. These are called "ponds" and can be manually created. Large lakes are called "seas".

Glacial lakes

A basin is a deep depression in Earth's surface. Lakes fill these basins. Giant glaciers created pits in the land as they slowly moved along the path. As the glaciers melted, the water collected into these pits and formed lakes. Such lakes are called "glacial lakes".

Lakes from volcanoes

The craters of inactive volcanoes get filled up with rainwater or water from melting snow. Some volcanoes erupt and leave behind a depression named "caldera". The water from the rains or melting snow fills up the caldera to form a lake.

WATER, WATER EVERYWHERE

The water present on Earth's surface can be found in oceans, seas, rivers, lakes and ponds. Water is also present in the air as water vapour and can be found beneath Earth's crust. So, the term "hydrosphere" refers to all of the water on Earth irrespective of if it is in solid (ice), liquid (water) or gaseous (water vapour) form.

The Water Cycle

The hydrosphere is in constant motion. Its movement might be visible to us or might be too subtle for us to notice. For example, we can see waves of water moving towards the shore of a beach, but we cannot see water vapour moving with the air. Earth's water moves upwards to the atmosphere and back down to the Lithosphere in a cyclical manner. This is called "water cycle".

Ocean waves

An ocean wave is a large mass of water that moves forward. It is a fold or bulge of water that moves the particles it contains to and fro in an oscillating manner. Ocean waves occur at the surface of the ocean when wind moves over the surface. We can see, hear and even feel ocean waves.

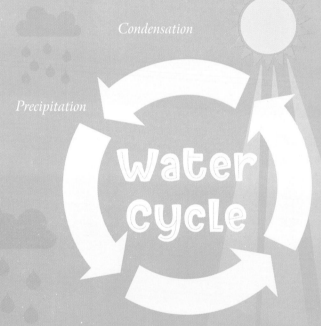

Condensation

Precipitation

Water cycle

Evaporation

Runoff

Groundwater

GEOGRAPHY

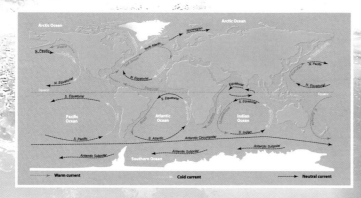

Ocean Currents

The water in the ocean is constantly moving. This movement of water can also be seen in the form of ocean currents. An ocean current is a continuous, directed movement of seawater generated by forces acting upon the water.

Tides

Tides are caused by the pull of the Sun and moon's gravitational force. As the Sun is farther away from Earth, the moon's gravitational force has a greater pull on the oceans. The tides that form on the ocean at this time are some of the tallest tides we experience on Earth. They are called "spring tides".

Tide falls away from bulge

Earth

Moon's gravity pulls at the Earth

Tides rise as Moon's gravity pulls at water

Moon

Sometimes, ocean currents are caused by the earthquakes or volcanic eruptions. They are driven by strong winds. These currents are caused by the temperature of the seawater. They are also caused by the density and salinity of the seawater. Earth's rotation and the gravitational pull of the moon also affect these currents.

Salinity

Salinity is the salt content of ocean water. Seawater amount of is salty water even though the water of the ocean mainly comes from freshwater sources such as rains and flowing streams and rivers. This is because flowing water carries eroded and weathered particles of rocks along with it.

CLIMATE

Climate is the long-term account of a place's weather. Climate has affected human life since the very beginning. We wear raincoats in the rainy season to protect ourselves from the rain. We wear cotton clothes in the summer season to protect ourselves from the heat.

Tropical Climate

Rainforests experience the tropical wet climate. They have regular annual rainfall as well as a warm, humid climate. The lowest day temperatures ranges from 20–23°C. The highest day temperature ranges from 30–32°C. The places lying 10° to the north and south of the equator have tropical wet climate. One of the main features of tropical rainforests is that they do not experience winter.

Rainforests have a tropical wet climate.

West Africa and South Asia experience the tropical monsoon climate. India has a tropical monsoon climate. Maximum rainfall is experienced during the summers. Tropical wet and dry climate experiences all three seasons.

Dry Climate

Dry climate is experienced in those parts of the world that have low precipitation. These places are mostly found in higher latitudes. Dry climate is further divided into arid and semi-arid climate.

Deserts have arid or semi-arid climates.

Arid and semi-arid climate

The annual rainfall in these places is low. A place that has arid climate receives less than 30 centimetres of annual rainfall. They experience the hottest climates. Semiarid sub climate zones have prairies and savannahs as they receive a good amount of rainfall.

Extremes of dry climate

The Atacama Desert is the driest place on Earth and lies in the dry and arid climate zone. A place called Arica which lies in South America has an annual rainfall of less than 0.05 centimetres.

WEATHER

Every day, we experience different temperatures. We might feel hot in the afternoon and cold at night. This daily change in temperature is called "weather". Weather is different from city to city. It changes suddenly.

Weather is defined as the short-term condition of the atmosphere at a given point of time. Wind, humidity, moisture, precipitation, cloud cover and air pressure are all factors that affect weather.

Weather and human life

Human life and human settlements are affected by weather and weather patterns. Weather also affects the production of crops and food. If the weather is extreme, meaning if it gets too hot or too cold, a person would feel uncomfortable. Weather could also cause sickness in a person. If a person stands out in the cold for too long, they might fall ill with fever or cold.

Changing weather

Weather does not have sudden changes all around the world. Some parts experience stable and calm weather with few sudden changes. The weather in the tropical areas changes at a rapid pace.

Predicting the weather

Predicting the weather is called "weather forecasting". Satellites have been launched into space for the specific purpose of predicting the weather. A meteorologist studies images from the satellite to predict weather.

Satellite images show a pattern of the weather. With these images, a meteorologist can tell where the warm air masses are and where they are headed. They can also predict where the cold air masses are, where they might intercept the warm air masses and what the air pressure is like.

Sudden changes in weather leads to a disruption in activities.

Phone displaying the weather

PRECIPITATION

A cloud is like a tap and precipitation is like the water flowing from it. There are different forms of precipitation at different places. Some places might see it as snow and some might see it as rain. But precipitation can also be in the form of hail or sleet.

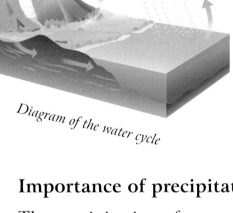

Diagram of the water cycle

GEOGRAPHY

Rain

Raindrops form in the atmosphere. When they grow in size, and the cloud cannot hold them anymore, they begin to fall towards the surface. Rainfall is the most commonly seen precipitation on Earth. Snow, hail and sleet are seen in fewer parts.

Rain is a type of precipitation.

Importance of precipitation

The precipitation of an area affects its vegetation. The types of plants that grow, what they grow and how they grow are all affected by precipitation. It even affects human life.

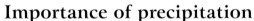

Formation of precipitation

Water vapour slowly forms water droplets or ice crystals, which then form clouds. Sometimes, they form fog. The water vapour collects dust and condenses to form cloud condensation nuclei. Precipitation forms along the cloud condensation nuclei.

Sleet

Around cooler areas, raindrops freeze on their way to the surface. These drops become thicker and have a more solid form. This is called "sleet" or "ice pellets". Sleet is wetter and mushier than rain.

Freezing cold temperatures

It can only snow in places that experience temperatures as low as 0° C. For it to snow, and for the snow to not melt as soon as it touches the surface, temperatures need to go below the freezing point of water.

Frost on a leaf

Frost gathering on windows

Hail and snow

Snow has a complex structure. On the other hand, hailstones are just water droplets that have frozen. They are like crystals of ice, somewhat similar to ice cubes. Hailstones are hard while snow is soft. Hailstones can be harmful. Snowfall is peaceful and calm.

Fog

"Fog" is a name given to clouds that float very close to the surface and even touch the surface. Fog is formed when water vapour condenses to make small water droplets close to the surface. These water droplets combine together so that we can see them.

Morning frost seen on the blades of the grass.

TYPES OF RAINFALL

Rainfall is the source of freshwater. It refills the waters in rivers and lakes. The water from rain is used for agriculture, in industries and in homes.

Types of rain

Two air masses flowing along the sky might meet over a certain area. A warm air mass cannot mix with a cold air mass. The warm air mass moves higher and the cold air mass passes below. The thinner, warmer air begins to cool and forms water vapour. This water vapour then follows the usual process and condenses to form a cloud and then raindrops.

Thunderstorms are a result of convectional rain.

Convectional rain

Instability in the atmosphere, caused by excess heat from the Sun, produces "convective clouds". This heat causes more water vapour to form. Also, the heat from the surface warms the air above it. Convection clouds form when the air cools and condenses. If the atmosphere is too unstable, it causes thunderstorms or heavy showers of rainfall. Convectional rains have a smaller range than frontal rain.

Orographic rain

In higher grounds, the humid and moist air rises upwards and slowly produce clouds. Over time, these clouds give precipitation in the form of rainfall. This rainfall is called "orographic rainfall" as it was produced as a result of the height of the land. Most mountainous regions experience orographic rainfall.

Mountains often get orographic rain

Acid rain

Drops of water falling from the sky are polluted by different factors. Nitrogen oxide and sulphur dioxide, two of the most common air pollutants in our planet, mix with the cloud condensation nuclei in the rainwater to make it acidic. This water then falls as "acid rain". Acid rain harms plants and animals that need this water for growth. It can even harm the soil.

Deforestation affects rainfall

NATURAL TREASURE

Gemstones are the most valuable minerals available on Earth. However, while looking at an uncut gemstone mineral, one might feel that they are very ordinary looking. Gemstones are cut, shaped and polished to form the beautiful, high-value precious stones we see in magazines and jewellery shops.

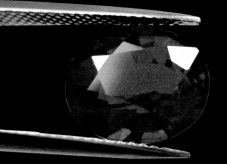

The deep red shade of the ruby is very popular and many lipsticks, clothes and shoes have this shade.

Precious stones

Diamonds, rubies and emeralds are precious stones. Diamonds are the hardest minerals and also the hardest naturally occurring substance on Earth. Made entirely of carbon atoms, they look unimpressive in the uncut form. There are only a few places in the world that have diamonds.

Quartz is also called silicon dioxide and is the most common silicate mineral.

Calcite is also called calcium carbonate and is found in limestone.

Rubies and emeralds

Rubies have chromium in small amounts which gives them their red colour. Emeralds are formed from beryl. Beryl is a mineral with the elements of beryllium, aluminium, silicon and oxygen. It has traces of vanadium and chromium which gives it its colour.

Diamonds have an extremely high value and are used in making jewellery.

Graphite

Graphite, like diamond, is a pure carbon mineral. However, the structure of graphite is very different from that of diamond. In the graphite structure, elements are arranged in layers. Because of this difference in structure, graphite is soft and has streaks in its appearance. It is not considered to be a precious stone like the diamond.

GEOGRAPHY

Even a single scratch on a diamond can bring down its value dramatically.

Making money with minerals

In ancient times, gold, silver and bronze were used to make currency coins. These metals can be beaten into sheets. They can be made into many shapes. Gold and silver are also used to make articles of jewellery.

Gold

Gold is a very valuable metal. In the past, many people have migrated to areas which have or had gold deposits in the past. They did this in the hopes of discovering gold deposits themselves and earning a lot of money by selling the deposit. This period of migration was called the "gold rush".

EARTH'S ATMOSPHERE

Atmosphere is a blanket of air surrounding Earth. The air is made up of gases like nitrogen, oxygen, argon, carbon dioxide, helium and neon. Other gases are present in small percentages. The atmosphere also has dry air and water vapour. The atmosphere protects Earth from harmful radiations emerging from the Sun.

This layer is known for absorbing UV rays.

Layers of the atmosphere

Troposphere

Troposphere is the layer which is closest to Earth's surface. It holds clouds in the sky. The weather systems change here so that we experience different weather through the course of a day. As we go higher into the troposphere, the air thins. The oxygen molecules greatly reduce in number. This is why mountain climbers are asked to carry oxygen cylinders.

Stratosphere

Air in the stratosphere flows horizontally. The stratosphere contains ozone, a form of oxygen. It blocks the ultraviolet rays of the Sun from reaching Earth's surface. These rays are harmful to the environment.

Exosphere
700-10,000km

Thermosphere
80-700km

Ionosphere

Mesosphere
50-80km

Stratosphere
12-50km

Troposphere
0-12km

2000 °c

1500 °c

-85 °c

0 °c

-60 °c

Mesosphere

Of all layers of the atmosphere, the lowest temperatures are seen at the mesosphere.

Thermosphere

It contains the lighter gases of the atmosphere such as oxygen, helium and hydrogen. It is said to be the thickest of all layers.

Exosphere

The exosphere is the outermost layer of the atmosphere. It lies about 500 kilometres above Earth's surface

The Hubble Space Telescope helped us learn more about this layer.

Only rockets can survive in the mesosphere

Ionosphere

The ionosphere is named after the ions that are present here. These ions are created from particles of sunlight. They contain a lot of energy. Radio waves travelled by bouncing off the ions in the ionosphere.

THE PUSH AND PULL OF AIR

Air has weight and this weight allows air to push and press against everything around it. This is called "pressure" or "air pressure". In terms of the air in the atmosphere, it is called "atmospheric pressure". Atmospheric pressure is the force that air exerts upon Earth's surface as it is being pushed down upon by gravity.

Barometer

A device called "barometer" is used to measure atmospheric pressure. This device has a glass tube with liquid mercury. As the weight of the air in the atmosphere increases or decreases, the mercury in the barometer rises or falls. The rising mercury helps determine the weight of the atmosphere.

An Aneroid barometer that can be kept at home.

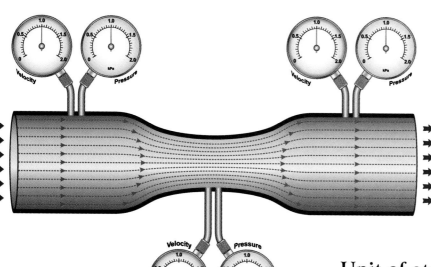

Unit of atmospheric pressure

Atmospheric pressure is expressed in a unit called "millimetre". An atmosphere (whose unit is "atm") is the average air pressure at sea level at a given temperature of 15 °C. One atmosphere is equal to 760 millimetre of mercury. Atmospheric pressure is measured in comparison to this unit.

Oxygen and atmospheric pressure

The oxygen in the air decreases with a decrease in the atmospheric pressure. At great elevations and altitudes, the atmospheric pressure is low. This is another reason that the amount of oxygen in the air is also low.

Oxygen cylinder

Artificial Pressure

The interiors of aircraft and aeroplanes have artificial air pressure so that the people within have enough oxygen and feel comfortable.

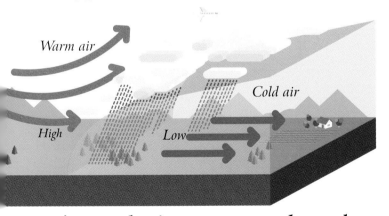

Warm air

Cold air

High

Low

Oxygen cylinders

Mountaineers carry oxygen cylinders while climbing because the air at high altitudes is thinner. Thinner air decreases the oxygen available for breathing and can lead to a condition called "hypoxia".

Atmospheric pressure and weather

There are two atmospheric pressure systems. These are "low-pressure system" and "high-pressure system". These systems determine the weather and weather patterns of any place. A place that has high-pressure systems will experience stable and calm weather. A place that has low-pressure systems will experience cloudy and windy weather with more precipitation.

THE MOVING BORDERS

Moving air is called "wind". Atmospheric pressure is received in different amounts in different areas. Wind is generated by these differences in atmospheric pressure. Wind begins to blow at areas with high-pressure systems and then moves to areas with low-pressure systems.

Diagram depicting the movement of air

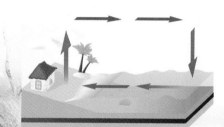 

Wind patterns

Wind patterns tell us in which direction the wind moves and what it contains. Heat from the Sun gives wind the energy to move. As the wind moves, it makes warm and cool spots around Earth in an uneven manner.

Sea and land breeze

As the evening approaches, the inland starts experiencing cool breeze. At night, the temperature in the inland areas cools down and the air begins to drop lower. This area receives land breeze. The air above the ocean now warms up instead.

Doldrums

An intertropical convergence zone is a formation that takes place in an area where trade winds from two directions converge. The prevailing winds that surround this area tend to be very weak. Due to this factor, the weather remains relatively calm throughout the year. This surrounding area is called "doldrums". The intertropical convergence zone overlaps the Equator.

Winds sweep over the Kalahari dunes in South Africa.

Horse latitudes

A horse latitude is a weather zone. The 30–35° N and 30–35° S latitudes have horse latitudes. This zone has a dry and warm climate. All horse latitudes have prevailing winds. However, they are light. These winds are only strong for some time. The Kalahari Desert of Southern Africa is a part of the horse latitude zone.

DROUGHT

If a place does not experience rainfall for a long time, and if it does not have other means to supply water to the land, it begins to experience a drought. A drought is an extreme water shortage. The lack of water begins to damage crops and reduces the flow of streams.

Droughts affect an entire region

Unpredictable drought

Some areas that experience sufficient rainfall might suddenly experience a lack of rainfall or any precipitation. The weather would become hot and the humidity in the air would decrease. Such a drought occurs in humid and sub-humid climate.

Permanent drought

Arid regions and other places with the driest climates experience a permanent drought. East Africa or the Atacama Desert, for example, are places which experience permanent droughts.

Seasonal and unpredictable drought

Seasonal droughts take place in areas with a rainy and dry climate. The tropical and subtropical climate areas experience seasonal droughts. They have plenty of water during the rainy season, but in the summer and winter, they might experience water shortage and drought.

Food shortage

Agriculture without any irrigation support becomes difficult during a drought. There is a definite shortage of crops. This creates a shortage of food. Import of crops and other food items might then become a necessity. These things would require lots of money. In poor countries, droughts have resulted in starvation and famines for this reason.

Declaring a drought

A drought is declared when the amount of dryness in an area is more than its average for a long period of time. There is no fixed length of time to declare a drought. The time for an arid region is shorter than the time for a place near the coast.

The California droughts dried up the wetlands over a few years.

TSUNAMI

Sometimes, waves as tall as 100 feet come surging from the ocean and crash onto the shore. These waves move faster than a jet plane. With their force and speed, the walls of these waves demolish the structures on the shore within minutes. This series of massive and destructive ocean waves is called "tsunami". "Tsunami" is a Japanese word which means "harbour wave".

Causes of a tsunami

The oceanic crust, and the part of Earth below it, undergoes lots of activity. Sometimes, this activity results in an earthquake (on or near the boundaries of tectonic plates), volcanic eruption or a landslide. As a result, the water above this part of the oceanic crust is displaced (forced into motion) in waves. These waves then reach the ocean with great force.

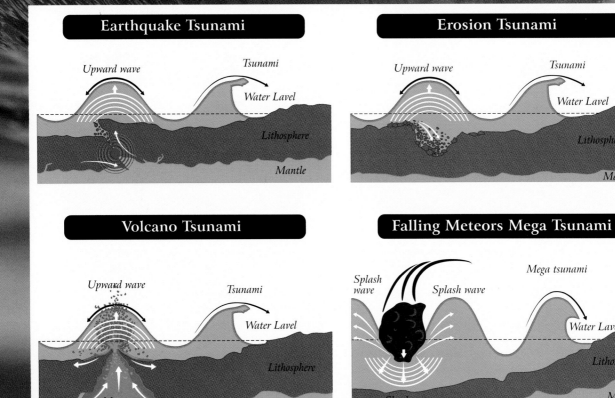

Approaching tsunami

Tsunamis travel across the ocean at a speed of 800 kmph. The tall waves gain more and more energy as they move. It is difficult to spot an approaching tsunami. While it approaches, the water at the coast retreats just a little. Then, the tsunami waves hit the shore within the next five minutes.

Signs for evacuation during a tsunami.

Tsunami warning tower

Pacific Tsunami Warning System

There are systems built to predict and give early warning of the tsunamis. The Pacific Tsunami Warning System is headed by 26 countries. It is based in Hawaii. It is equipment with technology to measure the seismic waves and find out the water level.

The growing wave

If seen in the middle of the ocean, a tsunami wave might look only one-foot tall. This is because it is surrounded by deep water. When it reaches the shallow water at the coast, it is at its tallest and more energetic.

VOLCANIC ERUPTION

A volcano is formed when molten rock or magma erupts through the surface of a planet. When magma reaches the surface of Earth it flows out through the volcanic vent as lava.

Lava flowing into the Pacific Ocean at Big Island, Hawaii.

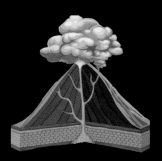

What causes a volcanic eruption?

Earth's crust is made up of enormous slabs called "plates". When two plates collide, volcanoes erupt.

Arenal Volcano at Costa Rica

Aftermath of an eruption

Eruptions are often accompanied by severe rains, which condenses in the atmosphere to form clouds. Explosive gases in the magma are let out into the atmosphere. A thick wave of ash, extremely heated gases and rock travels downhill at speeds of more than 100 kmph and collapses as it cools, and resulting in a rock formation.

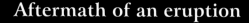

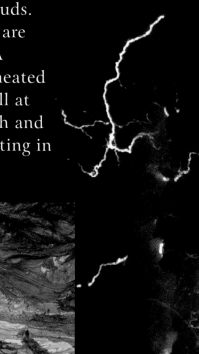

Flows of searing lava can reach upto 1250°C or more.

Types of Volcanic Eruptions

Volcanoes are classified as extinct (unlikely to erupt), dormant (not extinct but temporarily inactive) or active (experiencing frequent eruptions). They can also be classified on the basis of their shape.

Cinder cone volcanoes

They are highly explosive volcanoes with sharp hills shaped like cones. There is very little lava present in its composition.

Shield volcanoes

A shield volcano is extremely wide and extremely tall. The lower slopes contain lava which pile up during eruptions. Their eruptions are non-explosive.

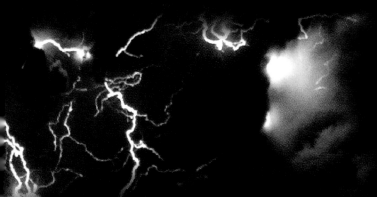

Submarine volcanoes

They are cone-shaped, mostly found under water and erupt under water. Most are active.

Stratovolcanoes

Stratovolcanoes or composite volcanoes are made up of lava flows, volcanic ash and cinders. The lava flows are arranged in layers which appear to be in pattern.

Caldera

If the top of a volcano collapses inwards, it results in the formation of a circular shape called "caldera", which might have a small lake present in it.

Lava domes

Some vents give out thick lava which accumulates in layers without flowing forward. This eventually forms a lava dome. They are wider than they are tall.

271

EARTHQUAKES

Earthquakes occur in the areas where two tectonic plates meet. Earthquakes occur when two plates are squeezed together or stretched apart. It is only when the stress between the plates is released quite suddenly and quickly that the vibrations or seismic waves occur. They travel thousands of kilometres from their position and reach the surface. An earthquake starts right below Earth's surface at a particular point called the "hypocentre" or the "focus". Another point which lies just above the hypocentre is the epicentre.

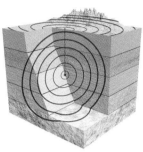

Diagram showing the hypocentre and epicentre of an earthquake.

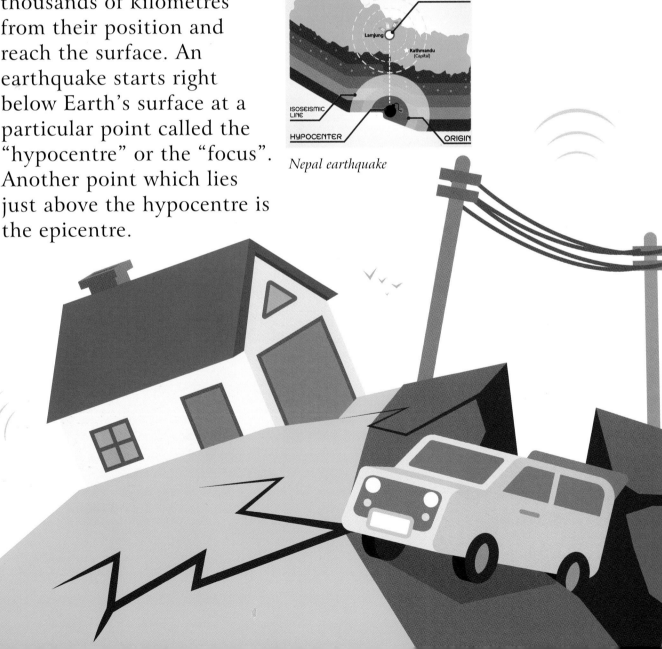

Nepal earthquake

Products of earthquakes

Though earthquakes are destructive, they have helped shape our planet. The islands of Japan, the Himalayas, the state of California and the oil drills are all a product of the earthquakes that have occurred in the past.

How are earthquakes measured?

The vibrations or tremors felt during the earthquakes are recorded and measured using a seismogram. These seismograms create zig-zag lines on paper. The lines made by the seismogram appear more frantic when the intensity of the tremors increase. Seismologists use the seismogram to understand the epicentre, focal depth and type of fault lines on which the earthquakes took place.

Seismograph instrument

Types of earthquakes

If the hypocentre is at a distance of 0–70 kilometres from the surface, then it is called a "shallow-focus earthquake". If the hypocentre is at a distance of 70–700 kilometres from the surface, it is called a "deep-focus earthquake". A shallow-focus earthquake is more powerful, and causes more devastation than a deep-focus earthquake. As they are closer to the surface, the seismic waves reach the surface faster and are stronger when they do. The rocks at the surface apply more strain on the hypocentre.

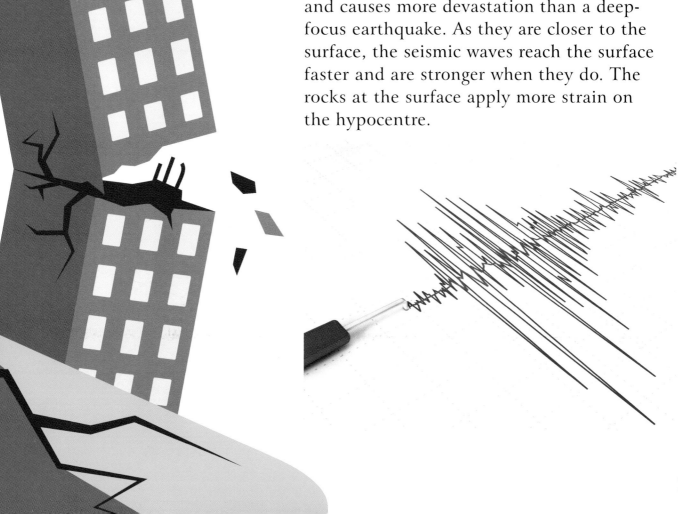

NATURE'S WONDERS

From deep blue waters with hidden treasures, to phenomenal islands with pretty white sand and the blinking northern lights, nature has many attractions for us to explore.

The Whitemouth eel is one of the species that lives in the Great Barrier Reef .

The Great Barrier Reef

The Great Barrier Reef, the world's largest coral reef, is located on the east coast of Australia. It consists of 2,100 coral reefs and 800 fringing reefs. It is a diverse ecosystem with more than 2000 species of fish, 4000 species of mollusc and 250 species of shrimp. The polyps and hydrocorals with the coralline algae and bryozoans have formed these reefs.

A geyser in Namafjall in Iceland

Geyser

It is caused due to pressure build up below Earth's surface. It erupts intermittently sending jets of water and steam upwards into the air.

The Great Barrier Reef has a co-dependent ecosystem.

Hot spring

A hot spring is a pool of water whose temperature is higher than the surrounding air temperature. It flows from an underground water source which is heated by magma or molten rock.

This is the Sea Hell hot spring in Beppu, Japan. It is one of the most popular tourist spots of the area.

The Yellowstone National Park was created in 1872 to preserve the thermal areas, hot springs and geysers here. It is spread across the states of Wyoming, Montana and Idaho in the USA. This park lies directly above a giant hot spot with magma rising towards the surface. It has more than 10,000 geysers and hot springs.

The Auroras

Auroras occur at Earth's magnetic poles. Aurora borealis occurs at the North Pole and is also called the "northern lights". Aurora australis occurs at the South Pole and is also called the "southern lights. Auroras also occur in dual bands, which appear like a forked ray of light.

Uluru

Uluru or Ayers Rock, made entirely of sandstone, stands tall and proud in the middle of the sandy plains of the Central Australian desert. It is nearly 348 metres tall. From left to right, it is 9.4 kilometres wide. This natural wonder is also rich in culture and heritage as it is home to the Anangu tribe, an aboriginal tribe. Not only is Uluru a sacred site for the aboriginal tribe, it is also an important Australian landmark.

AGRICULTURE

Agriculture developed around 12,000 years ago. The practice of settling down in one place began when people settled next to the crops they had cultivated. Starting from 2000 years ago, agriculture became the main occupation of the world population. Domestication developed alongside. The first wild animal to be tamed were the dogs, and they were used to hunt. Sheep and goat were tamed so that they could supply milk and wool. Cattle like cows and buffaloes were then tamed to work in the farm and to provide milk, butter and cheese.

Cattle used in the farm

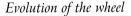
Evolution of the wheel

Development of agriculture

After domesticating cattle, people developed the techniques of ploughing and pulling. The invention of the wheel helped develop transport. People used modes of transport to send their crops to different places. People were able to grow more crops than they needed. They used the extra crops to trade for other items. People stayed close to their farms. With this, permanent villages began to develop.

Invention of farming tools

After axes were developed, farmers used them to cut down trees and clear out small plots of land on which to farm. They also found methods to store the crops. One example is the clay pots which were used to store and cook food in.

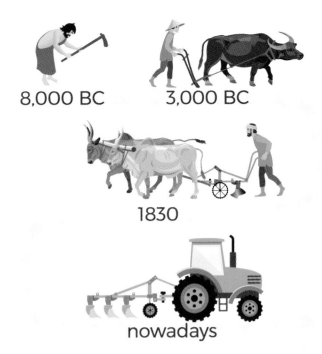

8,000 BC   3,000 BC

1830

nowadays

Cotton field during the time of harvest.

Irrigation

Irrigation systems are said to have developed in the Mesopotamian Civilisation in 550 BCE. Water from the Nile River and some nearby streams was directed to the fields in the inner parts of the civilisation. The entire community came together to build a proper irrigation system which could benefit everybody. Soon, with improved tools and methods, people were able to grow more variety of crops.

TECHNIQUES IN FARMING

By the 1950s, tractors replaced bullocks. Electricity powered water pumps, livestock feeding machinery and milking machines. With the introduction of pesticides, insecticides and fertilisers, the yield was better.

Slash and burn

Slash and burn is a technique of farming where land is first cleared with the help of a fire. The heat from the fire burns the soil and fertilises it. Then the farmer sows seeds of the new crop. When the fertility of soil is exhausted, the farmer moves to a new land.

Intercropping

Crops are planted in rows with large gaps between them. Different crops are planted in these gaps. For example, a farmer plants kernels of corn in rows, and a row of legumes and pulses between the rows. This reduces soil erosion and prevents loss of moisture in the soil.

Coffee plant

Slash and burn is carried out in small areas.

Cabbages grown in rows

278

Ranching

Herds of cows, sheep or buffaloes are let loose on big farms or ranches. Here, they graze upon the wild plants and grass grown on the land. They also crush some of the bigger plants and shrubs. This creates a grassland.

Herds of cows and sheep in the field.

Crop rotation is an important farming technique.

Rosemary and beetroot grown by crop rotation.

Mixed farming

Mixed farming is the growing of crops and the rearing of livestock on the same farm. Farm animals like sheep are sometimes kept in a field with strong fences. The matter excreted by them is used as fertiliser. The dung and manure which falls on the land fertilises it. Then, the animals are cleared and the field is used for farming.

Crop rotation

Farmers grow different kinds of crops. This practice reduces crop diseases. If a farmer continues to grow rice on a farm repeatedly, insects that attack rice would multiply and eventually destroy the crops. This is why the rice farmer must grow crop like legumes, beans and bulbs.

POPULATION DISTRIBUTION

The term "population distribution" describes where people of the world live and how they are spread across the world. It takes into account which places are most lived in by people and why those people have chosen to live there. This study of population is made to understand human behaviour and preferences.

Population density

Population density takes into account how many people live in one square kilometre. It is from this data that we know the total population of a place. It is surprising then to know that there are more "empty areas" (where humans do not live) in the world than "occupied areas". A large part of the world population is concentrated in developing countries like India.

Physical factors

Antarctica has a permanent zero population because of its harsh climatic conditions. Lack of fresh drinking water, extreme temperatures, low vegetation and low availability of food are some physical factors which discourage people from living in a place. On the other hand, places with fertile soils, plenty of available natural resources, pleasant climate and plenty of food encourage people to settle there.

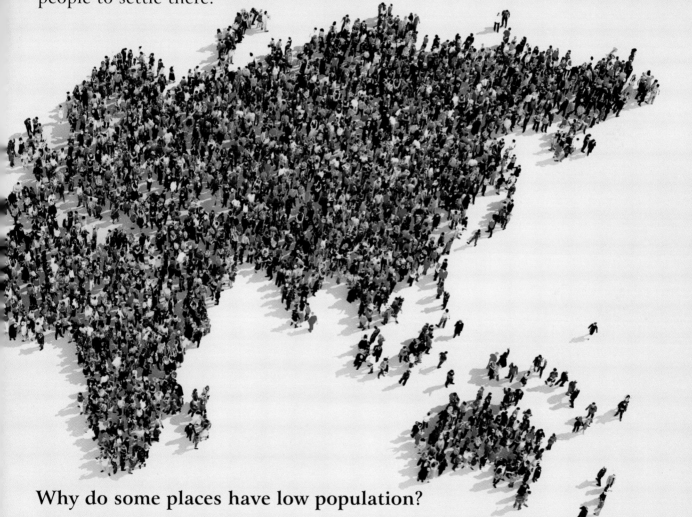

Why do some places have low population?

People flock to places with more employment opportunities as it allows them to earn money. They prefer places that offer good services like education, healthcare, entertainment and recreation. Hence, a place which does not provide enough of these services and requirements remains thinly populated. The people living in such places might choose to move away to seek more employment, entertainment or education opportunities.

MIGRATION

"Migration" refers to movement from one place to another "Human migration" specifically deals with the reasons behind why a group or individual might want to permanently change their location.

Internal and international migration

Migration can be of two types—internal and international. Internal migration is when people move within the same country. International migration is when a person moves from one country to another. A person who leaves their country to move to another is called an "emigrant", while a person who has moved to another country is called an immigrant.

A large group of people might migrate to another country together during crisis times like war or an epidemic.

There was a lot of migration during World War I and World War II.

Pull factors

A country or city which has more opportunities of employment, higher wages and offers more services tends to attract migrants. Farmers like to migrate to places that experience stable weather, fertile lands and a lower risk of natural disasters. Countries that have political and economic stability are also more attractive to migrants.

A sudden natural disaster can cause great loss to life and property. It forces the people of the area to move temporarily or permanently.

Push factors

If a country experiences a lot of crime or war, people of that country might feel unsafe and choose to flee. Farmers would not want to reside in an area that experiences too many floods, droughts or crop failures. People also tend to leave places that do not provide basic services or experience poverty.

Slave migrations

The imperialistic European nations, consigned nearly 20 million slaves from the continents of Africa and Asia to their colonies in the Americas during the sixteenth and nineteenth centuries.

Mass expulsions

Mass expulsion is carried out when the official bodies of a country believe that the presence of a certain group of people is illegal or damaging to the country. During World War II, Nazi Germany had deported close to eight million people from Germany.

Slave migration was a practice of the colonial era.

Farmers during a harvest

PLANNING THE CITY

A city planner or an urban planner designs the plans for the city. They keep a track of available space and make plans to utilise it. City planning is also called urban planning. It is the design and regulation of available space. Its main focus is the social, economic and environmental impact of constructing a certain structure in a spot in the city, or allowing certain activities there. City planning is a highly technical career which involves lots of study and regular updating.

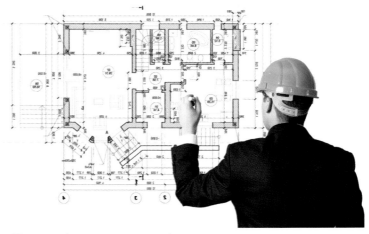

City planning and society

A city planner needs cooperation from political leaders. Cooperation and participation from the public is also needed. Each step taken by a city planner needs to have a long-term view. City planners also need to look at the available infrastructure and budget while planning for something. If the budget is exceeded, there might be backlash from political powers. Also, if the plan for a new building or activity does not please the public, the city planner would have to face lot of criticism and public protests against the plan.

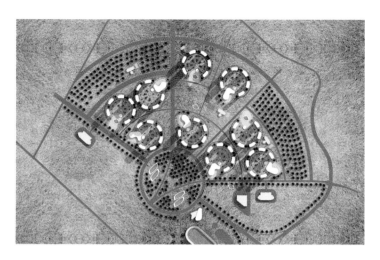

Construction and restoration

City planners do not just decide how the available space can be utilised. They also check the conditions of the structures in the city. If any building or public location is facing disrepair, city planners plan the funds and resources to repair it.

Master plan

During the early twentieth century, western countries saw lots of expansion and development. Construction was taking place everywhere at a speedy rate. This brought about the need for controlled and systematic development. The value of property also came down. To preserve this, city governments began to create master plans for the cities. Zoning regulations were started. They were used as a means to achieve master plan for city.

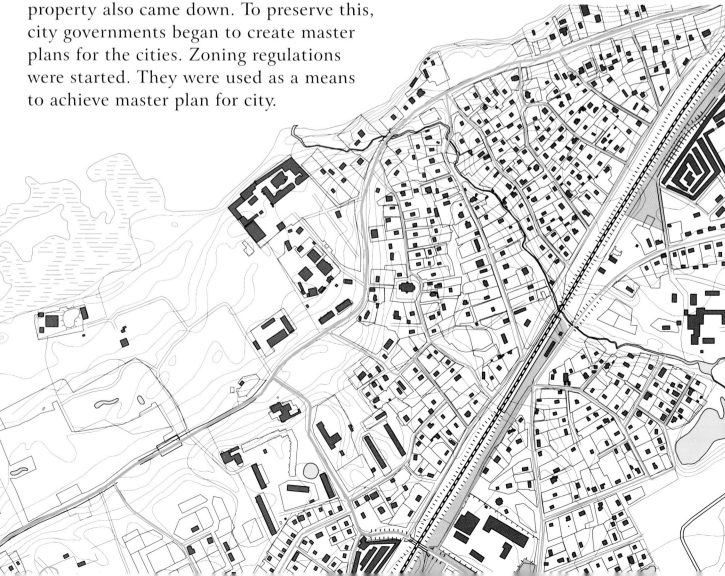

CITIES OF THE WORLD

Cities came about in the nineteenth century as a direct result of the industrial revolution. They are highly organised and more developed than towns and villages. By the year 2030, it is believed that about 60 per cent of the world population will be living in cities.

Barcelona, Spain

Barcelona is one of the most congested yet beautiful cities in the world. A seaport, it is located by the Mediterranean Sea. Due to its strategic location, this city was very heavily fortified until the nineteenth century.

The Barcelona skyline

Athens, Greece

Athens, the capital of Greece, is considered to be the birthplace of the western civilisation. This city has rebuilt itself several times after almost being destroyed by the devastation of wars.

The Parthenon temple is an important monument in Athenian and Greek history

Paris, France

Paris, the capital of France, is known for its food, entertainment, culture, art and literature. The Eiffel Tower is one of its main attractions, followed by the Louvre, the most popular museum in the world.

A view of Paris with the Eiffel Tower in the distance.

Shoreline view of the city of Istanbul, Turkey

Passing through the Grand Canal in Venice on a gondola is a major attraction

A lighthouse on a beach in Colombo.

Istanbul, Turkey

Istanbul, the capital of Turkey, shows glimpses of the famous empires that once ruled it. It serves as Turkey's economic and cultural capital. The city stretches across both Europe and Asia, making it a transcontinental city.

Venice, Italy

Venice is a major seaport of Italy. More than 200 canals make up its transport network. The most popular form of transport for tourists is the gondola. This city is considered an artistic and architectural treat for all travellers.

Colombo, Sri Lanka

Colombo, the national capital of Sri Lanka, is the principal port of the Indian Ocean. It has attracted many foreign travellers like the Arabs, British and Portuguese, and has always been a place of financial and political importance.

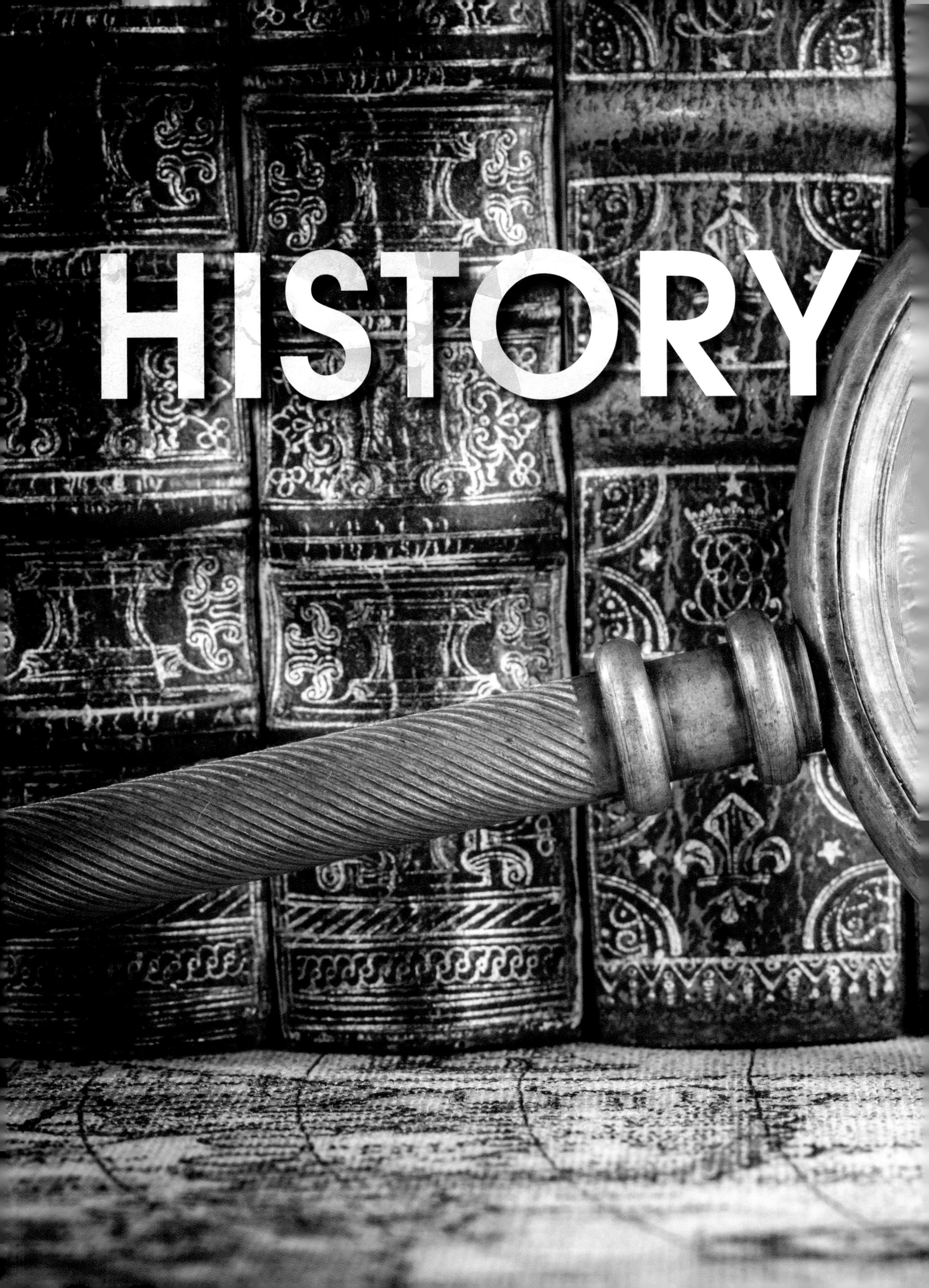
HISTORY

Moments and events in past make up history. History is the story of people on their planet and their changing cultures, politics, lifestyles, beliefs, and creativity.

WHAT IS HISTORY?

History is the study of past and future events. People know what happened in the past by looking at things from the past including sources like books, newspapers, and letters and artefacts (like pottery, tools, and human or animal remains.

Why do we study history?

Studying history is important because it allows us to understand our past, which in turn allows us to understand our present. If we want to know how and why our world is the way it is today, we have to look to history for answers. People often say that "history repeats itself," but if we study the successes and failures of the past, we may, ideally, be able to learn from our mistakes and avoid repeating them in the future. Studying history can provide us with insight into our cultures of origin as well as cultures with which we might be less familiar, thereby increasing cross-cultural awareness and understanding.

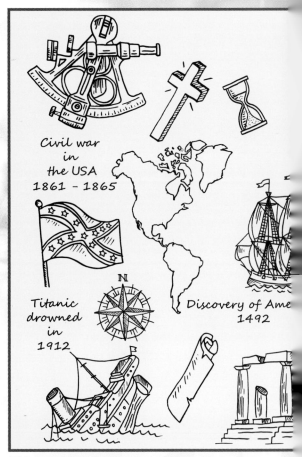

Civil war in the USA 1861 – 1865

Titanic drowned in 1912

Discovery of Ame 1492

Themes of History

Historians

A historian is a person who studies and writes about the past and is regarded as an authority on it. Historians are concerned with the continuous, methodical narrative and research of past events as relating to the human race; as well as the study of all history in time.

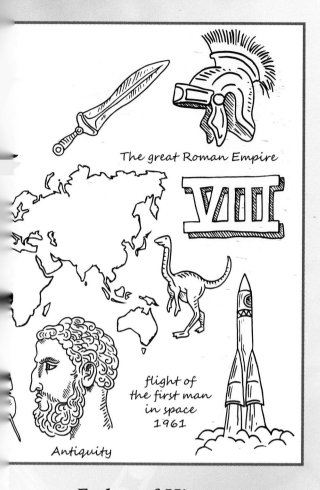

The great Roman Empire

VIII

flight of
the first man
in space
1961

Antiquity

Famous Historians

One of the most important historian is Fernand Braudel. He is well-known for the huge scope of his books on the history of the Mediterranean civilisation and capitalism. His focus on social and economic developments and on the lives of so-called 'ordinary' people have been tremendously influential.

Fernand Braudel's masterpiece, *The Mediterranean and the Mediterranean World in the Age of Philip II*, more than any other work of history published in the 20th century, showed just how immense and indeed almost Olympian, a historian's scope legitimately can be.

Father of History

In the fifth century BCE, a Greek historian, Herodotus, attempted to put down the events of the past to help people recall and remember the past, and hence is known as the "Father of History".

THE FIRST HUMANS

Almost six million years ago, the first humans appeared in East Africa. They walked on all four limbs and often swung from tree to tree. They began to hunt and run away from danger when they finally learnt to walk on two feet. Their bodies changed because they now walked and did not swing from trees. They had relatively smaller brains and were very hairy.

Fossil skull of Homo Erectus

Australopithecus

Life of the first humans

Early humans lived in caves. They ate nuts, roots, yams, insects, fish and meat. Gradually, they developed bigger brains, and to learned talk. They lost a lot of their body hair. Over time, they understood how to make fire. Soon, they learnt that fire could keep them warm and help them cook food, making it easier to eat.

In time, they learnt how to develop and make their own tools. Their tools were very basic, but more often than not, they used sticks and bones to dig and also defend themselves.

Homo sapiens

Dated to 30,000-
10.000 years ago

Homo neanderthalensis

Dated to 50,000
years ago

Homo erectus

Dated to 1,000,000
years ago

*Australopithecus
africanus*

Dated to 2,500,000
years ago

*Sahelanthropus
tchadensis*

Dated to 7-6
million years ago

Early humans and their survival techniques

Early humans mainly survived by hunting other animals for food. In order to hunt, they built and used different types of tools made of stones. The flint tools, as they were known, were quite useful to cut and scrape flesh from the hides of animals.

Later, humans began making hand axes, which were used to chop wood so that they could light a fire in order to stay warm. The first tools were rough and barely useful, but were improved over the years.

*Humans used tools
to defend themselves.*

*Primitive humans lived
outdoors and hunted food.*

PEOPLE OF THE PREHISTORIC AGE

The people that walked upright and straight are called "hominids". "Homo sapiens" is the Latin term for "wise human", owing to human beings' developed brains, bipedal gait (where one moves using the two rear limbs or legs) and opposable thumbs. Evidence of this species was found in Africa, Middle East and in Europe.

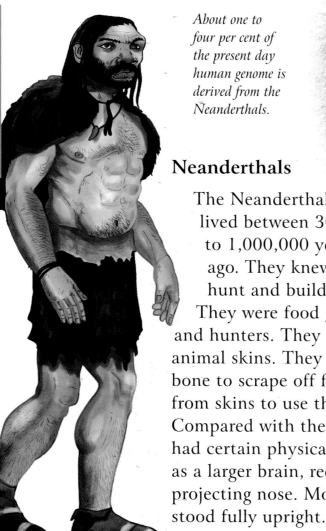

About one to four per cent of the present day human genome is derived from the Neanderthals.

Neanderthals

The Neanderthals lived between 300,000 to 1,000,000 years ago. They knew how to hunt and build shelters. They were food gatherers and hunters. They also wore animal skins. They used rock and bone to scrape off flesh and fat from skins to use them as clothing. Compared with the Early humans, they had certain physical differences such as a larger brain, receding chin and a projecting nose. Most importantly, they stood fully upright.

Climate

Much of the time Earth's climate was hotter and more humid than it is today, but climate has also been colder, as when glaciers covered much more of the planet. The most recent ice ages were in the Pleistocene Epoch, between 1.8 million and 10,000 years ago. Glaciers advanced and retreated in cycles, known as glacial and interglacial periods. With so much of the world's water bound into the ice, sea level was about 125 meters (395 feet) lower than it is today. Many scientists think that we are now in a warm, interglacial period that has lasted about 10,000 years. The drop in temperature led to the four periods of cold temperatures called the "Ice Age". Each age is known to have lasted anywhere between 40,000 years and 60,000 years. This impacted man's activities.

Culture

Towards the end of the second "Ice Age", many tribes of hunters and gatherers travelled to different parts of the world. They had no definitive literature, but burial chambers with artefacts in them have been found in numerous places including Great Britain.

A stonehenge in Great Britian

ART OF THE PREHISTORIC AGE

Various art forms have been discovered from Africa to Europe. From cave paintings in Lascaux and Chauvet in France, to the engravings of humans in Asia, to the rock art in Australia, the art during this age gives us a glimpse of the life of that period.

Different artefacts from the Palaeolithic Age.

Abalone shells, ochre, bone, charcoal, grindstones and hammer stones were used for different works of art in the prehistoric period.

Artefacts

Central and East Asia have numerous examples of art with carved figurines found in Malta. The archaeological site of Jiahu in China hosted bone flutes that represented the culture and their appreciation for music.

Prehistoric art is the oldest form of art, appearing much before literarure or sculpting.

In France, the Rouffignac caves have markings called "finger flutings" made by a child, where the art consists of simple lines. The lines have some symbolic meaning. These flutings or meandering lines depict the everyday lives of the people of this time. Some are shaped like animals or have a hut-like appearance called "tectiforms".

Cave painting

The Lascaux cave paintings were made with brushes made from the fur of animals. Artists from the Palaeolithic age used five different colours including black, violet, yellow, red and brown. Most art generally depicted animals, humans and certain symbols. With people engaging in farming activities, The art of domestic animals, maps and other landscapes made their presence felt. Pots with different decorations were also made.

Terracotta vases and goblet bowls are examples of this art.

ICE AGE

The Ice Age occurred during the Pleistocene Epoch (2.6 million to 11,700 years ago) when huge glaciers formed and spread from the North Pole towards the South Pole. During the Ice Age, such glaciers existed all over Canada, the USA and even the northwestern part of Europe.

HISTORY

Mammoths walked on Earth thousands of years ago.

A melting glacier

What made Earth cold?

Scientists have not been able to state what exactly caused the Ice Age, but some believe that the change in Earth's orbital pattern could be one reason behind this. A few others believe that the reason could be attributed to the huge amounts of dust and fewer gases that could have made Earth cold.

Sometimes, the ice was a thousand feet deep. But even in these sub-zero conditions, both plant and animal life existed. Animals like reindeer and giant mammoths roamed the Earth.

Rise and fall of sea levels

The most recent Ice Age entered its coldest period about 22,000 years ago, when ice sheets covered a great part of North America and Northern Eurasia. As the seas froze, the sea level fell exposing bridges of land between land masses, forcing animals such as mammoths and deer to move between Asia and North America. They were followed by human hunters, the first humans to colonise North America.

THE STONE AGE

The Stone Age began around 2.5 million years ago and continued till around 3300 BCE. The Stone Age is divided into three separate periods: the Palaeolithic Period, the Mesolithic Period and the Neolithic Period.

These pottery-making Mesolithic cultures can be found peripheral to the sedentary Neolithic cultures.

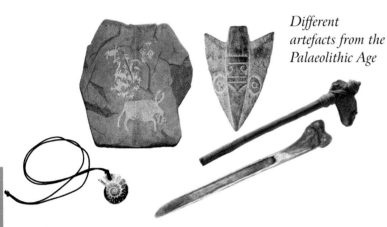

Different artefacts from the Palaeolithic Age

Palaeolithic Age

The Palaeolithic Age is also known as the "Old Stone Age". Stones were used to make fire and tools of wood, bone as well as stone were made. Some of the earliest known hand axes were found at Olduvai Gorge in Tanzania. Special tools were made from worked flakes of flint that were carefully shaped.

A group of Palaeolithic people living in a cave.

A Palaeolithic man using a spearhead against a wild animal for his defence.

Stone Age man making a stone tool. As humans became smarter, they started to make even more complex tools.

Mesolithic Age

In the Mesolithic Age, tiny chipped stone tools called "microliths" were used. They were used to make lightweight spears and arrows. The tools made from bones were used as fish hooks. Deer antlers were used for digging. The people hunted, fished and lived along rivers and lakes. Pottery and the bow were developed during this period. The nomadic Mesolithic people lived in temporary "tent houses" made from animal skins.

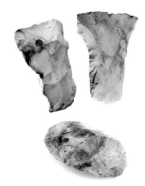

Flint axes of Mesolithic Age

A seamless pattern with petroglyphs.

Neolithic people began to cook food.

Neolithic Age

People used sophisticated tools that were made from stones such as jadeite or schist. In this period wood was made a building and hunting material. Canoes, paddles and other such materials were made during this period. Huts began to be made out of branches and stones. The people settled in communities. This was due to the emergence of agriculture. Animals like cow and sheep were domesticated during this period, to ensure a ready supply of meat, milk, wool and leather. Dogs would help humans and warn them of any dangers as well.

Collection of different types of stone tools

IRON AGE

Iron Age was a time when humans used tools and weapons made of iron. This age started somewhere in 1200 BCE in the middle and southeastern part of Europe.

Iron tools used for farming.

Tools and weapons

Iron was also used to make iron-tipped ploughs thathelped the farmers tackle heavy clay-like soil with ease. Iron was also used to make weapons and create armours like shields and helmets. Iron was also used to make coins.

Iron anvil and tools

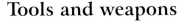

Shields were often decorated with a painted pattern or had an animal representation.

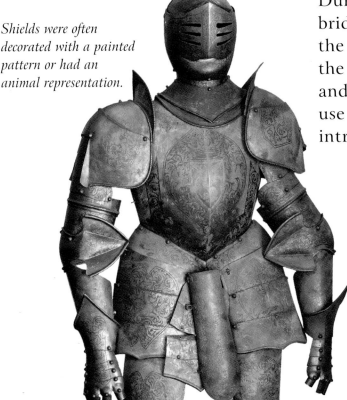

During the Iron Age forts and bridges were being constructed for the first time, humans discovered the concept of mining to find salt and other precious minerals. The use of horse chariots was also introduced.

A quern stone with grain

Life

During this period, the life expectancy of humans was just around 30 years. The Iron Age also marked the start of trading, when people began to sell and buy grains.

During this period, animals herded were kept close to human dwellings.

Occupation

Villages were made more secure during the Iron Age. As farming itself offered so many opportunities, everyone worked in the farms and very few chose to be artisans or take up another occupation.

Women during this period made skilled earthenware which were used for cooking as well as trading purposes. Women also did farm work.

ANCIENT GREEK CIVILISATION

Ancient Greece witnessed the Archaic Period, from the 700 BCE to 480 BCE, when democracy emerged; and the Classical Period, when philosophers like Socrates, Aristotle, Pythagoras and Plato lived. This period ended with the death of Alexander the Great in 323 BCE.

Athens

Athens, the largest city-state in Greece, was the one of the biggest democracies. Citizens met, chose members of the government and formed a small council. The council discussed public matters by laying it before the assembly.

The clothes worn by the men and women of Ancient Greece.

Olympic Games were held in elaborate stadiums.

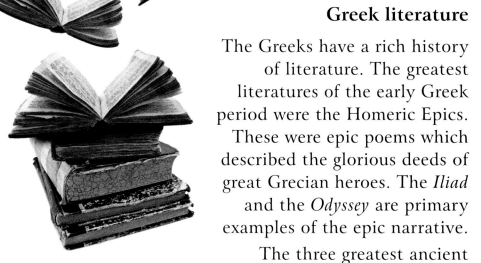

Culture

The Greeks built temples for their many gods. The first recorded Olympic Games were held in 776 BCE at Olympia in the Greek city-state Elis.

Greek literature

The Greeks have a rich history of literature. The greatest literatures of the early Greek period were the Homeric Epics. These were epic poems which described the glorious deeds of great Grecian heroes. The *Iliad* and the *Odyssey* are primary examples of the epic narrative.

The three greatest ancient Greek philosophers were Aristotle, Plato, and Socrates. Socrates taught Plato, then Plato taught Aristotle. These three thinkers turned early Greek philosophy into the beginnings of Western philosophy as it is today.

ANCIENT ITALIC PERIOD

Italy's first societies emerged around 1200 B.C. Around 800 B.C. Greeks settled in the south and Etruscans arose in central Italy. By the sixth century B.C., the Etruscans had created a group of states called Etruria.

Carvings of ancient Etruscans

The Etruscans

The Etruscan region bordered the Tyrrhenian Sea in the west, the Tiber River in the south and east, while in the north was the Arno River. This region was rich in metal ores such as copper, iron and tin. They traded lumber and fur to the east and purchased spices and perfume. The Etruscans had a government system, where the control was held by the central government.

Etruscan gravestones, "Pietra fetida" funerary sphinx, middle sixth century BCE

A commemorative plaque

The Toga

The Etruscans created the Toga, which became the official costume of the Romans. It was made from a semi circular white wool cloth piece. Only emperors or senators used purple coloured clothing. They were known for their gold and semi-precious stoned jewellery. They influenced Roman architecture, particularly the grid plan city system. The Etruscans followed a polytheistic religion.

Ancient Etruscan art

Etruscan warrior riding a chariot

Ancient Italic people and their customs

Religion became a uniting factor for the diverse Etruscan cities. These people had a strong belief in life after death. Unlike Greek and Roman societies, women sat with their husbands to eat at banquets and had their own possessions. They were also very active in politics.

Etruscan Roman archeology museum

Ancient Roman man and woman wearing Toga.

Downfall of the Etruscan cities

After 400 years of Etruscan rule, they could not withstand the force of the reorganised Romans, who had managed to unite themselves and gained over their opponents quite easily. By 265 BCE the Romans had already claimed the Etruscan cities.

THE ROMAN EMPIRE

According to legend, Rome was founded by twin brothers named Romulus and Remus in 735 BCE. Rome began developing during the sixth century BCE near the River Tiber. Till up to 117 CE, the Roman Empire had spread to include Italy, the Mediterranean, Europe, England, Wales and even parts of Scotland.

Sculpture of a mother-wolf feeding Romulus and Remus in the Capitoline Hill.

Technology

The Romans built aqueducts that could transport water for public baths and toilets. They used water mills, manure and mechanical reapers. They built fantastic roads.

The Romans invented concrete and they were the ones who used it to make the Pantheon that still exists even today. Their villas had bath suites, mosaic floors and under floor heating.

A picture from an archaeological site of Ancient Rome.

Religion

Emperor Constantine made Christianity the religion of the empire. Before the spread of Christianity, Romans believed in many gods and goddesses like the Greeks.

Decline

The Roman military slowly became inefficient. The internal rebellions plagued the government which was unable to collect taxes and safeguard the economy. Foreign powers such as the Visigoths also weakened the Roman Empire, leading to its decline.

Gladiators

Romans held gladiator contests. The gladiators would generally be prisoners or slaves. The gladiators would fight till either one of the men died. The contests were held in big amphitheatres and people would come to watch the fights. Men in armour would fight against animals like bears, bulls, alligators, lions and tigers.

Remains of the public baths in Pompeii

Antique illustration of Roman Forum, Italy

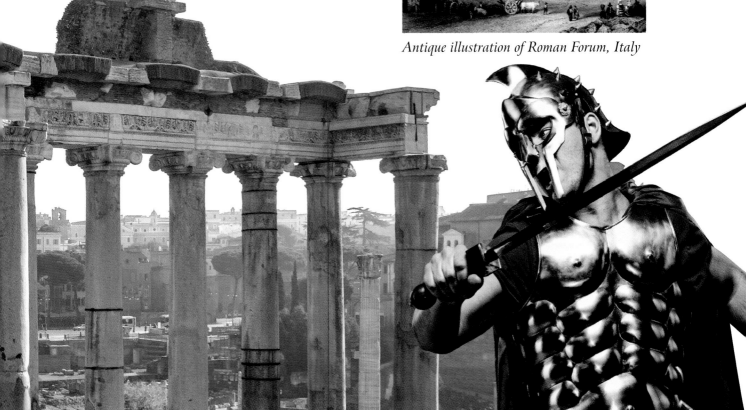

BARBARIAN INVASIONS

In 410, Rome was attacked by Germanic tribes who moved across the Roman Empire in a destructive and barbaric manner, earning them their name. These tribes settled down over the vast empire in different regions. For instance, the Angles and Saxons settled in England, while the Franks in France and Lombards made Italy their hometown. The Huns were a nomadic group who plundered the Roman Empire, but eventually lived in Eastern Europe, Central Asia and the Caucasus.

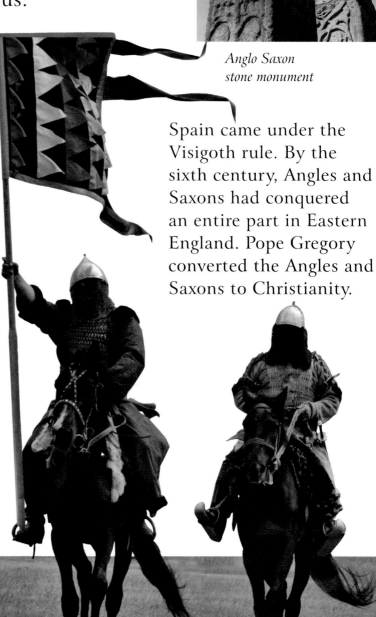

Anglo Saxon stone monument

HISTORY

The Franks, Angles and Saxons

The Franks ruled in the northern part of France from AD 481-511. Clovis ruled over the tribe and followed Christianity. The Alans, Sueves and Vandals occupied Spain after crossing the Pyrenees, but when the Visigoth King crushed the Sueves tribes,

Spain came under the Visigoth rule. By the sixth century, Angles and Saxons had conquered an entire part in Eastern England. Pope Gregory converted the Angles and Saxons to Christianity.

An artist's imagination of the Franks, Angles and Saxons.

Attila the Hun

Led by King Attila, the Huns devastated the Gaul region. The Burgundians joined hands to defeat the Huns at the "Battle of the nations"—as the battle was called. Attila did not give up; he marched through Italy, leaving in his wake a devastated Rome. Pope Leo I, assisted by St Peter and St Paul, ensured that he did not go further with his plundering . The Huns found themselves troubled by famine and plague and their numbers began to drop. Attila's retreat was soon followed by his death—he died after he choked to death from a nosebleed. His sons split the empire amongst them, but the Huns never returned to their former glory.

Painting of the Huns attack in Turkey

A mosaic depicting the Sword of God, the legendary weapon of Attila the Hun.

Old map of Barbarian kingdoms before Clovis I.

311

ANCIENT JAPANESE CIVILISATION

Different periods marked the history of ancient Japan, each leaving behind a legacy that impacted the culture of the Japan as we know it today.

Remains from the Jomon Period

A famous Shinto shrine

Jomon Period (13,000 BCE to 300 BCE)

This period was known for its pottery and ceramics, which had a unique "cord marked" pattern. It is believed that the Jomon people were semi-sedentary and obtained their food through hunting, fishing and gathering. The Kimono came into existence during the Jomon period. The word kimono means "thing to wear".

The kimono is a traditional Japanese dress worn by women, that is popular even today.

Kofun Period

(250 CE to around 538 CE)

The documented history of Japan starts in this period. The Shinto culture prevailed during this period and still exists in Japan.

Sumo wrestling is an ancient Japanese art which originated in the Shinto religion.

Yayoi Period (300 BCE to 250 CE)

This period saw the use of bronze and iron. People also discovered newer techniques of agriculture (wet rice cultivation) and weaving. They began to live in permanent communities.

Asuka Period (552 CE to 645 CE)

During this period, Empress Suiko and Prince Shotoku, spread the teachings of Buddha. Other ideas that appeared were the using of coins as currency, standardising weights and measures, and a central bureaucratic government.

Nara Period (710 CE to 782 CE)

The golden era of Japanese history, the Nara period, was named after the city of Nara, which became the base of culture and political power.

Heian Period

Almost 400 years of peace was overseen by the Fujiwara family. The *kana* script, which became the Japanese writing system; the waka style of poetry; the monogatari, or narrative tales, evolved during this period.

The painted Japanese fan is indicative of the delicate artistry prevalent in Japan.

The samurai warriors of ancient Japan.

Kamakura Period

(1192–1333 CE)

The royalty became figureheads with the real power being vested in the samurai, shogun and military aristocracy.

Karate, an ancient martial art, is widely practiced even today.

Muromachi Period (1392–1573)

Zen Buddhism impacted all aspects of life – art, commerce, education and politics. The shoguns performed the elaborate tea ceremony. Flower arrangements, calligraphy and preparing and serving food gained importance.

The tea ceremony is an elaborate ritual that takes years to master.

Azuchi-Momoyama Period

The internal conflicts of Japan came to an end with this period. This was followed by the Edo period (1603–1868) where Japan began to isolate itself from the rest of the world in terms of trade and missionaries.

Martial arts

Ancient Japanese were great students of weaponry and combat techniques. Judo has its origins in Jujutsu. Karate, is believed to have originated from Okinawa.

The Noh dance drama.

THE MESOPOTAMIAN CIVILISATION

Mesopotamia includes areas that are more commonly known as eastern Syria, southeastern Turkey and a large part of Iraq today. Evidence of people occupying this land goes back to 6000 BCE. As the population grew independent "city-states" emerged. Later, there was unification under the rule of King Lugal-zage-si of Uruk (a city in ancient Sumer). Finally, Babylon established a state in the south and Assyria, in the north.

Relief of an ancient Assyrian king

Tablet with cuneiform script

3500 BCE

The evolution of writing begins. At first, it appears in the form of pictograms, but it took about a thousand years to evolve into a full cuneiform script.

The Code of Ur-Nammu, the first complete law code

2100 BCE

The city of Ur becomes the centre of a powerful Mesopotamian state. It soon fell into decline as the Amorites, a nomadic tribe, started moving into Mesopotamia.

Map of Babylonia, Mesopotamia

5000-3500 BCE

Sumerians set up the first city states in southern Mesopotamia.

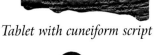

2300 BCE

King Sargon of Akkad starts conquering the first empire in world history. The empire reaches its height in 2220 BCE.

Statue of King Sargon

Major achievements

Mathematics and astronomy flowered during this period. Some concepts used even today include the 12 "double-hours" day; the zodiac, etc. Legal theory flourished and much of it was documented in various collections termed as "codes" by historians. The most famous of these is the "Code of Hammurabi". These codes focussed on concern for the weak, widows, orphans, etc. The Etruscans had a government system, where the control was held by the central government.

Changing life over centuries

The move from a nomadic to sedentary life was followed by the emergence of an agricultural economy. The construction of permanent houses, temples and burial grounds indicated the organisation of society. Specialised craft, division of labour, use of new materials like metals were indicative of the transition from the late Neolithic to a Chalcolithic period.

King Cyrus at a Babylonian temple.

1530 BCE

Babylonia is conquered by the Kassites, who rule the area for 400+ years.

Portrait of an old Chaldean man.

1100 BCE

Nomadic peoples such as the Aramaeans and the Chaldeans overrun much of Mesopotamia. The kingdoms of Babylon and Assyria go into temporary decline.

Law code of Hammurabi.

1792-49 BCE

King Hammurabi of Babylon conquers a large empire. Hammurabi is famous for the law code which he issues. His empire begins to decline immediately after his death.

1500 BCE

The Mitanni (Indo-European people) conquers northern Mesopotamia and areas of Syria and Asia Minor. After 200 years, the kingdom of Assyria conquers northern Mesopotamia from the Mitanni.

Map of Syria.

ANCIENT EGYPTIAN CIVILISATION

The ancient Egyptian civilisation lasted for more than 3000 years from 3150 BCE to 30 BCE. The monuments and tombs of the Pharaohs of Egypt, called pyramids, which are over 4000 years old, continue to stand even today.

An image showing the size of the Nile River flood that hit the capital, Khartoum.

The Great Nile

Every year the Nile, which flowed through Eygpt, would flood. The floods brought in the rich soil of the mountainsides, causing the land to be extremely fertile, and giving life to Egypt's civilisation.

Practices of the afterlife

The afterlife was very important to the Egyptians. They preserved their dead bodies by mummifying them. The bodies of the dead would be oiled and their internal organs would be removed. The bodies would then be wrapped in long strips of cloth. The dead were buried with their personal belongings, which the Egyptians believed would be needed in the afterlife. The Pharaohs were given a more elaborate burial. Pyramids were built for them, where they would be buried with all their riches.

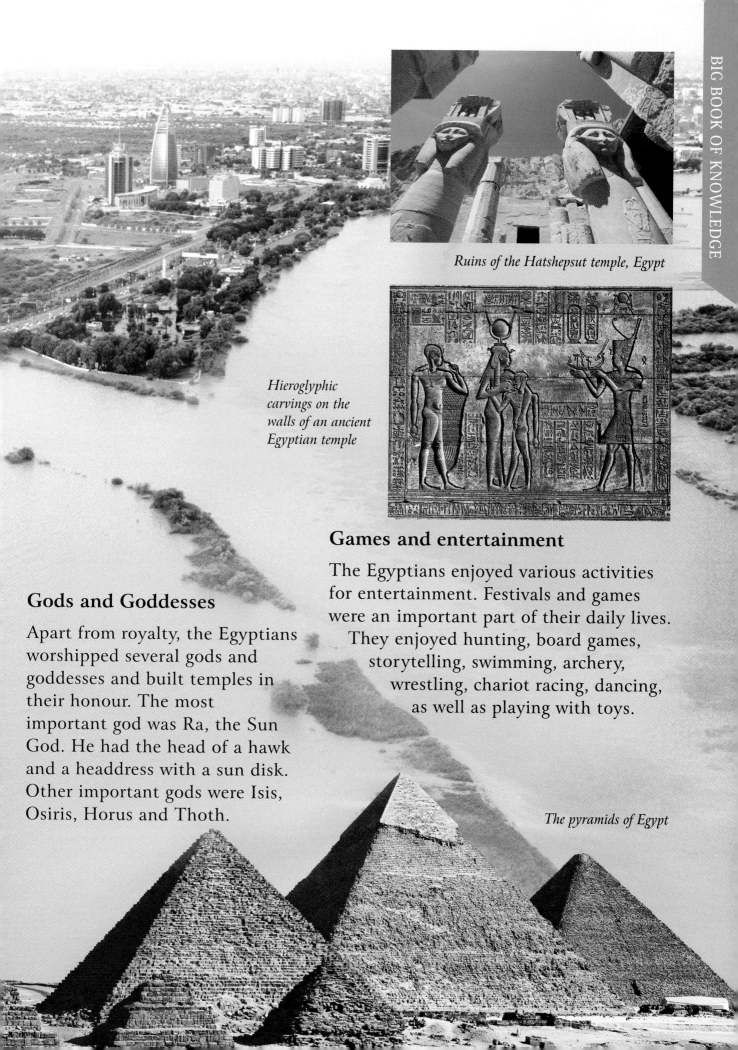

Ruins of the Hatshepsut temple, Egypt

Hieroglyphic carvings on the walls of an ancient Egyptian temple

Games and entertainment

The Egyptians enjoyed various activities for entertainment. Festivals and games were an important part of their daily lives. They enjoyed hunting, board games, storytelling, swimming, archery, wrestling, chariot racing, dancing, as well as playing with toys.

Gods and Goddesses

Apart from royalty, the Egyptians worshipped several gods and goddesses and built temples in their honour. The most important god was Ra, the Sun God. He had the head of a hawk and a headdress with a sun disk. Other important gods were Isis, Osiris, Horus and Thoth.

The pyramids of Egypt

MAYAN CIVILISATION

The Mayan Civilisation primarily existed in and around the lowlands of the area that is present-day Guatemala. The Mayans are believed to have been an advanced people and were known for their hieroglyphic writing, mathematics, agricultural techniques and calendar-making.

Architecture

The Mayan cities had names like Tikal, Uaxactún, Palenque and Río Bec. These cities were supported by agricultural communities and villages. The Mayans followed modern techniques of agriculture like terracing and irrigation. The evidence of the architectural brilliance of the Mayans is visible in the palaces, pyramids, temples and plazas that have been discovered during archaeological excavations.

A visual depiction of the Mayan calendar.

Evolution

The earliest known Mayan settlements have been said to exist around 1500 CE. During their Golden Age, the Mayans built over 40 cities, each with a population ranging from 5000 to 50,000 people. At its height, the Mayan population is believed to have crossed 2,000,000 people.

A pyramidical temple from the Mayan period.

Mayan Culture

The Mayans excelled in pottery, hieroglyphics, mathematics, calendar-making, and agriculture. The Mayan people left behind magnificent stone cities, meaningful artwork and amazing architecture.

Statue of a Mayan god

Attire

The Mayans had vibrant dance outfits, elaborate armour for protection and simple flexible clothes for everyday wear. During public events, the ruling class would wear elaborate headdresses, jewellery made of jade and clothes made from the skin of animals that were considered to be "dangerous". Their clothes were embellished with jewellery like bracelets, anklets and neck pieces. Their hair was often tied together with bands and decorated with feathers.

Ancient mayan warrior in red and white war paint and golden mask.

Decline

The Mayans inexplicably collapsed and disappeared by AD 900. Their disappearance remains a mystery till today and historians have been researching the reasons why this happened since the 19th century.

319

INDUS AND SARASVATI CIVILISATION

The Indus valley civilisation was one of the largest civilisations of the ancient world. Its two great cities were Harappa and Mohenjo Daro. Each had a population of more than 40,000.

Old map of the Indian sub-continent, 1867 showing rivers

Sarasvati

The Indus valley civilisation developed on the banks of the river Indus—Sarasvati. Mohenjo Daro is a city in the Indus valley civilisation that was built around 2600 BCE and flourished till 1900 BCE.

Mohenjo Daro is a city in the Indus valley civilisation that was built around 2600 BCE and flourished till 1900 BCE. It was discovered in the 1920s.

Cities

The Indus Valley Civilisation spanned across present-day Punjab, Haryana, Gujarat, Uttar Pradesh and Sindh and Baluchistan in Pakistan. Artefacts from this civilisation show that its inhabitants followed a number system. This civilisation was perhaps the first of the settlements in the Indian subcontinent. Cities such as Mohenjo Daro and Harappa also had citadels (fortress above a city), proper drainage and sewage system.

Life of the people

The people of the Indus Valley Civilisation reared cattle, pigs, sheep and goats. They also practised hunting and fishing. They grew wheat, cotton, chickpeas, mustard and sesame among other crops. They also traded gold, copper and silver, pots, gems like turquoise, seashells, gold and silver.

The toys made of clay and terracotta such as toy carts, rattles, whistles, pull-along animals, etc. were there. They played dice games and board games. Both men and women wore jewellery, such as beads. Indus valley seals have been found in Mesopotamia, suggesting that they had trade relations with Mesopotamia.

Evidence of writing

Artefacts, such as seals found at these sites, prove that the people from this civilisation were literate. Unfortunately, the Indus Valley writing has still not been deciphered. The writing has around 400 picture symbols.

Decline of the civilisation

Unfortunately, from 2000 BCE, the Indus valley civilisation began to decline. This is attributed to the devastating floods that destroyed the crops or because the river Indus changed its course making the once fertile land barren.

ARYAN MIGRATION, HINDUISM AND THE VEDIC PERIOD

German linguist and Sanskrit scholar, Max Muller's Indo-Aryan migration theory suggests that the Indo-Aryan group of languages were introduced in the Indian subcontinent when people from central Asia, that is, the Indo-Iranians migrated here around 1800 BCE and brought the Indo-Aryan languages with them. The Indo-Aryan languages are a part of the Indo-European group of languages.

Migration to India

The Aryan migration is believed to have occurred during the Indus valley civilisation. Coming from Central Asia, these large groups of nomadic cattle herders crossed the Hindu Kush mountains. In fact, some researchers believe that this settling down near the Indus valley civilisation could be one of the reasons for its collapse.

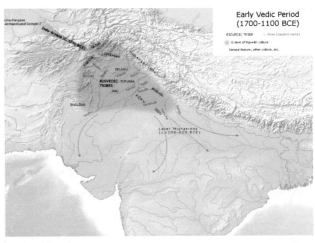

Map showing early vedic India and the extent of the Aryan migration.

Rigveda was written during the Vedic period somewhere between 1500 and 1000 BCE

Illustration of Aryans entering India during the Indus Valley Civilisation.

Hinduism and Vedic Period

Hinduism refers to many different beliefs, philosophies and perspectives that originated in India. It is a polytheistic religion, that is, it involves worship of several gods.

Temple in Karnataka state, India

Vedic period (1500–500 BCE)

The Vedic period laid an emphasis on religious sacrifice or yajnas and other religious rituals. This period saw the worship of various Gods, such as *Indra, Vayu, Marut, Varun, Rudra* and *Agni*. The *Vedas* were written in Vedic Sanskrit. They are ancient texts that contain Hindu teachings. There are four *Vedas*: the *Rigveda*, the *Yajurveda*, the *Samaveda* and the *Atharvaveda*. Collectively the four Vedas are known as *Chathur Veda*.

Palm leaf manuscript (top). Dried palm leaves were used as writing materials in ancient India to record events, right from horoscopes to mythological stories (left).

The *Rigveda* means, 'Veda of praise' It is supposed to be the main *Veda*. It contains 1028 hymns or *suktas* and 10,600 verses. The *Samaveda* is a collection of melodies. The *Yajurveda* explains various mantras to be sung and religious rituals to be followed by priests. The *Atharvaveda* is a collection of spells and charms to treat diseases.

JAINISM

Jainism rose as a voice against orthodox religion, which followed rigid rituals and rites. Jainism originated between the seventh and fifth centuries BCE. Jainism does not have one founder, but 24 tirthankaras or teachers who have surmounted the cycle of birth and death, and who show others the path to attain *moksh* (salvation).

Caste system leading to rise of Jainism

The four castes were Brahmins, Kshatriyas, Vaishyas and the Shudras. The upper castes lived a life of privilege while the lower castes were discriminated against and denied many resources. This led to resentment against the upper-castes.

Carvings in a Jain temple in Ranakpur, India

Statue of Jain god Gomeshvara in Shravanabelagola, India

The one who leads

The twenty-fourth and final *tirthankara* was *Vardhamana*, also known as Mahavira (great hero).
Mahavira was a Kshatriya chieftain's son who renounced his princely status at the age of 30 to live the life of an ascetic. Mahavira spent around 12.5 years as a devout ascetic and attained enlightenment (*kevalnyan*). He had 11 disciples or *ganadharas*. Of these disciples, Indrabhuti Gautama and Sudharman were the founders of the historical Jain monastic community.

Principles of Jainism

As per Jainism, right knowledge, right faith and right conduct can help a person attain moksha. For this, the five great vows—non-violence (*ahimsa*), truth (*satya*), non-stealing (*asteya*), celibacy (*brahmacharya*) and non-attachment (*aparigraha*)—should be followed.

Rockcut statue of Jain tirthankara in rock niches near Gwalior fort, India.

Hutheesing Jain Temple, constructed in 1848 AD, is one of the best known Jain temple located in Gujarat, India.

Time of social flux

It was a time of great social, political and intellectual flux. Some groups, known as republics, came into existence. The old social order began to slowly disintegrate. Further, many complicated rituals and sacrifices during the late Vedic period remained . All these factors led to disillusionment amongst the common people. They wanted a simple way towards salvation in a language that was known to them. Mahavira managed to do just that.

Chaumukha Mandir–Jain Temple, Ranakpur, India.

BUDDHISM

Buddhism aims to achieve *nirvana* by following the path laid down by Gautam Buddha. It is believed that if we do good in this life, we will have a better life when we are reborn. Although Buddhism originated in India, it presently has more followers in countries like Thailand, Japan and China. Gautam Buddha was the founder of Buddhism. His real name was Siddhartha and he renounced his life as a prince after witnessing human suffering.

Buddhist monks praying.

Young Buddhist novices pray at Shwezigon Pagoda near Bagan

Old Buddhist Temple Wat Yai Chai Mongkhon in Ayutthaya Province, Thailand

Becoming the Buddha

At the age of 35, he meditated under the Bodhi tree and gained enlightenment; thus becoming the Buddha (awakened one).

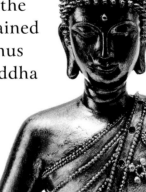

Red and golden Buddha statue

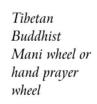

Tibetan Buddhist Mani wheel or hand prayer wheel

First sermon at Sarnath

Gautam Buddha delivered his first sermon at Sarnath to five monks. This was the beginning of the Buddhist sangha or community of monks.

Four noble truths of Buddhism

Buddhism revolves around the four noble truths: (1) suffering, (2) origin or cause of suffering, (3) cessation of suffering and (4) the path to the cessation of suffering. The Buddha prescribed the eightfold path to end suffering. It includes right views, right intention, right speech, right action, right livelihood, right effort, right concentration and right mindfulness of the Buddhist sangha or community of monks.

Ashoka

King Ashoka was a follower of Buddhism. He used oral announcements to spread Buddha's teachings and also had them inscribed on rocks and pillars at various sites, such as Sarnath.

Tibetan prayer wheels in a Buddhist temple

The Buddhist council

Ashoka organised the Third Buddhist Council and supported Buddhist missions that travelled as far as Greece, Egypt and Syria. There is a mention in the Buddhist Theravada tradition of a group of Buddhist missionaries who were sent by Emperor Ashoka to a Buddhist school in Sri Lanka in 240 BCE. Due to his efforts, the religion gained prominence, particularly after he made Buddhism, his state religion.

The different colours of the lotus represent the different stages of the spiritual journey.

Ashokan pillar with four Asiatic lions on top.

327

THE MAURYAN DYNASTY

Alexander's campaign in northwest India lasted from 327 to 325 BCE. A few years later, in 321 BCE, Chandragupta Maurya founded the Mauryan dynasty.

Statue of Chandragupta Maurya

Mauryan Empire

After Alexander's death, Chandragupta Maurya, the founder of the Mauryan dynasty, created an empire that would go on to include most of India. The empire had a well-organised army and civil service. Chandragupta was assisted by his advisor Chanakya, who was a teacher at Takshashila. Chanakya authored the treatise, *Arthashashtra* that explains the duties of a king, methods to manage the economy and administration of the Mauryan Empire and steps to maintain law and order.

HISTORY

Chandragupta Maurya and his bride from Babylon

भारत सम्राट् महाराजा चन्द्रगुप्त मौर्य

Ashoka the Great

The Buddhist Mauryan emperor Ashoka ruled from 265 to 238 BCE. He was the third ruler of the Mauryan empire. After the Kalinga war, Ashoka maintained friendly relations with his neighbouring kingdoms. He worked towards extending Buddhism and spreading Buddhist teachings across the world. He commissioned some of the finest works of ancient Indian art.

He built several Buddhist monuments, such as *stupas*, *sangharama*, *viharas* and *chaityas*. Ashoka set up clinics for people and animals, and had wells dug out for the benefit of his people. Further, he abolished hunting and fishing. After Ashoka's death, the Mauryan empire began to decline. Brihadratha was the last Mauryan ruler, who was assassinated 50 years after Ashoka's death.

The Great Stupa (Stupa 1) at Sanchi

PERSIAN EMPIRE

The Persian Empire rose in Western Asia after the fall of the Babylonian Empire. Lasting less than 250 years, it was the largest empire in the ancient world.

Cyrus the Great

The Achaemenid Empire was founded by Cyrus the Great. His name was derived from Kuros, meaning "like the sun". He founded Persia by uniting the Medes and the Persians - two original Iranian tribes. He then went on to conquer the Lydians and the Babylonians. Under his rule, the people were allowed to practise a religion of their choice. They could keep their customs as long as they paid taxes and obeyed the rulers.

Stone bas-relief of Persian soldiers in Persepolis, Iran.

The Cyrus Cylinder, now preserved at the British museum, London

The Great Cylinder

Cyrus the Great was known for creating the first Charter of Human Rights known to humankind. It was written on a clay cylinder, which was excavated in 1879. It is said that the script on the cylinder was written by Cyrus himself. It was written in the Akkadian language with a cuneiform script. Passages in the text express the emperor's humanity, religious tolerance and freedom. Today, Cyrus the Great is remembered as a wise, peaceful leader and a liberator of his people.

Ruins of the city of Persepolis, the capital of the Persian Empire

Fighting the Greeks

After the death of Cyrus the Great, the next strong emperor to come into power was Darius I. Under his rule, the Persians tried to expand their empire by conquering Greece. King Darius first attacked Greece in 490 BCE. However, he only managed to conquer a few city-states, before he was defeated at Athens. His dream of conquering Greece was fulfilled by his son Xerxes I in 480 BCE when he won the Battle of Thermopylae against a strong army of Spartans.

THE VIKINGS

Large numbers of Scandinavian seafaring warriors, known as Vikings or Norsemen, raided and colonised several settlements between the eighth and eleventh centuries. For three centuries, they made their mark on large parts of England, Europe, Russia, Iceland, Greenland and Newfoundland.

Longships were seagoing vessels used by the Vikings for their seafaring adventures.

The Viking legacy

The Viking society believed in law and democracy. The "Althing" was believed to be Europe's first national assembly, with powers akin to parliament. Though women could not vote, they did enjoy tremendous equality, running farms and businesses while their husbands were at sea. They could inherit property and even initiate divorce. The Vikings wrote with a set of alphabets called "runes". The Vikings also appeared to have high hygienic standards, as is evident from excavations of tweezers, razors, ear cleaners and combs that were made from bones. The importance of boats in the Viking way of life is evident from the fact that sometimes they buried their dead on boats or wagons.

Landowners and farmers take to the sea

The Vikings comprised heads of clans or landowners who, on their own lands, were farmers; but once they set out, they turned into violent raiders and pillagers. They would organise bands of armies, set forth on seagoing vessels called longships and raid coastal cities and towns, plundering, burning, and killing at will.

Making inroads into England and Europe

By the middle of the ninth century, the Vikings had made significant inroads into Ireland, Scotland and England. They brought much of Scotland under their control; they established Ireland's early trading towns of Dublin, Waterford and Limerick. They attacked and occupied large parts of France (the name Normandy comes from The Land of the Northmen), Italy, Denmark, Greenland and Iceland.

CHINESE CIVILISATION

The Chinese Civilisation is one of the oldest civilisations of the world. Bounded by oceans, mountains and deserts; it was inaccessible to outsiders. The first recorded Chinese dynasty was the Shang Dynasty, which is said to have ruled China from 1766 to 1122 BCE.

Mongols and the Great Wall

To keep the Mongols from invading, the Chinese built a huge wall on its northern border. Started by the Qin dynasty, most of the wall was built by the Ming dynasty. It is the longest man-made structure in the world, stretching up to 8900 kilometres.

The wheelbarrow was invented by the Chinese.

Portrait of Emperor Qianlong of the Qing dynasty, the last dynasty to rule China.

Chinese technology and inventions

Printing was first practised in ancient China on wooden blocks. Their other inventions include gunpowder, crossbows, hand fans, fireworks, ploughs, kites, umbrellas, paper money, the compass, silk, paper and the abacus.

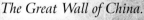

The Great Wall of China.

HISTORY

Traditional Chinese medicine

They devised various healing methods such as acupuncture or the science of healing through needles pierced at critical points and acupressure which is the science of healing by applying pressure at key points.

Needles are used for acupuncture

The Chinese Terracotta warriors

Ying Zheng unified a number of warring kingdoms and became the first Emperor of the Qin dynasty at the age of 13 in 246 BCE. The standardisation of coins, weights, measures, building of canals and roads, etc., are attributed to him. He commissioned the creation of an army of terracotta warriors to accompany him into the afterlife. Over 700,000 workers were involved in the creation of the famous Terracotta Warrior Army. Archeologists excavated four pits that were filled with over 6000 terracotta soldiers, weapons and horse-drawn chariots.

Languages in China

The many languages and dialects in China are known as Sinitic languages. The main language group, Chinese Han, comes from the Sino-Tibetan area. Other languages are Mandarin, Wu, Gan, Hakka, Xiang and Cantonese.

Calligraphy is a known art in China with elaborate and delicate strokes creating virtual pieces of art

The army of terracotta warriors was intended to serve the emperor in the afterlife.

A terracotta horsedrawn carriage as a part of the terracotta army

THE INCA CIVILISATION

Inca icon

The Inca Civilisation came into being during the twelfth century. With Cuzco (now Peru) as their capital, the Incas brought almost twelve million people in the region of Western South America under their control.

Expanding boundaries

It was during the reign of Topa Inca Yupanqui (AD 1471–93) that the Inca empire was the most widespread. Huayna Capac came to power in AD 1493–1525, but his death brought about another succession struggle. This remained unresolved when the Spanish arrived in Peru in 1532. By 1535, the Inca Civilisation came to an end.

Inca's water canal in the archeological site of Ollantaytambo, Sacred Valley, a major travel destination in the Cuzco region of Peru. Inca terraces can be seen in the background.

Machu Picchu, an Inca site built during the fifteenth century, is a World Heritage Site. It means "Old Peak".

Advanced society

At the helm of the Inca society was the emperor, who ruled ruthlessly and harshly with the help of an aristocratic bureaucracy. Technology and architecture during this period were fairly advanced. Excavations have unearthed evidence of fortifications, places of worship, palaces and irrigation systems from this period. Evidence of the advanced architectural abilities of the Incas lies in the vast road network they built.

The Inca economy was primarily agricultural, with a predominance of crops like maize, potatoes, peanuts, cocoa, cassava, cotton, etc. Domestic animals were raised and utilised in farms. Clothing was largely made of llama wool, as well as cotton.

View of the ancient Inca City of Machu Picchu, often called the "Lost city of the Incas".

The Inca religion

The Incas worshipped animals and nature gods. Inti, the Sun God; Apu Illapu, the Rain God; and Viracocha, the God of creation were among the chief Gods they worshipped. The official ruler of the Incas was said to be Sapa Inca, which meant "Son of the Sun". They conducted elaborate rituals that included both animal and human sacrifice. Many of these rituals were discontinued after the Spanish conquest.

Ancient Inca circular terraces suggest organised farming.

RISE OF ISLAM

After Prophet Mohammed's death in 632 CE, the Muslim armies had captured large parts of the Middle Eastern cities like Baghdad, Damascus and Cairo. All of these were ruled by the Caliph. It was also a period where great works of Greek, Indian and Iranian origin were translated into Arabic. This was a period of several inventions including the soap, windmills, the numerical system and even an early version of a flying machine. The Islamic world was created during the seventh and eighth century Arab conquests, and Islam spread far and wide from Turkey and Middle East to India.

Prophet Mohammed stamp on a metal ring.

Concerns of the Church

The rise of Islam brought forth concerns among the people of the Catholic Church who began to authorise military crusades against the Muslims. These began in 1095 when Pope Urban urged the Christian Army to fight its way to Jerusalem. While no one won the crusade, it did bring about a feeling of purpose to the Catholic communities.

The new caliph

After the death of Prophet Mohammed, the united tribes of Arabia and the followers of Islam were faced with a dilemma—who would be their next leader? They had two people to choose from. One of whom, was a man named Ali, Prophet Mohammed's cousin and son-in-law. The other was Prophet Mohammed's father-in-law and longtime friend, Abu Bakr. The latter of the two received support from many of the elders and he was chosen to become the first caliph of Islam. Although Abu Bakr died two years later, he managed to convert the entire Arabian Peninsula to Islam with his words, knowledge and wisdom.

NORMAN CONQUEST

In AD 1066, William the Conqueror and his army defeated King Harold in the Battle of Hastings. That was when power shifted to the Normans from the Anglo-Saxons. The nobles were expected to collect taxes. Historians opine that the root of feudalism started when William confiscated all the land from the Saxons and then distributed the same to the Norman Barons.

Detail of the famous Bayeux Tapestry depicting the Norman invasion of England in the eleventh century.

King William I of England

King William introduced the tradition of building castles. He ensured the supremacy of the Church in England. His Norman legacy remained etched into the English aristocracy and royalty. He was credited with having altered land tenures.

Scene of the Battle of Hastings of 1066.

King William I of England

The Domesday Book was ordered by William the Conqueror in 1085 to assess England's wealth to help the tax system. Close to 13,000 places were covered in the book. It shows how advanced their methods and technologies must have been to collect this "Grand Survey".

The Normans

The Normans were Vikings who had settled along the coast of France where they were known as the "Norseman from Norway". Eventually, they came to be known as "Normans" after they settled down in Normandy.

The Battle Abbey medieval gate building.

Art during the Norman legacy

The Norman architectural style found its way in cathedrals across Ely and Durham in England. It was in the Norman legacy that Latin as a language was introduced. Soon, after the Norman invasion of England, after winning the Battle of Hastings, the Normans marked the event by making the Bayeux Tapestry. It was a large embroidery made up of small stitches that showcased the events of the Battle of Hastings.

The Normans were great organisers, and excellent city planners. They were patrons of art and music. They took forward the culture and beauty left behind by the Anglo-Saxons, also called the founders of England as they contributed greatly to its culture.

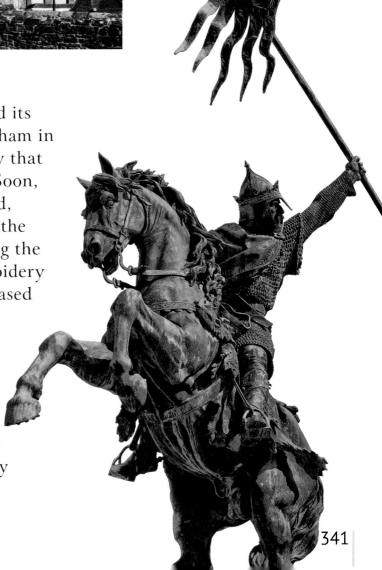

MAGNA CARTA

The Magna Carta or 'Great Charter' was an agreement imposed on King John of England (r. 1199-1216 CE) on 15 June 1215 CE by rebellious barons in order to limit his power and prevent arbitrary royal acts, especially those of land confiscation and unreasonable taxes. Thus, the Magna Carta became a symbol of the rule of law as the ultimate sovereign. Although not entirely successful in its aims, the charter did permit further constitutional developments in England in subsequent centuries and it provided inspiration for similar models of limited monarchy in other European states.

Doors of the Milan Cathedral depicting conquest of Jerusalem by crusaders.

Magna Carta Memorial at Runnymede, Surrey, England, UK

Magna Carta Libertatum, is an English legal charter that required King John of England to proclaim certain rights, respect certain legal procedures and accept that his will could be bound by the law.

The Magna Carta had 63 clauses that outlined the laws, which the barons wanted the King to put into practice. The rights included the church rights, ability to avail justice quickly, no imposition of new taxes without agreement from the barons, feudal payment limits and so on.

If there was were a corrupt king, these laws could limit his word or could overthrow him. The Barons were keen on this charter as before it, the daughters and widows of Barons could be sold for profit.

Shield of King John (XIV century), From the Dictionary of Word and Things, 1888.

The Magna Carta being signed by King John, 1215

The Magna Carta was written in Medieval Latin on parchment paper. The writing was made by scraping a sharp knife against dry parchment. As this process and paper was expensive, scribes would abbreviate words and write in small letters.

MAGNA CARTA

EUROPE IN DARKNESS

The term "100 years' war", refers to the conflict between the kingdoms of France and England. The War actually lasted for 116 years, beginning in 1337 and ending in 1453.

Joan of Arc

In 1428, as the English began to invade Southern France, a peasant girl called Joan of Arc decided to battle it out with the forces based on a vision she had from God. She won the battle at Orleans in 1429 and remained unbeaten in many such victories until she was captured by the Burgundians who sold her to the English and they executed her.

King of England, Henry V

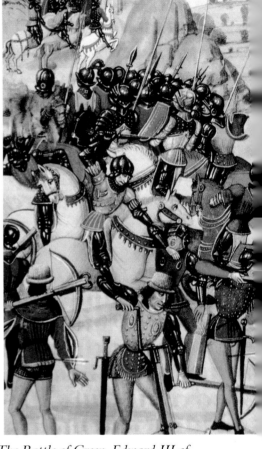

The Battle of Crecy, Edward III of England defeats Philip VI of France, 26th August, 1346.

The Hundred Years' War did not have any set winners or losers. The Hundred Year's War re-evolved the two kingdoms into looking more internally and into setting things in order before seeking expansion.

The famine

In the backdrop of the terrible wars between the kingdoms of France, the climate had taken its toll on farming and the scarcity of grain led to acute starvation. Around 15 per cent of the population suffered and finally succumbed to diseases like bronchitis, tuberculosis and pneumonia.

A painting showing the people of Europe suffering from the "Black Death"

Artist's imagination of the Black Death.

The Black Death

The Black Death was the name given to the pandemic that spread across Europe from 1347 to 1350. At the time, the plague was a disease that had no cure and unfortunately was very contagious.

The carriers of the disease were essentially fleas that travelled with or lived on the bodies of rats. As the plague began to hit a large number of the population, it spread panic among the people who mostly experienced nose bleeds and began to grow paler, experiencing swellings in the groin and armpit.

Joan of Arc statue, Blois, France

RENAISSANCE

The Renaissance emerged in Europe during the late fourteenth century, when there was a rebirth and a reawakening of philosophy, literature and particularly art. Many European thinkers moved away from the Church and promoted investigation and observation. This aspect was called as "humanism".

During this period there was a considerable growth of cities. Trade flourished between states and even countries. It was during this period that Columbus sailed across to the other side of the continent in search of India.

The Arts Movement

During this time, a lot of religious artwork was made for churches and chapels. However, artists also started getting inspired by Greek and Roman mythology and also began developing portraits of real people.
Michelangelo was a painter, sculptor and an architect par excellence. His frescoed work on the ceiling of the Sistine Chapel is among his well-known works.
Raphael, known for his Madonna paintings, was also the chief architect when the St. Peter's Basilica was rebuilt.
Leonardo da Vinci's celebrated art works include—*Mona Lisa* and *The Last Supper.*

A building inspired by Renaissance architecture

Literature

The Gutenberg Press invented by Johannes Gutenberg was the first movable printing press. People began to translate and share great works for the education of the masses. Niccolo Machiavelli's *The Prince* was a handbook for rulers everywhere. Dante Alighieri penned *Divine Comedy* in Italian. Soon native languages replaced classical languages like Latin and Greek. Martin Luther published the German translation of the Bible.

Intellectual works during the Renaissance

This era witnessed new approaches to the various sciences, medicine and philosophy. Copernicus observed that Earth and other planets revolved around the Sun. Renaissance medical scholars studied different body parts. Many universities were established during this period. The Bible was translated into several European languages during this period.

Protestant Movement

During the sixteenth century, the Protestants rejected the authority of the Roman Catholic Church. Theirs was essentially a literary movement, as it stressed on an individual reading the works of the Bible rather than passively receiving sermons from the priests.

Statue of Johannes Gutenberg

CROZATIER FUDIT
PARISIS MDCCCXXXVII

DISCOVERY OF THE NEW WORLD

The age of exploration started in the 1400s. European nations began exploring the world by travelling even further than the regular routes. It began by discovering new routes to India, then to the Far East, and finally, the Americas. Trade was one of the primary reasons behind these expeditions.

Christopher Columbus received by King Ferdinand and Queen Isabella on his return from the New World in 1493.

Christopher Columbus: The explorer

Christopher Columbus wanted to find a sea route to India, but he made it across the other side and discovered America instead. The King and Queen of Spain sponsored Columbus's journey. On 3 August 1492, he set sail from Palos and travelled for over two months. He set foot on the Caribbean islands of Bahamas and named the island San Salvador. He thought he had reached India, and he called the natives "Indians".

Illustration of Ferdinand Magellan (1480–1521). He was the first to start the expedition around the world.

HERNANDO DE MAGALLANES.
Cavallero Portugues, descubridor del
Estrecho de su nombre.

Discovery of America

Italian explorer Amerigo Vespucci set sail to the new land and, since he had realised that the new land was not Asia, German map maker Martin Waldseemuller decided to call the new region "America" after Vespucci's first name. Juan Ponce de Leon was the first explorer to land in North America in 1513.

Map of Panama in Central America.

Statue of Amerigo Vespucci at the Uffizi Loggia in Florence, Italy.

AMERICA

AMERIGO VESPUCCI

Age of exploration

Panama was the first Spanish colony in the Pacific and was soon known as "the door to the seas and key to the universe". The job to assess the extent of Earth's expanse was first started by Ferdinand Magellan around 1519, but it was fully completed by Juan Sebastian around 1522. During these explorations, Europeans actually used the term "East Indies" for all of South East Asia, including India.

Illustrations from the manuscript of Baburnama (Memoirs of Babur)—late sixteenth century

THE MUGHAL EMPIRE

Dagger and flintlock pistol from the Mughal dynasty

The Mughal dynasty began their rule in India in AD 1526. Under the Mughals, roads were built, trade prospered and the arts flourished. This glorious dynasty that ruled India for over 300 years, came to an end during the reign of emperor Bahadur Shah. The advent of the British reduced the later rulers to mere puppets.

Emperor Babur

The Mughal dynasty

Babur the first Mughal Emperor, was the descendent of Genghis Khan and Tamburlaine. He became a ruler at the age of 12. In 1526, he captured Delhi after ousting the forces of Ibrahim Lodhi in the first Battle of Panipat and defeated Rana Sanga of Mewar. Soon, Babur controlled the entire northern India from the Indus river to present-day Bihar, from Bengal in the east and Himalayas in the north to Gwalior in the south.

Diorama of Battle of Panipat (1526) displayed at Indian War Memorial Museum, Naubat khana, India

Tolerance policy

Emperor Aurangzeb

Akbar expanded the empire and established an efficient administrative system. His son, Emperor Jahangir, followed his father's policy of religious tolerance. He was followed by Shah Jahan. The Taj Mahal and the Great Mosque of Delhi were built under his patronage. Emperor Shah Jahan was succeeded by Aurangzeb, who annexed the Deccan states of Bijapur and Golconda, which were under the rule of Muslim leaders.

During his reign, he plundered and destroyed several temples and schools attended by Hindu children. Those who followed Sikhism also suffered under his reign. This caused several rebellions to break out against him. The Rajputs, Sikhs and Marathas were at the forefront of these rebellions. Aurangzeb also levied heavy taxes on farmers who were already suffering. All these factors added to the slow decline of the Mughal Empire. Bahadur Shah II, the last Mughal emperor, was exiled to Yangon, Burma, by the British for his participation in the Indian Mutiny of 1857.

OTTOMAN EMPIRE

The Ottoman Empire was created by Turkish tribes and lasted for 600 years, ending in 1922. At its peak, it had taken over the gates to Vienna from South Western Europe, from Hungary to Serbia and Bosnia, from Romania to Greece and Ukraine. It had taken over Iraq, Syria, Egypt, Israel and Africa, including Algeria.

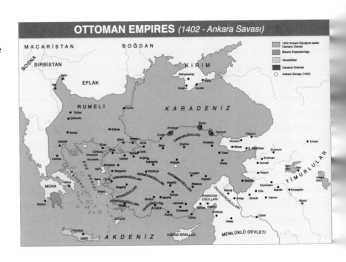

Expansion of the Ottoman Empire

After the defeat of the Mongols in 1293, Osman became the prince of Byzantine Bithynia in North Western Anatolia. His successors focussed their attacks on territories near Bosporus and the Sea of Marmara. Mehmet II captured Constantinople, converted it into his capital and called it Istanbul.

An illustration of a port in early Constantinople.

Statues of an Ottoman Pasha and Janissary, Istanbul, Turkey.

The Ottoman Empire

Statue of Suleiman the Magnificent at Edirnekapi, Istanbul, Turkey

It was during the reign of Suleiman the Magnificent, that the Ottoman Empire was said to have been at its peak. It was due to Suleiman's superior military planning that he could invade more territories and conquer new lands. He was also the caliph—the religious leader of his people. He put in place a big bureaucratic set up that was led by a vizier who followed Suleiman's commands. Suleiman the Magnificent also had a supreme army who were called "janissaries". The janissaries had unwavering faith and loyalty towards their Sultan.

Decline of the Empire

Suleiman grew tired of his administrative duties at some point and chose to spend more time devoted to pursuing the pleasures of life instead of focussing on the betterment of his people. The grand vizier did not have enough power or even the loyalty of all the Ottoman subjects, which brought about a lot of division within the empire itself. The empire also began to face economic competition from India and Europe. Internal corruption and poor leadership led to its decline until it was abolished and Turkey was declared a republic in 1923.

Battle of Mohacs, 1526, Ottoman victory over Hungary, led by Suleiman the Magnificent, Askeri Military Museum in Istanbul, Turkey.

The Blue Mosque, Istanbul, Turkey

REFORMATION

Reformation was a religious revolution that occurred during the sixteenth century, led by Martin Luther and John Calvin, among others. With the invention of the printing press, new ideas spread quickly and scriptures like the Bible were printed and distributed easily to people. A monk by the name of Martin Luther began to question the Catholic Church and its various practices. He published his writings as the *95 Theses* in 1517 and nailed it to the door of a Catholic Church.

Martin Luther

The *95 Theses*

The *95 Theses* stated that the Bible was the central authority and that people attained salvation through their faith, not their deeds. This was the basis for the Protestant Reformation.

HISTORY

Lutheran Church Dresden Frauenkirche in Dresden, Germany.

Reformation Movement, St. Peter's Basilica, Vatican City, Italy.

King Henry VIII statue

Beginning of the Reformation movement

Many new churches were established and were called the Lutheran Church and the Reformed Church. In Switzerland, John Calvin also spoke out against the Catholic Church's corrupt practices. King Henry VIII split from the Catholic Church. A few rulers converted to Protestantism, while some continued to support the Catholic Church. The religious divide led to the 30 Years' War which involved most of Europe.

Counter Reformation

The Counter Reformation was the result of the efforts of the Roman Catholics against the Protestant Reformation. It occurred around the same time as the Protestant Reformation. Pope Paul III requested for the prohibition of the luxurious living of the clergy. The Jesuits, known for their role in education, missionary work and theology, were founded in 1540 by St. Ignatius Loyola. The Roman inquisition started in 1542 and involved the army and political leaders against the protestant movement. Counter Reformation brought many people back to the Catholic Church in Austria, Poland, Holland, Germany and Hungary.

Lutheran Church of the Redeemer in Jerusalem.

Martin Luther's translation of the Bible into German.

Reformation wall in Parc Des Bastions, Geneva, Switzerland. Sculptures of the four great figures of the Geneva protestant movement: Guillaume Farel, Jean Calvin, Theodore de Beze and John Knox.

FRENCH REVOLUTION

Years of feudal oppression and economic problems led to the French Revolution. The bourgeoisie in France felt excluded from power. The peasants wanted to end the feudal setup, and philosophers wanted to reform the political and social scene. On 14 July 1789, the common people stormed the Bastille Fortress.

The Arc de Triomphe de l'Étoile in Paris, France

The reasons

The royal treasury was empty. For more than 20 years the country had suffered bad harvests. Inflation was at an all time high. King Louis XVI lived an extravagant lifestyle and Queen Marie Antoinette had frivolous spending habits. Heavy taxes were imposed on the working class in order to pay for the extravagances of the royalty.

The peasants grew tired of being exploited. Soon, they refused to pay taxes. The bourgeoisie were hardworking, educated men and were subjected to the same taxation as the poor peasants. The bourgeoisie would soon become the catalyst for the Revolution. The people were frustrated by their conditions and it was this unrest that caused the great French Revolution.

A portrait of the Peasant War that called for the abolishment of the feudal system.

Formation of a new constitution

On 26 August 1789, the Declaration of the Rights of Man and of the Citizen was introduced, which claimed liberty, equality, inviolability of property and the right to resist oppression. It was committed to the replacement of the ancient regime with one that focussed on equal opportunity, freedom of speech, sovereignty, and, most importantly, a representative government.

The motto of French Revolution

The French Revolution:scene in the throne-room of the Tuileries, Feb. 24th, 1848.

Reign of terror

Louis XVI was executed for treason in January 1793. Maximilien de Robespierre took over. The fear of counter-revolutionary forces made him start a reign of terror. From 1793 to 1794 he executed more than 15,000 people at the guillotine for being alleged enemies of the revolution.

INDUSTRIAL REVOLUTION (1700S–1800S)

The use of iron and steel as raw materials, the discovery of coal and improved transportation, such as with the steam engine, kick-started the industrialisation of Europe. New machines enabled the mass production of goods. From Britain, this revolution spread to Europe and North America, followed by the rest of the world.

The Industrial Revolution was a time of invention.

Technological change

The factory system came into existence. Means of communication improved with the introduction of the radio and telegraph. The textile industry improved with inventions like the spinning jenny by James Hargreaves. James Watt enhanced the efficiency of steam engines.

A cotton mill in Lancashire, England using power looms in 1835.

Transformation of transportation

The Industrial Revolution saw stronger roads, the building of canals and the introduction of railway lines. Raw materials were now transported using faster means. Manufacturers were also able to find and travel to new markets.

Migration to cities

Rural workers started moving towards cities to get jobs in factories. The population increased and cities expanded. The cost of labour for factories became cheap.

Employment of cheap labour

Machines were doing everything, so factories employed unskilled workers. Entire families worked in the same factory. Most factories had 15-hour working days. These conditions led to many people falling sick or dying. Factory owners grew rich, while the labourers remained poor and lived in slums.

Gender bias

Prior to the Industrial Revolution, both men and women worked together in cottage industries. Farmers involved their entire families, thus making it a "family business". The roles of men and women began to change as women entered factories as workers. Men were paid more than women and children. Women could not vote or even own property.

A steam engine with the intricate parts below.

WORLD WAR I (1914-1918)

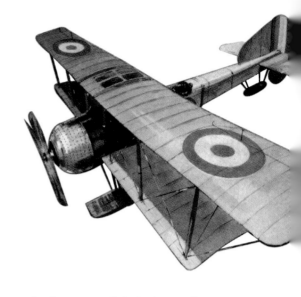

The assassination of Franz Ferdinand, the archduke of Austria-Hungary, by a Serbian nationalist propelled European powers towards the Great War. Austria-Hungary declared war on Serbia, Russia supported Serbia, and Germany joined Austria and Hungary. France allied with Russia and so Germany declared war on France.

Improved weapons

German troops used machine guns, fortifications, trenches, poisonous gases and barbed wires. Submarines or German U-boats attacked ships with torpedoes. Fighter aircrafts with machine guns and planned bombings were initiated.

Rest of the world joins the war

US had joined the Allied Forces, and made financial contributions in purchasing armaments and supplies. It sent food to the nations and armies of the Allies. It dispatched more than 10,00,000 soldiers and its navy focussed on the construction of destroyers and submarine chasers to protect the allies from German U-boats. Japan and China joined the war. China sided with the Allies and so did Japan.

Troops ride on World War I tanks going forward to the battle line in the Forest of Argonne, France.

French helmet of World War I

A French military helmet donated by the French Republic to the soldiers of Serbian army during World War I

The Allies Emerge Victorious

Germany signed a peace treaty with Russia. It deployed its forces against the allies on its western border. But the allied troops pushed back the Germans. By September 1918, German army leaders met with German chancellor Kaiser Wilhelm and reported that they had lost the war. Germany had to withdraw its forces from all the territories it had occupied. It had to give up its weapons including airplanes, submarines and battleships.

World War I and the destruction left in its wake

The monarchies of Hohenzollern, Habsburgs and Romanovs came to an end. It is estimated that eight million soldiers died, while nine million civilians died. The war destroyed 3,00,000 houses, 6000 factories, 1000 kilometres of railway lines and 112 coal mines. This war brought Germany towards the brink of an economic collapse. The war upset the European economies, making USA the chief creditor and industrial power.

Two German U-boats washed up on the rocks at Falmouth, England, in 1921. Both were sunk during World War I.

Luxemburg women wave allied flags from their windows to greet the Occupation of the American Army at the end of World War I.

16 soldiers leaving Camp Dix, New Jersey, in a car after 11 November 1918.

RUSSIAN REVOLUTION

The Russian Revolution was a movement started by the Bolshevik Party of Russia. This revolution aimed to end the Tsarist system followed in Russia and led to the formation of the Soviet Union. The Russian Empire came to an end with the abdication of Tsar Nicholas II. A temporary government was formed in February 1917 which had members of the Bolshevik Party.

Formation of a new republic

By March 1917, nationalist uproar in the Russian Empire quickly spread and there was widespread support for the efforts made by the moderate socialist revolutionary, Aleksandr Kerensky. By April, the National Moldavian Committee insisted on autonomy, land reforms and the use of the Romanian language. A move towards complete sovereignty was further pushed due to the events in Ukraine, where a council called as the "Sfat" was formed based on the model of the Kiev Rada, which proclaimed Bessarabia as an autonomous republic of the Federation of Russian Republics.

Bolshevik parade in St Petersberg during the Russian Revolution in the spring of 1917.

Military help

The Sfat appealed to the allies for military help. The Bolshevik Revolution of November 1917 put an end to the provisional government formed by the Bolshevik Party and got the Marxist Bolsheviks under the leadership of Vladimir I. Lenin came to power and put an end to Russia's contribution to the war. Acknowledging the possibility of isolation and taken aback by the affectation of the Ukrainian government, the Sfat voted for conditional union with Romania in April 1918. Reservations about the union were deserted with the defeat of the Central Powers and the creation of Greater Romania. An unconditional union was voted at the final session of the Sfat in December 1918.

Bolshevik revolution, 1917

WORLD WAR II (1939-1945)

World War II was fought between the Axis Powers comprising Germany, Italy, Japan and the Allied Powers comprising Britain, USA, Soviet Union and France.

An old hand grenade and bullet

Nazi award - Knight's Cross of the Iron Cross

Adolf Hitler in Nuremberg to attend a Nazi Party Convention in September 1934.

German Nazi flag demonstrates historical reconstruction of combat between Soviet and German armies during World War II.

Hitler's role in World War II

Adolf Hitler took over the reins of Germany by 1933. Germany attacked Poland in 1939 and this sparked off World War II. By 1941, Hitler's troops had occupied much of Europe and north Africa. Hitler established concentration camps to imprison Jews, leading to the death of more than six million people in the Holocaust.

Adolf Hitler

Battles of the war

The Battle of Britain lasted for three months with Germany bombing England. The operation by Germany to invade Russia in 1941 was named "Operation Barbarossa". In a week's time the German army had advanced 322 kilometres into Soviet territory. However, the German Army was caught in the midst of freezing temperatures, which affected their advance. The 1941 Japanese bombing of the US Pacific fleet at Pearl Harbor ensured the entry of USA into World War II. The Battle of Normandy in 1944 led to the freedom of western Europe from Germany's control.

Vintage American M24 Tank

Soviet aircraft of World War II

German soldiers invade Poland in armoured and motorised divisions in September 1939. It was the beginning of World War II.

The European World War ends

Hitler committed suicide and the German forces surrendered. By midnight of 8 May, 1945, the war in Europe was formally over. US dropped atomic bombs on the Japanese cities of Hiroshima and Nagasaki in August 1945. The Hiroshima bombing killed more than 70,000 people and many more died due to radiation exposure. The bombing on Nagasaki killed around 40,000 people. The bombings led to Japan's surrender.

Emergence of superpowers

After World War II, two major powers emerged — USA and Soviet Russia. Soon, they would delve into the Cold War that would last for the remainder of the twentieth century.

Helmet and rifle monument dedicated to dead soldiers on a shell-blasted beach

INDIA'S STRUGGLE FOR INDEPENDENCE

Queen Victoria became the ruler of India in 1858. Indians paid for the maintenance British army and bureaucracy. The British made Indians poor with heavy taxations, which resulted in famines. Thus, the 1900s saw revolutionary groups emerge in different parts of India to fight the British. Political groups like the Congress came together to negotiate with the British Empire in a peaceful manner.

A painting depicting the Mutiny of 1857

William Hodson presented the heads of the two princes Mirza Mughal and Mirza Khizr Sultan. A scene in The Indian Mutiny, 1857.

Statue of Rani Laxmibai of Jhansi.

Memorial to those who died in the siege of Lucknow during the Indian Mutiny of 1857.

Revolt of 1857

The revolt of 1857 was the first united rebellion against the British in India. Mangal Pandey started the revolt, when new cartridges for the Enfield rifle were coated with animal grease, offending both Muslims and Hindus. The Bengal army and the armies of Awadh, Rohilkhand, Bundelkhand, Bihar and East Punjab joined in. The Mughal Emperor, Bahadur Shah, supported the revolt and so did leaders like Rani Laxmibai and Tatya Tope.

Indian National Congress

Indian National Congress was formed in 1885. It wanted the creation of a secular and democratic national movement. It wanted the Indian Civil Service Examination be held in India and the age limit for appearing in the Examination be increased, and to have elected members in legislative assemblies. Later, the Congress began the "Swadeshi" movement, wherein people were asked to boycott all British goods and use indigenously produced goods.

THE FIRST INDIAN NATIONAL CONGRESS, 1885.

Mahatma Gandhi became a global symbol of peace due to his peaceful methods of solving disputes of which one was the Boycott of British Goods.

Jallianwala Bagh

On 13 April 1919 thousand of unarmed men, women and children gathered at Amritsar's Jallianwala Bagh, despite a ban on public meetings. General Dyer ordered his soldiers to fire into the gathering, killing 400 civilians and wounding another 1200. The Jallianwala Bagh massacre caused a wave of anger and outrage across India.

Bullet-marked wall at Jallianwala Bagh, Amritsar, India

1600 rounds were fired by British troops from here on 20,000 innocent people.

Monument of Rabindranath Tagore in Kolkata, India

Close-up of a bullet mark from the massacre at Jallianwala Bagh

Non-cooperation Movement

The Non-cooperation movement was launched in 1920. The movement urged people to resign titles, boycott government educational institutions, courts, government services, foreign goods, elections, refuse to pay taxes and to use the *charkha* and *khadi*. Muslim leaders formed the Khilafat Committee to fight the British.

Gandhi and Sardar Patel, Bardoli Satyagraha, 1928.

Civil Disobedience Movement

This movement began with the Dandi March. Gandhi marched with his followers to protest against the taxes levied on salt. People all over the country boycotted British goods and services. Peasants started refusing to pay taxes.

Gandhi during the freedom struggle in 1930

Illustration of spinning wheel which became the symbol of the boycott of foreign cloth.

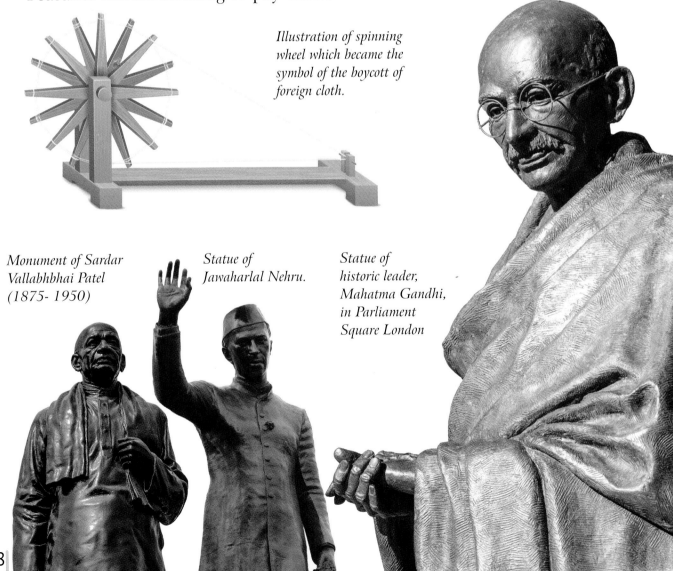

Monument of Sardar Vallabhbhai Patel (1875- 1950)

Statue of Jawaharlal Nehru.

Statue of historic leader, Mahatma Gandhi, in Parliament Square London

HISTORY

Quit India Movement

Quit India Movement was launched in 1942. It called for mass non-violent protest. The British declared the movement and the INC illegal. Leaders like Maulana Abul Kalam Azad, Netaji Subhash Chandra Bose, Mahatma

Discussing the "Quit India" movement with Nehru, 1942

Gandhi, Muhammad Ali Jinnah, Asoka Mehta, Jaya Prakash Narayan, Jawaharlal Nehru, and Chakravarti Rajgopalachari were involved in the movement. British arrested over 100,000 Indians. Riots and revolts began, and "do or die" became the mantra of Indians. The Quit India Movement showed the British that their time as the rulers of India was at its end. India gained its independence on 15 August 1947.

Netaji Subhash Chandra Bose

Netaji Subhash Chandra Bose addressing a rally in Tokyo, 1945.

Role of Indian National Army

Captain Mohan Singh came up with the INA or the Azad Hind Fauj ("the Free India Army"). The Japanese gave Indian prisoners of war to Mohan Singh, who trained them. The INA captured large parts of Manipur. Later, many INA soldiers were arrested and died while fighting the British. Subhash Chandra Bose tried to escape, but he is said to have died in an air-crash.

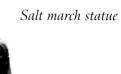

Salt march statue

369

PARTITION OF INDIA

The Muslim League was founded in 1906 under Aga Khan III to preserve the rights of Indian Muslims. Independent India would mainly comprise of Hindus, and India's Muslims would be a minority. Thus, Jinnah and the Muslim league spearheaded the struggle to partition British India into two different states, Hindu and Muslim.

Lord Mountbatten swears in Pandit Jawaharlal Nehru as the first Prime Minister of free India at the ceremony held at 8.30 am on 15 August, 1947.

Appeal for a unified India

Britain wanted India to be a part of World War II and provide soldiers. Since the Muslim League supported Britain, British authorities favoured the Muslim League when it demanded a separate state for Muslims. Nehru was against the Partition, but finally accepted the Muslim League's plan to divide India.

Policemen trying to control protestors

Earl Mountbatten

Lord Mountbatten meets Nehru, Jinnah and other Leaders to plan the Partition of India.

HISTORY

The Partition

More than 500,000 people on both sides lost their lives in the Partition. Around 10 million people fled from either side to avoid the violence that came with the Partition. Thousands of women were abducted. Cities swarmed with refugees, as over 14 million people crossed over the borders. Train compartments comprising thousands of refugees were destroyed and passengers were killed. Pakistan was formed as a new country on 14 August 1947. On the next day, India was granted its freedom and emerged as an independent country.

Nathuram Ghodse

Overcrowded train transferring refugees during the partition of India, 1947. This was considered to be the largest migration in human history.

Fixing of the border

On 30 January, 1948, Gandhi was shot by Nathuram Ghodse because of his acceptance to create a multi-religious state.

Before the partition, the Muslims were living in two main regions that were on the opposite sides of the country. Between these sections remained a huge Hindu population. Northern India also served as home to several other religions including Sikhs and Christians. To split the nation would also involve splitting the populations of these communities. While the talks of Partition were in progress, the Sikh community also asked for a nation of their own, but their demand was rejected.

371

GLOSSARY

GLOSSARY

Acceleration: In physics, this is a term that means rate of change of velocity.

Acupuncture: This is the science of healing by piercing needles at critical points of the human body.

Acupressure: This is a form of healing pain by applying pressure at key points.

Adaptation: This is a way in which a living species, such as an animal or plant, has developed in appearance or behaviour to fit in with its environment.

Agriculture: This is the use of land to grow food crops and/or raise domestic animals.

Algae: This is a simple, often single-celled organism, some of which look like plants; they are found in various habitats but occur most commonly in water.

Amphibians: This is a cold-blooded animal, such as a frog or a newt, that can live in both water and land.

Artefacts: These are objects made by a person, especially something of historical or cultural interest.

Antenna: This is a sensitive feeler on the head of an insect or a crustacean.

Atharvaveda: This is one of the holy books of the Hindus from the Vedic period and is a collection of spells and charms to treat diseases.

Arthropod: This is an invertebrate that has a joined outer-boned case. Arthropods include insects, spiders, and crustaceans such as crabs and lobsters and scorpions.

Asteroid: This is a small object in space, made from a mixture of rock and metals that orbits around the Sun.

Arthashatra: This is a treatise that was authored by Chanakya, the founder of the Mauryan dynasty.

Atmosphere: This is the layer of breathable gas, mainly oxygen and nitrogen, that surrounds the Earth.

Atom: This is the smallest particle of an element that has the same chemical makeup as the element.

Aurora: These are bands of light in the sky caused by high-energy particles from space meeting particles in the atmosphere.

Black Death: This was the name given to the pandemic that spread across Europe from 1347 to 1350.

Bacteria: These are microscopic, single-celled organisms, some of which are helpful.

BCE: This refers to Before Common Area: the years before 1CE (start of the Common Era). This abbreviation has largely replaced BC (Before Christ).

Biome: This is a large-scale biological community with a particular climate and certain types of plants.

Black hole: This is a body of matter in space of such intense gravity that even light cannot escape from it.

Bourgeoisie: The refers to the middle class in any society.

Calligraphy: This is a known art form in China with elaborate and delicate strokes creating virtual pieces of art.

Camouflage: This is a way an animal blends in with their background or uses a disguise to escape notice from predators.

Canopy: This refers to the topmost branch of a tree in a forest; canopy also means the part of a plant showing above ground.

Cavalry: This refers historically to military troops mounted on horseback. The term now also means army units that move around in vehicles such as cars and tanks.

Cellulose: This is a substance found in plant cell walls that give plants their structure.

Chlorophyll: This is the green colour in plants that enable them to absorb sunlight, which they use during photosynthesis.

Chloroplast: These are special structures in plant cells containing the green pigment chlorophyll.

Citizen: This is a person who belongs to a city or a bigger community such as a state or a country.

City-state: This is a city, together with its surrounding territory that has its own independent system of government.

Chromosome: These are threadlike structures, found in the nucleus of a body cell, that is made up of coiled strands of DNA.

Chrysalis: This refers to the hard, protective case, also called a pupa, which encloses the larva of an insect such as a moth or a butterfly as it develops into its adult form.

Code of Hammurabi: These are codes put together during the Mesopotamian civilisation and were aimed at protecting the rights of the weak, widows, and orphans.

Democracy: This is a political system in which people have power to control their government, usually by electing politicians to represent their view.

DNA: This is an abbreviation for deoxyribonucleic acid, the material packed inside chromosomes that holds all the instructions for making and maintaining a living body.

Dynasty: This refers to a family or group that rules over a country for several generations.

Ecosystem: This is a community of animals and plants that share, and interact with the same habitat.

Electron: This is one of the tiny particles inside an atom; electrons have negative electric charge.

Element: In chemistry, this is a simple substance made of atoms that are all of the same kind.

Embryo: This refers to the earliest stage in the development of an animal or a plant. A human embryo forms when sex cells join.

Empire: This is a group of countries or states united under one ruling power.

Enzyme: This is a substance in animals or plants that speeds up a chemical reaction.

Erosion: This is a process by which Earth's surface rocks and soil are worn away by the action of winds, water, and glaciers (moving ice).

Eruption: This is a violent discharge of lava, hot ashes, and gases from a volcano. Eruptions are the result of molten rock, or magma, working its way from the inside of the Earth to the surface.

Exoskeleton: This is the hard outer skeleton, such as that of insects and crustaceans, which supports and protects the body.

Extinction: This refers to the disappearance from Earth of the last living representative of a species.

Fault: This is a crack in the Earth's surface where the rocks on either side have shifted in relation to each other, either upwards or downwards, or sideways. The continuing movement of the rocks can cause earthquakes.

Feudalism: This is a social system that developed in medieval times, when people of the serving classes (such as labourers and peasants) pledged support to their overlord in return for his protection.

Fission: This is the process of splitting apart; nuclear fission is the splitting of the nucleus of an atom.

Fossil: These are preserved remains of life from an earlier geological time.

Friction: This refers to the dragging force that occurs when one object moves over another.

Fusion: This is a scientific process of joining together; nuclear fusion is the joining together of two atomic nuclei.

Galaxy: This is a gigantic group of stars, dust, and gas. Our own galaxy is the Milky Way.

Ganadharas: This term refers to the 11 disciples of Mahavira, the founder of Jainism.

Gene: This is one of the tiny units found inside cells that determine what a living thing looks like and how its body works. Genes are passed on from one generation to the next.

373

Gills: These are small slits that fish have at the front of their heads. They are placed right behind or next to the mouth.

Glacier: This is a moving mass of ice, formed from accumulated snow. Some glaciers flow like rivers, while others are vast ice sheets such as those covering Antarctica and much of Greenland.

Gravity: This is the force that attracts one object to another and prevents things from floating into space.

Habitat: This is an area where an animal naturally makes its home.

Hominid: A word meaning 'human-like', which refers to humans and all our extinct ancestors. It can also include the great apes.

Hormones: These are natural chemicals that are produced by glands and which circulate in the bloodstream to have an effect on particular parts of the body.

Hurricane: This is a type of violent tropical storm with torrential rain and high winds that reach more than 119 kph.

Indigenous: This refers to something occurring naturally in a particular environment or country.

Invertebrate: This is an animal without a backbone: for example, an insect, a worm, or a crustacean.

ION: This is an atom that has lost or gained one or more electrons and as a result has either positive or negative electrical charge.

Ionosphere: This is an area of the Earth's atmosphere through which radio waves can be transmitted.

Iron Age: This is the historical period characterised by the use of iron for making weapons and tools. The earliest known iron implements were found in the Middle East and Southern Europe, and date to about 1200 BCE.

Janissaries: This was the name of the supreme army of Suleiman, the great king of the Ottoman empire.

Kármán Line: This is the starting point of outer space. It starts at an altitude of 100 kilometres above sea level.

Kimono: The Kimono came into existence during the Jomon period in Japan. The word kimono means "thing to wear".

Lava: This is hot liquid rock forced out of a volcano during an eruption.

Light Year: This is a measurement used by astronomers, based on the distance that light travels one year.

Magma: This is a hot liquid that is found underneath Earth's surface.

Mammal: This is a warm-blooded animal that has a backbone, feeds its young on milk, and usually has a covering of fur.

Mantle: These are rocks that lie beneath Earth's crust, extending almost to the inner core, and making up most of our planet's weight.

Marsupial: This is a mammal that carries it's developing young in a pouch, usually on the stomach.

Mass: This is the amount of matter in an object.

Medieval Period: This refers to the Middle Ages, the period in European history that lasted from about the 5th to the 16th century.

Meteorite: This is a small body of rock or debris that falls to Earth from space.

Microliths: This is a tiny blade tool especially of the Mesolithic period usually found in a geometric shape (such as that of a triangle) and often set in a bone or wooden shaft.

Migration: This is the seasonal mass movement of animals from one place to another in search of food and places to breed.

Mineral: This is a solid, inorganic material occurring naturally in Earth. Different minerals are classified according to their elements and crystal structure.

Mitochondria: These are tiny organs inside a body cell that create energy to keep the cell alive.

Molecule: This is a group of atoms bonded together.

Monarchy: This is a type of government in which a king or queen is recognised as the head of a country, even though he or she may have no real power.

Nebula: This is a cloud of gas and dust in outer space; some nebulas are the debris from dead stars, others are where new stars form.

Neutron: This is one of the tiny particles inside an atom. Neutrons have no electric charge.

Nomadic: This describes people who move from place to place, usually according to seasons, but never establish a permanent settlement.

Nucleus: This is the control centre of a body cell, where information about living organisms is held in the form of genes. It is also the central core of an atom.

Nutrients: These are food substances that are necessary for life and growth.

Orbit: This is the path taken by an object, like a planet circling around another planet or star.

Organism: This refers to any living thing, including an animal, a plant, or a microscopic life form such as a bacterium.

Pharaohs: This was a title given to a king in Ancient Egypt. People believed that the pharaohs had sacred powers.

Photosynthesis: This is a chemical process by which plants use the energy from sunlight to make their own food.

Phylum: This is one of the major scientific divisions that group together living things according to what their ancestors were like and the way their bodies are made.

Plasma: This is a gas-like cloud of electrically charged matter.

Plate Boundary: This is an area where the edges of the vast moving plates that make up the Earth's crust come together.

Polyp: This is a form taken by some marine animals, such as jellyfish, sea anemones, and corals. Usually tube-shaped, polyps have a mouth at one end, and are attached firmly at the base to a rock or the seabed.

Predator: This is an animal that hunts other animals for food.

Prehistory: This is the time before the development of civilizations, when people did not write things down.

Prey: This is an animal hunted by other animals for food.

Propaganda: This is information spread publicly to put forward ideas or political views; propaganda is sometimes used to create deliberate harm to a person or group.

Proton: This is one of the tiny particles inside an atom; protons have positive electric charge.

Pupa: This is the hard protective case also called a chrysalis, which encloses the larva of an insect as it develops into an adult.

Reactants: This is one of the ingredients that join together to cause a chemical reaction.

Reptile: This is a cold-blooded, scaly-skinned vertebrate (animal with a backbone); reptiles include snakes and birds.

Republic: This is a country without a royal family that is headed, usually, by a president, who may or may not have been freely chosen by the people.

Retina: This is a layer of light sensitive cells lining the inside of an eyeball.

Rigveda: This word means 'Vedas of praise.' It refers to one of the main religious books of Hinduism from the Vedic period and contains 1028 hymns and 10,600 verses.

Samaveda: This is a holy book of the Hindus from the Vedic period and is a collection of melodies.

Sfat: This is a council formed based on the model of the Kiev Rada, which proclaimed Bessarabia as an autonomous republic of the Federation of Russian Republics.

Solar System: The Sun together with its orbiting groups of planets, including Earth, and other smaller bodies such as asteroids form the solar system.

Stomata: These are tiny openings on the undersides of leaves that control the amount of gas and moisture passing into and out of a plant.

Stone Age: This is a period of prehistory, lasting more than 2 million years, when humans and their ancestors made most of their tools out of stone.

Subduction: This is a geological process in which one of the vast plates that make up Earth's crust is pushed beneath another.

Sultan: In some Islamic countries, this is the traditional title given to the ruler.

Sunspot: This is a dark, cooler patch on the surface of the Sun.

Space manufacturing: This is the production of manufactured goods outside a planetary atmosphere.

Space race: This refers to the competition between the US and the Soviet Union in the 1950s and 60s to be the first to explore space.

Supernova: This is an exploding giant star.

Space warfare: This refers to combat that occurs in outer space.

Terraforming: Otherwise known as "earth shaping" this is the theoretical process of deliberately modifying a planet's, moon's, or any other body's atmosphere, temperature, surface topography, or ecology to make it habitable for Earth-like life.

Tectonic Plate: This is one of the large, slowly moving slabs into which Earth's crust is divided.

Tentacles: These are long, elastic structures, like arms, that some animals use for feeling ,moving around and picking up food.

95 Theses: This is a document stated that the Bible was the central authority and that people attained salvation through their faith, not their deeds. This was the basis for the Protestant Reformation.

Toga: This was the official costume of the Romans. It was made from a semi-circular white wool cloth piece.

Tsunami: This is an enormous, rapidly rising ocean wave caused by an earthquake or volcanic activity under the sea. Tsunamis travel far and fast, causing widespread devastation inland.

Velocity: This is the speed at which something moves in a particular direction.

Vertebrates: This is an animal who has a backbone.

Vikings: These were Scandinavian seafaring warriors who were also known as Norsemen.

Virus: This is a tiny life form that is a collection of genes inside a protective shell. Viruses can invade body cells, where they multiply causing illnesses.

Viscous: This is a measure of a liquid's ability to flow.

Vizier: This title was once given to a chief official in some muslim countries.

Volcano: This is an opening in Earth's crust that provides an outlet for magma (hot, liquefied rock) when it rises to the surface.

Warm-blooded: This describes an animal that can keep its body heat at an almost constant level, regardless of whether the outside temperature is hot or cold.

Yajurveda: This is a holy book of the Hindus from the Vedic period and explains various mantras to be sung and religious rituals to be followed by priests.

INDEX

INDEX

INDEX